How to Run a Small Factoring Business

Make Money in Little Deals the Big Guys Brush Off

Jeff Callender

DASH POINT PUBLISHING

Federal Way, Washington

How to Run
a Small Factoring Business
Make Money in Little Deals
the Big Guys Brush Off

by Jeff Callender

Published by:
Dash Point Publishing, Inc.
P.O. Box 25591
Federal Way, WA 98093-2591 U.S.A.

Website: www.DashPointPublishing.com

Library of Congress Control Number: 2012943556
ISBN: 978-1-938837-02-9 (Paperback)
ISBN: 978-1-938837-14-2 (PDF)
ISBN: 978-1-938837-20-3 (Kindle)
ISBN: 978-1-938837-08-1 (ePub)
Printed in the United States of America.

Dedication

This book is dedicated to my parents,
who have always been there.
Always.

Contents

Preface

This is the third book in The Small Factor Series, which opens the door to the remarkable investment of factoring small business receivables.

The first book, *Factoring Wisdom: A Preview of Buying Receivables,* is a compilation of many quotes from not only from the Small Factor Series, but from the other books and ebooks listed on the "Also by Jeff Callender" page. It serves as an excellent introduction to and summary of these books, providing both a look ahead to the other works, as well as a review when you've completed them.

The second title, *Fundamentals for Factors: How You Can Make Large Returns in Small Receivables,* introduces the reader to the basic concepts of factoring. *Fundamentals* describes what factoring is, how it works, businesses which can benefit, the remarkable returns possible, risks involved, and how to minimize those risks. It helps the reader define the meaning of "success," whether factoring is an appropriate move for his or her circumstances, and closes with a look at four small factors who enter the field from very diverse backgrounds, with quite different purposes.

The third book and the one you are reading, *How to Run a Small Factoring Business* is the "nuts and bolts," hands-on manual for running a small factoring operation. It includes first-hand lessons from the factoring industry, identifies where to find operating capital, provides marketing strategies, and describes numerous common mistakes small factors all too often make. In these pages you'll find discussions on due diligence, credit reports, factoring software, a chapter on record keeping, a sample factoring transaction from start to finish with an accompanying flowchart, and numerous resources available to small factors.

While *How to Run a Small Factoring Business* is the third book in sequence in the series, it was actually the first written, with the first edition published in 1995 under the title *Factoring Small Receivables*. The current edition has been completely revised to provide many updates and new material, as each edition has before it.

The purpose of the next book, *Factoring Case Studies: Essential Lessons from 30 Real Factoring Clients* is to illustrate the many principles and instructions provided in the two preceding books. While *Fundamentals* and *How to Run* are filled with chapters of instruction, training, and how-to information, *Case Studies* demonstrates how these actually work in real situations with real people.

The case studies are written by smaller factors from across the country, and provide unique and powerful lessons in running a factoring operation. They paint personal portraits of the people factoring involves, in what otherwise might be assumed to be a business of procedures, forms, numbers, and finance. The *Case Studies* book clearly shows the human side of factoring, and how both the risks and benefits play out in the real world. If you want to really know what a small factor's life is like (good, bad, and ugly), read *Factoring Case Studies.*

The last book, *Marketing Methods for Small Factors & Brokers*, provides the perspectives of eight contributors (seven small factors and one broker) who have worked in the industry for many years. They address the issue of marketing: what methods work, what methods don't work, and what advice they have to offer to those starting in the factoring world. It speaks to the very first matter anyone faces when starting in this business: how to obtain new clients.

I present this book – and this series – not just for your benefit, but for the benefit of the countless number of small business owners whose companies, and all the individuals whose lives they impact, can be greatly improved by your factoring service.

Jeff Callender

Part 1

The Basics

1
Introduction

For Whom This Manual Is Written

This manual is for two types of people: the factoring professional who would like to increase business by acting both as a factor as well as a broker, and the individual who would like to learn to factor small receivables as a supplement to other income and/or investments.

There is a large amount of business right in your back yard with clients whose receivables are too small for big factors to find profitable. This creates a perfect niche and a big market for the little guy: you and me.

The next chapter, "What Is Factoring?" is for those new to this form of alternative financing. You'll find a general description of factoring, what businesses it can help, and how it can help them. While the factoring industry is sophisticated and competitive, there is a huge market for factoring small receivables. Small factors who are aggressive, prudent and knowledgeable can make good income. This manual is intended to help the beginning factor get his or her business under way and further develop those who have already started.

This book has one theme: you can have a successful business by factoring small clients that larger factors won't accept. The pages that follow show how.

My Story

In the early 1990's I had been a Presbyterian parish pastor for 14 years and served three different congregations in Washington state. I was in my early 40's and realized parish ministry was not what I wanted to do with the rest of my working life. At the end of 1992, I left the security of a monthly paycheck and a familiar, significant role in the community to look for something I was missing: time with my family, a different way of helping people, a chance to work for myself at home, and a means of providing better income.

After nearly a year of working for myself, I received a letter inviting me to a free seminar that described something called "factoring" – a term which was completely new to me. I went, heard an interesting, smooth presentation and decided to enter the industry. The introductory tape from an organization (which is no longer in business) said you needed three things to succeed: a genuine liking of people, a desire to help them, and being in a transition in life. These described me perfectly and I was more than ready to get started.

I attended training in January of 1994 and began working the business part-time. In August I went full-time and continued this way for the next five years. Over that time I experienced great success, but also very significant factoring losses. I came to painfully appreciate the risks that lie in the underbrush, alongside the treasures that await small factors.

Smarting from my "education," I left factoring other companies' receivables and then owned a sign shop franchise for a year. Soon I was factoring my own receivables, which showed me personally how factoring helps small businesses when used correctly. Later I worked for a year as an account manager in the operations division for a large factor. There I learned first-hand how the "big guys" manage accounts, which further refined my factoring procedures.

Then, suddenly and unexpectedly, the operations office in which I worked was significantly downsized (and later closed), and several co-workers and I were summarily laid off. We went to work as usual one day, were called into the manager's office, and without fanfare given our two-week severance checks and told to take our things "and go home now."

This was my final look back at working for corporate America, and in particular for someone else. I started Dash Point Financial Services, Inc. as my new factoring business, incorporating all the lessons learned. I also began a new publishing company, Dash Point Publishing, Inc., having learned first-hand the value of self-employment with multiple streams of income. I set about writing several books, which combined with factoring, have produced very satisfying success and personal fulfillment.

I have been factoring my own clients since 2001. Running my three businesses simultaneously, my time is an enjoyable blend of factoring, running a software company, working with small factors, and writing.

In 2003 I took on the challenge of developing web-based software for (at the time) smaller factors. This project evolved into a product and company called FactorFox which now is available for the greater factoring community, and includes several services in addition to its database tracking software for subscribers. This experience has further instructed me in the nuances of how other factoring companies run their organizations, set rates, perform due diligence, etc., and taught me further how to run a smooth, successful factoring business. It's also shown me…well, how *not* to.

The book you are reading is the culmination of all these experiences.

How This Manual Came to Be Written

Back in the mid 1990's, about a year after working part-time and then full-time as a broker, I spent a LOT of money on advertising and running the business and still had nothing to show for it. I ran across an ad on the Internet – a far cry from what it is today! – that caught my eye. It was a "Factoring Manual" entitled *Accounts Receivable Factoring Manual* (©1993) and written by Joseph Casano of Gulf Coast Factoring in Pass Christian, Mississippi, who had worked as a small factor for five years.

I was amused that the only mention of brokering (compared to my training manual's exhaustive tome) was one paragraph that said, in effect, you can get nice finder's fees from large factors by referring bigger deals you can't fund yourself. End of brokering education. The rest of the manual provided the basics of what you need to know to factor small deals. I found it very helpful for it gave me the courage to dabble in this on my own.

Factoring a few small deals quickly showed me that brokers who have experienced the same problems I did, can nevertheless be successful as small factors. So can people who are interested in entering the factoring business to supplement regular, investment, or retirement income, if they are willing to learn and do what it takes to make the business work. What it takes is some guts, bucks, common sense and a healthy dose of caution.

What's New in This Book

This book was originally published under the title *Factoring Small Receivables*; its seven editions stretched from 1995 to 2005. The present book was given a new title which more accurately describe its contents, and provides extensive updates to my own factoring procedures which continue to evolve and always will. Also included are many updates to technology tools as well as factoring resources.

The sections have been reorganized and renamed, and several chapters moved to better fit the segments. Four new chapters have been added: "How to Become a Factor," "Factoring Franchises," "Checklists," and "Factoring from a Virtual Office." The first two answer one of the most frequent questions I am asked: "How can I get into factoring?"

The "Checklists" chapter is in response to a very common request and provides step-by-step procedures for planning and implementing your due diligence process. The "Virtual Office" chapter describes how I use technology, available to anyone, to work from anywhere and how I have co-workers across the continent. The chapter describes how we each work from home without a centralized (and expensive) office, and how remarkably efficient the operation is day to day.

The "Banking and Funds Transfers" chapter has been updated to keep pace with current technology and banking practices. Likewise the "Marketing" chapter has been extensively updated with the more arcane methods deleted and several new ones added. The chapter "Common Mistakes" has been reorganized, the mistakes are now numbered for easier reference, and four new common mistakes have been added.

The chapters "UCCs," "Credit Reports," and "Factoring Software" have been updated and shortened considerably, since this information quickly becomes outdated. The new material provides a means for the reader to keep current on this information using simple internet searches. Additionally, like the "Factoring Franchises" chapter, a series of questions has been added to the "Factoring Software" chapter to help readers know what to consider when selecting a platform.

Finally, this and the other books in the *Small Factor Series,* as well as all my other books and ebooks (previously only available in PDF format), are now available in ebook formats for iPad, Kindle, and Android tablets.

You will find within this manual the nuts and bolts of factoring small receivables, and some practical wisdom that has helped my business. Let's roll up our sleeves and get started.

2
What Is Factoring?

Factoring Defined

The Latin word "factare" means "to make" or "to do." Obviously the word "factory," the place where products are made, comes from this Latin root. Likewise, "factor" comes from the same word, so a factor is someone who "makes it happen" – who "gets it done." As we'll see below, this has been true for some time.

Factoring, by definition, is the purchase of accounts receivable at a discount – for less than their face value – for immediate cash. When a business sells a product or service to a customer, that business provides an invoice stating what products or services were sold and the amount the customer has agreed to pay. It is an IOU from the customer to the business. Sometimes these invoices are paid immediately. Sometimes they are paid over the course of 15, 30, 60, 90 days, or even more. Quite often, larger customers take longer to pay. An unpaid receivable or invoice has value. Factors are investors – individuals or businesses – who pay cash now for the right to receive future payments on a client's invoices to their customers. Customers are often called "debtors" in factoring parlance.

Because so many customers wait weeks or even months to pay their bills, a cash flow problem can arise for the companies to whom they owe money. Instead of having to wait for payment on a product or service that has already been delivered, a business can factor – sell – its receivables for cash at a discount off the face amount of the invoice. This almost instant cash offers a number of benefits to cash-starved companies: they can meet payroll, fund marketing efforts, have working capital, pay taxes, or meet many other needs. This cash can provide the means for a manufacturer to replenish inventory and make more products to sell without having to wait for earlier sales to be paid.

A typical business that extends credit will have ten to twenty percent of its annual sales tied up in accounts receivable at any given time. Just think for a moment about how much money is tied up in 60 days' worth of receivables, and then think about what a business could do with that cash if it were on hand. You can't pay the power bill or this week's payroll with a customer's invoice; but you can *sell* that invoice for the cash to meet those obligations.

Factoring is not a "loan" – it is the sale of an asset. A loan places a debt on a balance sheet, and it costs interest. By contrast, factoring puts money in the bank almost as soon as an invoice can be created. Thus having more cash on hand and fewer receivables strengthens one's balance sheet. Loans are largely dependent on the borrower's financial soundness. With factoring, it is the soundness of the client's customer that matters most – a real plus for new businesses without an established track record.

Because factors do not lend money but rather buy invoices, they look at prospective clients differently than a bank. A bank makes a loan with the assumption that the business to which the loan is made will be stable enough to repay. Factors look to the stability of the *customers* of the business, because the *customers* will be paying the factor – not the client. Thus the focus on repayment is different; and because the focus is more on the customer than the client, factors often accept clients that banks turn away. In fact, bank referrals provide factors some of their best leads.

So factoring is not only an excellent means for expanding a business, it may provide the only means when traditional loans aren't available…which, for many, many owners of very small businesses, is most of the time.

The History of Factoring

Today, the most common form of factoring fits conveniently in your wallet – the credit card. A consumer makes a purchase from a merchant, who in turn sells this "receivable" to the credit card company at a discount. The credit card company, acting just like a factor, receives its money by charging the merchant a few percentage points for collecting payment and depositing funds, less a discount, into the merchant's bank account. It also accepts the responsibility for collection of the debt. While we may not call this factoring, it is, in essence, what factoring is all about – selling accounts receivable at a discount for immediate cash.

Aside from credit cards, the practice of factoring has been largely unknown in North America (though this trend has changed with the Great Recession). But it has been around for a very long time: the Romans issued promissory notes at a discount.

Do you know how the Pilgrims financed their trip to America? Since the Pilgrims did not have enough capital for their journey, they negotiated an agreement with a London businessman named Thomas Weston. An iron merchant, Weston advanced money for repayment at a future date, using as collateral the Pilgrims' accounts receivable for the raw materials the colonists shipped to London. However, he probably bought the receivables at a great discount because of the high risk involved with transporting and receiving the raw materials from America. For a fascinating depiction of the Pilgrims' challenges in the New World, and a very human picture of their relationship with Weston, read Nathaniel Philbrick's book *Mayflower*. You'll come away with a deep appreciation of the courage and fortitude of these remarkable settlers.

Factoring, as it is now practiced in the United States, began in the garment industry in the 19th Century and has grown steadily and expanded to other industries. Up until the 1980's, factoring was limited to mostly large corporations involving very large dollar amounts. That decade brought a change in the factoring industry. With the savings and loan crisis during those years, banks became much more regulated and cautious about lending money, especially to businesses. Since then, standard practice for banks has been to require at least two or three years' of financials from a business before they will even consider a loan request. Consequently, newer businesses or those who don't meet a bank's often rigid requirements need an alternative source of financing for their business. More and more therefore are turning to factors.

This is especially true since 2008 when the Great Recession started, and continues to the time of this edition. Bank lending has been seriously constricted for small businesses since then; but "constricted" is an antiseptic financial term. To put it in normal language, bank lending to small businesses has essentially *vanished.*

As a result factoring has become much better known because factors are financing businesses that banks are not. While this economy makes for tough times for business, many consider it a boon to the factoring industry as it not only increases our business, but makes factoring more mainstream and known to those who need it. In short, it's becoming more legitimate in the eyes of the world.

As we come out of this difficult economic period in the coming years, factoring will continue to be needed and used – banks will still turn down companies seeking loans even after the "constriction" is over – and factors will be there to fund them.

How Factoring Works

An Example

Let's say a business has a $10,000 invoice. It could be for $100, $1,000, $100,000 or $1,000,000…the principle is the same. This invoice is billed to a good customer who will take 30 days to pay. Rather than waiting that length of time, the business factors the invoice and receives an 80% advance, or $8,000, in cash the next day from the factor through various means: a bank wire, electronic funds transfer, or perhaps a check. The invoice is delivered to the customer who 30 days later pays the factor the full amount of the invoice, $10,000. With that $10,000, the factor reimburses himself the $8,000 advanced, keeps his discount of 5%, or $500, and pays back the balance, $1,500, to the client.

In essence, this is what happens with just about all factoring transactions (though advance and discount amounts vary widely). A business pays, in this example, $500 to have $8,000 tomorrow, and gets the other $1,500 in a month. Meanwhile, what has the $8,000 in hand enabled the business owner to do? He can buy inventory to make more sales, he has cash on hand to take advantage of discounts or simply pay bills, meet payroll, pay taxes, or whatever the business might need. The company has accessed instant cash for an otherwise non-performing asset: receivables. No debt is generated, the discount is paid after the cash advance is received, and the cash has enabled the company to increase profits with greater sales volume. Further, the discount has more than paid for itself.

You're probably beginning to see how a business can grow from factoring receivables.

Recourse and Non-recourse Factoring

As all business owners know, any time credit is extended to a customer there's a chance that customer, for a variety of reasons, will not pay the bill. What happens when a factor buys an invoice which the customer doesn't pay? The answer depends on whether a recourse or non-recourse factoring agreement is in place, and the reason for nonpayment.

When the factor and the client establish their financial relationship as one with **recourse**, the factor determines how long he will wait to be paid by the client's customers – usually a period of 60, 90, or 120 days. If the customer does not pay in that length of time for whatever reason, the factor has "recourse" to the client to recoup whatever amount is owed the factor. In essence, the client "buys back" the invoice previously sold. This can be done by:

- swapping the old invoice for a new one
- taking a deduction from new invoice advances or rebates due the client
- tapping a reserve account

- the client simply paying the factor in cash
- or a combination of any or all of these.

The buy back, or "charge back," covers the factor's unpaid advance, expenses and discount.

In **non-recourse** factoring, the factor does not have a claim against the client if the customer cannot pay. In such arrangements, the factor is assuming the risk of nonpayment (essentially offering credit insurance to the client) which provides an added bonus to the client along with the other advantages of factoring. Non-recourse factoring, according to the language of most factoring agreements, is in effect when the customer is *unable* to pay; that is, if the customer goes bankrupt, goes out of business, or otherwise can't pay the bill. However, if there is a dispute and a customer *won't* pay, the factor *will* have recourse. The client is required to do what is necessary to satisfy the customer so the invoice is paid.

Some larger factors who purchase invoices totaling $100,000 or more per month may offer both recourse and non-recourse factoring, but others provide strictly non-recourse funding. This is of benefit to the client; but keep in mind, non-recourse factors must be even more careful about which customers they will factor as they are at greater risk of losing money. Thus, they may be much more selective about the clients and customers they will accept.

Smaller factors who deal in sums less than $100,000 per month are usually strictly recourse factors. Recourse factors may be especially careful and prefer clients who are financially stable (which very small clients needing financing usually are not), and/or who have a large number of customers or very stable customers which tends to limit risk. If an invoice isn't paid and goes to recourse, the client must be able to make good on the loss or the recourse factor will lose money. If a recourse factor ends up with bad invoices from a client who can't make good on them, the recourse nature of the relationship does the factor little good and money can be lost.

When a business owner decides to factor, he should factor only those customers whom he is absolutely certain will pay in a dependable manner. A common mistake with clients new to factoring is to want to factor poor-paying or non-paying customers. However, this is one of the worst things that can be done. Why?

1) Factors' discount rates are usually based on the length of time a customer takes to pay. The longer an invoice is unpaid, the higher the discount. The discount for an invoice that is unpaid after 90 days will be far higher than that for an invoice paid within 30 days.

2) When recourse occurs, the client must reimburse the factor for the amount advanced plus the discount; thus, factoring non-paying customers may temporarily help the client's cash flow problem. But a few months later when recourse kicks in, the client will have a greater problem than he did when he factored the non-paying customer's invoice. In the long run, the client has harmed his cash flow more than helped it. If a client has poor paying customers, a collection agency is the best resource, not a factor.

3) A bank makes money on interest as a loan is repaid. A factor makes money on discounts generated as the client makes money. The more a client's business grows and he factors his invoices, the more the factor makes. Hence a client and factor are business allies. If a non-paying customer harms a business, this will in turn harm a recourse factor because the client's cash position is weakened. A non-recourse factor is simply out the money. In any case, everyone's better off to factor good paying customers who pay from about two weeks to two months (30 to 45 days is best) and pay dependably.

Types of Businesses
Which Benefit from Factoring

What types of businesses can benefit from factoring? The list is surprisingly long and can include industries which you probably don't even know exist. Let's review the kinds of companies who can benefit from factoring and the kinds of customers they need to have.

Any company, whether starting out, in a growth phase, or mature in years, needs good cash flow. If a company's cash flow is good and always has enough to pay its bills, meet payroll and taxes, and can expand to its desired size unaided, factoring isn't necessary. However, if improved cash flow is needed, factoring can be one of the best ways to get it.

A company considering factoring will need to have at least one customer whose invoices can be factored. Young companies a few months to a few years old, as long as they have good receivables, are often good candidates. Their customers need to be other businesses or government bodies such as school districts and city, county, state or federal branches whose receivables are assignable. The receivables should be with dependable, good-paying customers who simply take longer to pay than the client can wait.

Customers who are very large corporations often make their vendors wait 60 or more days to pay as part of the terms for doing business with them. These customers are usually good to factor. Companies that sell strictly to consumers won't factor those receivables; however, if a company invoices both the general public as well as businesses or government, the latter can be factored. A good strategy to improve a company's cash flow is to accept credit cards from consumer customers and government branches who pay that way, and factor their invoices to business and other government customers. They get paid immediately (for a small price) either way.

The best customers to factor are creditworthy, solid firms who regularly take approximately two weeks to two months to pay. Accounts which fall outside of this window may not be cost effective to factor.

The Cost of Factoring

A moment ago we spoke of an 80% advance rate and a 5% discount fee. These percentages will vary a great deal depending on several things.

The first consideration in establishing a factoring rate is to assess the stability of the customer – the business or government body that will pay the invoice. The more stable and dependable the customer is, generally the better the rate a factor can offer. If the customers are financially sound government bodies, Fortune 500 companies and/or businesses with a high credit rating, the factor's risk of not getting paid is considerably less. If a client sells only to "Mom & Pop" companies who operate on a shoestring, to companies with a history of not paying their bills in a timely manner (or at all), or to those who are in financial trouble, the factor is more likely to charge higher rates, give lower advances or both, or turn down the customer or client outright.

Another consideration in determining rates is in assessing the stability of the client's business, especially for recourse factors. Are company or personal assets sufficient to cover bad invoices? How long has the company been in business, how well does the owner know her business, and how well does she manage her company? How many bad debts has she had? How long do her customers typically take to pay?

Further, what is the character of the business owner as gleaned from a personal as well as business credit report? Are there numerous judgments, tax liens, criminal history, collection agency write-offs, or other public records indicating the person is not an upstanding citizen, a person of integrity, or is a person who is simply unable to manage money responsibly? Did she tell you there are no judgments or liens outstanding against her, but the credit report indicates otherwise? In short, was the person honest with you? These are issues the factor must consider before even accepting a client, let alone determining rates for her.

Further, the volume of receivables to factor monthly, the length of time one wishes to factor and the size of the individual invoices to factor all play a part in determining rates. Generally, the larger the volume factored each month – spread among creditworthy customers in balanced concentrations, with a stable payment history and reasonably-sized individual invoices – the better the rates will be.

Why? Lower risk and lower administrative cost to the factor make the client more attractive. If a business "spot" factors (factors only once or just an occasional invoice here and there), it will take as much time to set up the account, perform the due diligence, and manage the account as it does if one factors a steady stream of invoices, week in and week out, over a span of several months or years. The factor won't make as much in discounts from spot factoring and thus may charge more. Some factors require clients to factor a certain volume of invoices for a certain period of time. Rates are then calculated on this basis.

The size of invoices also can make a difference. Suppose Business A wants to factor $30,000 a month. This total is made up of 3 invoices of $10,000 each between 3 different customers. Business B also wants to factor $30,000 a month but his invoices are for $100 each between 300 different customers. It doesn't take a rocket scientist to realize that the time involved for the factor to process the invoices for Business B will be much longer, and thus more expensive, than those for Business A.

Obviously, a business owner wants a factor who will agree not only to rates he can handle, but one who will take on the size and kind of customers he has. Therefore, it's almost impossible to say what a factor will charge in discounts and provide in advances. Each client must be considered unique, with rate and advance calculations based on each situation. However, there are some general standards that are common across the industry.

Unless a business is in the medical, construction, or transportation (specifically trucking) industry, factoring advances for clients with stable customers will typically fall in the 75 to 90% range. If customers have tenuous credit histories, the advances may drop to between 40 to 60% if they are approved at all. If customers are exceptionally strong or the client has been factoring for some time, advances may enter the 85% or even 90's range. It's rare for them to go much higher than low to mid-90's. Overall, 75% to 85% is a good rule of thumb for most receivables.

Trucking is an industry that is heavily factored today, and as a result the rates are more competitive among trucking factors. It's not unusual to see advances well into the low to even high 90's, with discounts quite low and often fixed (i.e. they don't increase as time passes, but are the same no matter how long an invoice takes to pay).

Outside of trucking receivables, however, the discount will usually depend on how long the invoice takes to pay; consequently, rates can be all over the playing field. Some factor's discounts are based on the first 30 days the invoice is out. Then they increase the rates every 15 days thereafter. For example, a factor might charge 5% for the first 30 days and an extra 2% for each 15 days after that. If an invoice is out for 31 to 45 days the discount becomes 7%. If it's out 46 to 60 days, it's 9%; and, if it takes 61 to 75 days to pay, it becomes 11% and so on. This helps illustrate why companies don't want to factor invoices that take a very long time to pay as they can become quite expensive. On the other hand, they also wouldn't want to factor an invoice that will only be out a few days: the discount wouldn't usually be cost-effective for such a short wait.

Calculating the discount can be done with a variety of combinations. Some factors base it starting with the first 30 days, some on the first 15, some on the first 10, others on the first 7, and some on just one day. Some increment the times thereafter every 30 days, some every 15, some every 10, some every 7, some every day, with various percentage rates for each of these. Each factor has his or her own way of calculating discounts; some are very flexible and will work with the client to reach an agreeable rate. Others are fairly strict about rates and offer discounts based on charts or fixed time tables on a "take it or leave it" basis. Both the factor and client have overhead expenses and desired profit margins, so negotiating fees must be done with respect for the needs of both parties.

It is not uncommon to see factors outside of trucking who advertise rates on the internet that are extremely low, with advances that are extremely high. You might find companies who say they give 100% advances, or charge 1-2% rates (or less). As the old saying goes, if it sounds too good to be true it probably is.

How can a company give a 100% advance and charge a discount (that is, make any money)? Actually they're deducting the discount (whatever it is) from the 100% advance, which means it's not a true 100% cash advance. As to the discounts, read their words carefully: are the *total* discounts 1-2% or less, or do they *start* there, and increase as time passes (which is the norm)?

While marketing needs to make them sound attractive, factors who advertise extremely low "teaser" rates have the same expenses and profitability requirements that everyone else does. The teaser rates are just to grab attention; they make up their other costs with hidden fees that aren't advertised, and are buried in the fine print of their contracts. Let the buyer beware.

It's not uncommon for many business owners, and especially accountants, to find normal factoring rates (when all the costs are included) compared to standard loans to be rather shocking. "After all," they reason, "if I borrowed money from a bank at 5% a month, that works out to an Annual Percentage Rate of 60%! That's outrageous!" There are several answers to such a reaction, and each must be considered carefully.

First, if a business can get a bank loan, they are usually better off to do so. But if one is unable to get a loan, the interest rate at which loans are made becomes moot. Moreover, remember that factoring is not a loan; it's the purchase of accounts receivable. A business is not borrowing money at an interest rate: it is selling an asset at a discount for cash and receiving a service. Factoring is generally comparable to 2% net 10 rates many businesses routinely offer customers (2% discount if paid in 10 days). People don't annualize a 2% net 10 discount because it's a discount deducted from the invoice amount – not a loan. Thus, comparing factoring rates to interest on bank loans is the proverbial comparison of apples to oranges.

Also, if someone borrows, say $500,000 from a bank, they typically must pay it back on a monthly basis for a period of several years. This is where the familiar annualized percentage interest rates occur. However, if a small business owner factors a month's worth of receivables that are, say, $25,000, the discount they're going to pay will be based only on the period of time the invoice is outstanding – usually a month, not a whole year. They may not factor that amount every month, or may not factor at all some months; therefore you can't annualize a factoring discount quite as simply or accurately as a loan with required monthly payments. While in truth factoring is generally more expensive than a bank loan (*if* a business can get one), annualizing discount amounts can be rather misleading.

It is helpful for a business owner selling his receivables to consider the cost of factoring as an operating expense needed to run the business, rather than interest on a loan. Just as a business can't exist without office or shop space, lights, phone, and employees, businesses also can't exist without adequate cash flow. Business owners don't think twice about paying rent, utilities, phone bills and payroll. If factoring is what it takes to get cash flow under control, they should consider the cost of factoring as part of the normal costs of running their business.

In time, some will eventually have enough cash on hand so as not to need factoring any more, and dispense with it. Others find the conveniences and other services factoring provides to be well worth the cost, and choose to factor over the long term and make it a standard way of doing business.

Calculating Profits

How can you calculate whether factoring will improve one's bottom line? Below is a simplified Income Statement to determine if factoring will help.

Chart 2-1: Sample Income Statement XYZ Manufacturing Company				
	Before Factoring		With Factoring	
Gross Revenues	100,000		200,000	
Cost of Goods Sold	60,000	60%	120,000	60%
Gross Profits	40,000	40%	80,000	40%
Less:				
Variable Expenses	15,000	15%	30,000	15%
Fixed Expenses	20,000	20%	20,000	10%
Overhead	35,000	35%	50,000	25%
Cost of Factoring	0		5,000	
Total Expenses	35,000	35%	55,000	28%
Net Profit	5,000	5%	25,000	13%

Study this statement (the Cost of Factoring is based on $100,000 worth of invoices at 5%). Then insert a real company's figures, and see if factoring can significantly improve the bottom line. In order to estimate what Gross Revenues might be with factoring, ask: "How much could this company make if it had an unlimited supply of cash on hand?" Perhaps it could double revenues as XYZ has in the example; perhaps they would be less, perhaps more. At any rate, run the numbers and see if factoring makes sense. If it does, you might ask: "Can this business afford *not* to factor?"

Other Services Factors Offer

Factors can quickly run credit checks on prospective customers, saving the potential disaster of unknowingly accepting a customer who might never pay. Most small business owners don't have the know-how or inclination to check customers' credit reports themselves, but jump at the idea of a factor doing it for them.

Many factors take over a business' billing responsibilities or even management of all their accounts receivable. This enables the owner of a small business to concentrate on growth, and saves a larger company the expense of such a department. Factors commonly verify invoices before making advances, which provides a built-in means of quality control and speeds up customer payments. Because factors normally report payment histories to credit agencies (and receive a lower rate on their cost of credit reports for doing so), some customers pay factors more quickly than vendors.

Many businesses offer discount terms to companies to pay quickly. If a business offers 2% net 10, or a 2% discount if a customer pays in 10 days, it's already discounting for quicker cash. Factoring can make such discounts unnecessary and cost about the same or even less, while offering many more benefits.

Especially for smaller and younger companies, factors can be a source of business leads, networking connections, and vendor sources. As an interested third party, often with years of business experience, the factor can make observations and suggestions to enhance the daily operations of a business, trim costs, and increase income.

As you can see, factors provide a great deal more than simply improved cash flow. They bring services and expertise from which nearly any business, and certainly a young and growing business, can benefit.

3

What I've Learned about the Factoring Industry

The First Lessons

Costs. If you intend to become a factor as a supplement to your regular income and want to have only one or two clients at a time, your startup costs will be minimal – especially if you already have the office equipment mentioned below. However, if you plan to make factoring your full-time business, your first consideration is start-up costs.

Regardless of the number of clients you expect, you'll want a computer with a high speed internet connection and a phone; starting with just a computer and cell phone is fine. Then there's office space if you don't work at home, office furniture, business license, office supplies and the like. You should carefully think through what you really need and keep overhead to a minimum. My rule of thumb: don't buy something until you experience the need for it at least three times; never buy ahead of time what you only *think* you will need.

Another expense you must also keep in mind is marketing. There are many ways to market your service and an entire chapter – and other books – are dedicated to this (see "Marketing: How to Find Clients"). If you are factoring part-time and want just one or two clients, marketing may be easy: you very likely know a few small business owners who can benefit from your service. However if you plan to factor more than lightly, you should allocate enough of your operating budget for marketing efforts that will work effectively, especially to start.

Expect to spend some time and money to launch your factoring service. If factoring will be your full-time work, you need to look at several aspects of the business you might not have considered. Book 2 in this series, *Fundamentals for Factors: How You Can Make Large Returns in Small Receivables* is written to help those contemplating becoming a small factor. That book looks at the subject from several standpoints: financial, time availability, tolerance for risk, family considerations, and more. Several questions are posed to help the reader "look" before "leaping" and decide if this is a wise move for his or her circumstances – *before* a dime is invested in receivables.

If your factoring business will be full-time, be sure you have enough socked away – both to live on and with which to run your business – to carry you for at least two years. It also helps enormously to have a spouse with an income to help in the short run. I would not have made it if this were not true in my case. Several other small factors I've known have said the same thing; they couldn't have stayed in business when their companies were young without the income from their spouse's job. If you don't have this security for at least a year or more (not to mention your spouse's and/or other family members' support), you'll have a tough row to hoe as a full-time factor.

It may take anywhere from six months to two years to really get your factoring business off the ground and profitable. Like anything worthwhile, expect there to be moments of discouragement and even a few times when you feel like throwing in the towel. You must know your tolerance for such dips in the road, and determine ahead of time you will hang in there when they come.

Start Gradually. I started with the impression that if I worked full-time, making $100,000 a year is not only possible but fairly easy in this business. My experience has been that it is possible after you have been at it a while; but starting full-time is anything but easy, especially the first year. Therefore, for many people starting gradually is not a bad idea.

When I was just starting as a factoring broker, the success stories I heard of other newcomers making numerous deals their first month or two, left me feeling like a failure and more discouraged than hopeful. I had worked extremely hard for several months and had nothing to show for it. It took close to a year before things clicked. For me, that started when I began factoring small, local deals in addition to operating as a broker. After working in the business part-time for six months and then full-time for another six months, I had made less than $300 brokering (all of which came in about the ninth month – not exactly what I expected). Two other brokers I knew made zero the first year. However, after factoring small local deals for about three months, I had grossed $3,000 with far less effort than I spent brokering and it steadily improved from there.

If you have a related business and/or financial background, experience in a specific factorable industry, and excellent contacts, you will have a far easier task than if you don't. Whom you know is at least as important as what you know in this business.

The Stigma of Factoring. Unfortunately you will find that some people familiar with factoring view it negatively and factoring does not have the stellar image we might wish. A bank manager once told me his colleagues consider factors to be "the used car salesmen of the financial world." Isn't that inspiring?

Regrettably, the people who often could be good sources of leads – accountants, bankers, attorneys – are too often the ones with negative opinions about factors. Almost predictably, those who view it negatively are almost always the ones who don't really understand factoring or have very limited experience with it. Not all such professionals are against factoring, but several either look down their noses at it or just don't mention it to clients who would benefit.

There is a need to re-educate people who think factoring is only a last-gasp effort to save a sinking ship. Most of the businesses that factor today do it because they are growing, not because they are dying, and because traditional loans are not available. This needs to be impressed on everyone you talk to, both the uninformed as well as the misinformed.

Full/Part Time. If you wish to factor only a small, limited number of clients as a means of supplemental investment or retirement income, factoring small receivables can be quite rewarding. As discussed in *Fundamentals for Factors,* part-time factoring can be a great move for investors with a regular job, retirees, and those wanting to create another income stream as an add-on to their current business.

In my case, after attempting to do the business part-time I had more success working it full-time. I found most business people you need to contact work regular business hours, and you usually can't prospect successfully on evenings and weekends. It's hard enough doing that during regular working hours. I used various marketing methods that could be done at odd times, but eventually I had to talk with these people during normal working hours.

You can get started while you do something else, but be aware that factoring takes time, energy and focus. Unless you keep your client load intentionally small, it can be tough to split a busy factoring business with another demanding job.

Why Big Factors Don't Want Small Deals

One of the first lessons brokers and prospective factoring clients learn is that factors have minimums. That is, most say, "I don't want deals that are less than $10,000 or $25,000 or $100,000 per month." This very important fact not only tells you where you can and can't take clients as a broker; it creates your niche as a small factor.

Some larger factors say they have "no" minimums or "low" minimums, often putting $5,000 or $10,000 as the lowest they'll accept. However, when presented with bona fide prospects with monthly volumes under $10,000 they usually turn them away because they will not make enough with such clients (see Chart 2 below). Why then do they claim to accept such deals when in fact they reject those that come along? They do this to attract more business, particularly if a smaller "borderline" prospect appears to be ready to grow rapidly. If other factors know you really will accept such small clients they turn away, these factors can be a source of referrals.

Many of the deals you'll find, especially at a local level when you start, are small. When you're new at this game, these are best because your inexperience will be evident to bigger companies with bigger needs. However, if you find a young, growing company with a struggling business owner, you may form a quick camaraderie with such a person because you're both in a similar situation.

Sadly, larger factors with $25,000 or higher minimums put factoring out of the reach of many of these very small companies. These potential clients could benefit from factoring but can't get it (nor bank loans, nor anything else). The reason big factors don't want them is not because they're selfish or mean-spirited; it's simple economics. Big factors, by virtue of the volume they do, must pay staff to find new business, manage accounts, and run the operation. This labor isn't cheap. Each factor's minimum represents what they must make to break even to factor an account. Factoring a client below their minimum causes them to lose money. How?

Suppose a factor takes on an account with $5,000 in invoices per month. If these invoices produce a 5% discount, the factor makes $250. However, out of that $250, staff costs to service the account may be $150. Add to this the factor's cost of money, broker's commission, taxes, overhead, other operating expenses, and they might break even – or even lose money. They're better off spending their staff resources on $50,000 to $2,000,000 accounts that will be worth their time and investment.

Chart 3-1 is a simplified explanation of factors' expenses, which vary according to their size and overhead costs.

Chart 3-1: Break Even Points			
Monthly Expenses	Beginning Factor	Small Factor	Larger Factor
Rent	0	500	2,000
Phone/Utilities	50	500	3,000
Operat'g Expenses, Taxes	250	1,000	15,000
Payroll	700	6,000	30,000
Total	1,000	8,000	50,000
Above expenses = 5% of:	20,000	$160,000	1,000,000
	Monthly invoice volume needed to break even (based on 5% avg. discounts)		
Typical number of clients:	4	20	50
Avg. monthly volume needed per client	$5,000	$8,000	$20,000

As you can see, each factor has monthly expenses (overhead) which must be covered by their business income (factoring discounts received). In order to make this amount, the factors must have sufficient monthly invoice volume which will produce income of at least the size needed to break even. Divide the monthly invoice volume by the number of clients each factor has and you have the average monthly volume each factor needs per client to break even.

Why You and I
DO Want Small Deals

One reason you don't want to bother brokering small deals is that you probably can't, at least to bigger factors! Bigger factors don't want small deals. Another is simple: your commission from a small factor who'll accept the deal is going to be very small.

For example, say a factor makes a 5% discount and pays you a 15% brokering commission (i.e. 15% of his discount; 10-15% is standard[1]). On a $1,000 invoice the factor makes $50 then pays

---

[1] Factors who pay more than 15% may not be able to offer competitive rates if a client is seriously shopping for and comparing costs.

your 15% commission of $7.50. How much have you invested in time, effort, and expenses to make that $7.50? Too much. If you're going to broker, go after bigger accounts of at least $20,000 or more; it's the only way to make money – as a broker (see Chart 3).

Chart 3-2: Referring Small Transactions					
Invoice Size	80% Advance	Factor's Discnt	Factor's Gross Inc.	15% Bkr's Comm.	Factor's Net Inc.
1,000	800	5%	50	7.50	42.50
5,000	4,000	5%	250	37.50	212.50
10,000	8,000	5%	500	75.00	425.00
20,000	16,000	5%	1,000	150.00	850.00
50,000	40,000	5%	2,500	375.00	2,125.00

However, as a small factor, going after smaller accounts is a different story. Factoring $5,000 worth of invoices generates $250 every month. Once this account and a number of others like it are set up, it becomes more valuable for you. Why? You don't have the staff and overhead to pay that the larger factors do, nor do you pay a broker's commission. This is money going into your pocket, not to employees. The only person you have to pay is you; and starting your factoring business this way is a good way to begin (see Chart 4). Furthermore, your risk is limited to the $4,000 advance ($5,000 x 80%). If one such loss occurs you should be able to recover.

Chart 3-3: Factoring Small Transactions					
Invoice Size	80% Advance	Factor's Discnt	Factor's Gross Inc.	0% Bkr's Comm.	Factor's Net Inc.
1,000	800	5%	50	0	50
5,000	4,000	5%	250	0	250
10,000	8,000	5%	500	0	500
20,000	16,000	5%	1,000	0	1,000
50,000	40,000	5%	2,500	0	2,500

What about using brokers yourself to obtain small deals? It's good to have a broker bring you a few deals to get started; after that, obtaining new clients from word-of-mouth and your own marketing efforts are very rewarding. On the other hand, if marketing isn't your forte, accepting broker referrals can be preferable. You don't pay brokers until their referred clients have generated income for you. This has worked well for me over the years, and even now nearly half of my active clients are referred by brokers.

Brokers just don't make much on very small invoices as you can see in Chart 3 above. Assuming a 5% factoring discount, you will make more factoring a $5,000 invoice ($250) than you will referring a $20,000 invoice even if you make a 15% commission ($150). A 10% commission is common, and that would only equal a $100 commission. Thus you can realistically make 2½ times as much factoring $5,000 as you would referring $20,000. However, you must always remember the flip side: as a broker, you have no funds at risk. As a factor, you do.

One of your greatest advantages as a small factor – and one of the most enjoyable aspects of factoring over brokering – is the fact that you're the boss! If you've referred deals to larger factors, you have no doubt experienced the frustrations of slow response time, an unwillingness to factor a prospect you find promising, rates or advances the client doesn't find appealing, and the sense that the factor's only in it to make a buck and protect him/herself. Because you're in the trenches with your small client and also making the funding decisions, you can act extremely quickly to set rates, negotiate terms and close a deal you otherwise might lose if it were in the hands of someone else.

Because you don't have the bureaucratic hassles of someone looking over your shoulder, a committee who must make a decision, or a mile of red tape to work around, you can fund someone based on as much due diligence as you think you need, or simply a gut feeling. (However, you also live with the consequences!) If snags develop, you rely on your own creativity to overcome them. This can be an exciting part of your business, but one you must treat with great respect, because it can both make and break you as a factor.

Used well, your flexibility can land you many new accounts, earn you good money, and make you a hero in the eyes of clients who otherwise would be turned down – and possibly go out of business. Used poorly, *you* can be out of business very quickly with some painful losses and perhaps nasty debts that are difficult to repay.

The other reason you want small clients is quite logical: as they grow, so do you. There is a strong possibility that a client's business will grow because of factoring. An account that starts factoring $2,000 a month can grow to $4,000 in three months, to $10,000 in six months, to $25,000 in a year, to $75,000 or more in a couple years. Handled carefully, you will profit handsomely from and with a client like this and grow right along with him. Best of all, because you've gained this client's trust and loyalty, he will stay with or return to you when he is bigger and needs a factor on a regular or occasional basis for those $100,000 to $500,000 receivables.

There are very few large factors who will take on clients with monthly volumes of $3,000 or $4,000. Lucky for you and me!

Small Numbers Add Up

How much money can you make factoring small deals? It depends on how much money you have with which to factor and your rates; more on these in later chapters. It's not hard to calculate...it's simply a matter of small numbers adding up. If you factor four clients at an average of $5,000 each per month and charge an average discount of 5% on each one, your gross profit is $1,000. Factoring ten clients at $5,000 per month each you'll make $2,500. Double the number of clients to twenty and you make $5,000. Double these twenty clients' average monthly volume to $10,000 and you're making $10,000.

That's not a bad monthly income for a one-person business. Meanwhile, when you run across accounts larger than those you can or want to factor yourself – and you will – participate with another factor or refer them. Add several hundred if not a few thousand dollars in broker commissions to your factoring discounts, and you have a very nice income indeed.

Just remember it takes a while to build up to these "small" numbers. Rome wasn't built in a day.

4

Bits of Wisdom for the Small Factor

Why You're in the Factoring Business

Let's get something clear from the beginning: why do you want to be in the factoring business? The quick response for many people is "to make money." Fair enough. But if that's the only answer you have, you're missing the boat and probably will be either less than successful or not have many friends as you grow your wealth from factoring.

The overriding reason to be in the factoring business is to help your clients. If your only purpose is the money you make, your clients will sense this quickly or eventually learn it, and their trust in you will become shrouded. But if you make it clear by everything you say and do that your first and major concern is the success of their company, you will earn devoted and loyal clients, even friends, for years. Many will more than gladly give you referrals and recommendations. My approach with clients is, rather openly, "I'm here, first and foremost, to help with your cash flow and make your business what you want it to be. If I can make a good living this way, then so much the better." You'll need to prove this over and over.

This is not to say that you should help clients at the expense of your own financial security; no one expects that. Besides, if you take on an account you shouldn't just because you want to help someone, you may be out of business yourself in no time. The point is this: who's first on your list of priorities? If it's not the client, you will have far fewer.

Factor Small Deals, Refer Big Ones

Because most bigger factors don't want small deals, a niche is created which you, the small factor, can fill nicely. Filling this niche is the key to growing your factoring business, and leads to the recurrent theme of this book – and to the motto of the small factor. Repeat it over and over; make it your mind set: "Factor small deals, refer big ones. Factor small deals, refer big ones...."

Factoring small invoices with very small companies is the best way to learn first-hand what factoring involves and requires. By being a factor for small accounts, you'll be a much better broker for big ones. When you've gone through the set-up procedures, done background checks, made verification calls, paid advances, kept the necessary paperwork, called slow paying customers, received customers' payments, paid the rebates and done everything else necessary, you'll know exactly what larger factors need and want, and why. You'll be a favorite referral source when you bring them the six- and seven-figure deals with all the i's dotted and t's crossed, because you think like they do and will be able to help them close larger deals more easily and quickly.

To be a successful small factor, you'll need to set some standards as to

- the maximum size of invoice you will factor
- how much total monthly volume you'll do
- how much monthly volume you'll do with a specific client and/or customer
- how much total money you'll have invested with a specific client and/or customer, and
- at what point you prefer referring instead of factoring

To a large degree, these selections will depend on 1) how much money you have to factor; 2) the level of risk you can tolerate, i.e. how much money you can afford to lose at a given time; and 3) the time you wish to devote to factoring.

Decide the maximum advance you will give a new client to start, and the average monthly amount you wish to factor with a client. If someone wants to start with more than your limit, you may simply refer him. However, if he is able to start small and build up to some larger amount, and it's an account you want to keep rather than refer, find another small factor with whom to participate. This way, not only will you keep in close contact with a loyal client, you'll make more income by splitting a factoring discount and risk than by getting only a broker's commission.

For example: a client factors $5,000 a month. At 5%, you make $250 as her factor. Her business grows and she wants to factor $10,000 a month. Now you make $500 as the factor. She continues to grow until she wants to factor $20,000 a month. Not wanting that much invested in a single client or not having enough money to factor her now, you could refer the account and make a 15% commission ($150). This is less than you made when she started factoring; however, you could now participate with her. You and a participant would each contribute half the advance payment and you would continue to make $500. (See Chart 5.)

Chart 4-1: Participating in Small Transactions					
Invoice Size	80% Advance	Half of 80% Advance	5% Factor's Discount	0% Broker's Comm.	Half of Factor's Discount
5,000	4,000	2,000	250	0	125
10,000	8,000	4,000	500	0	250
20,000	16,000	8,000	1,000	0	500

Participations can be good arrangement for the small factor. They can also be better for the client-factor relationship and trust. Such clients will usually rather stay with you than begin a relationship with a new, unknown factor who might operate differently. Further, the client need not be aware you are participating with another factor, as all the paperwork continues to go through your books, and the outside funds you're using are transparent to her.

Clearly, it's beneficial to have other factors you know and trust with whom to participate. Keep in touch with other brokers and small factors you meet at conventions, seminars, networking meetings, etc. whom you like, trust, and with whom you want to do business. It can pay handsomely for you both.

Keep It Local

As a general rule when starting out, it's not a bad idea to factor businesses in your local area. A "local area" in Montana can be geographically a lot larger than one in New York City; but the point is, deal with people you can meet face-to-face on a regular basis. This will provide an ample number of clients, as well as some built-in safeguards.

You'll Know Your Client Better. When you see where a client works and/or lives, you quickly get a feel for his personality, the kind of business he runs, his strengths and weaknesses as a business person, perhaps his family demands and many other worthwhile facts. You'll see for yourself how (un)sophisticated his bookkeeping is and (un)organized his office space may be. You're more likely to be familiar with his customers and can learn first-hand what his relations with customers are. In a word, you can enter your client's world and see how to best help him, as well as be aware of potential or actual problems that may impact your investment.

Trust. Mutual trust can be built more quickly. As the chapter "Reducing Your Risk" mentions, trust is the name of the factoring game. Your client is trusting you with some very private and very important information, which is the lifeblood of his business: receivables. From his perspective he is trusting you with his money. You can earn his trust more quickly in person when he sees how you operate. You can demonstrate that you sincerely are there to help his business by your attitude and efforts to do what's best for him and also prudent for you. Likewise, you can get a reading of his trustworthiness when you deal personally with a client regularly, tour his facility, see what his office looks like (messy or neat as a pin), meet his employees or spouse, have lunch occasionally, and so on.

Problems. Should a problem arise (say a customer disputes a charge), you can discuss it immediately and get things cleared up right away. If you want to make a change in your factoring methods or if your client doesn't understand something, you can discuss the matter with a quick, local phone call or work it out over a cup of coffee. Finally, in a worst case scenario, if your customer or client doesn't pay, you know where the client lives and works and how to find him. If he's disappeared, you'll know that a lot sooner if his office is 3 miles away than if it's 3,000 miles away.

Referrals. People are more likely to do business with people they know, like, and trust, than with a stranger. Being in a community where you are known automatically creates a circle of influence by virtue of people you know, and people they know. What's more, when local clients know you personally and trust you, and you've proven to be an asset to their companies, your name will get around as being someone good with whom to do business. People will call hoping you can help them like you helped their friends; and this will, in turn, benefit your business in every way. This can enable you to trim your advertising budget to a point where you only work from referrals.

In short, keep your factoring clients local when you start. It's much easier and will enable you to be successful more quickly. It will also lead to contacts with bigger clients whom you can refer for nice commissions.

If you run across small clients in other areas and want to fund only local clients, see if there's a colleague there who will factor them. They'll appreciate the referral and may return the favor. Alternately, the factor in that area may agree to participate with you. Let the local factor make the contacts, do the underwriting, record keeping, etc., while you make nice participation income for simply providing half the funds. Just be sure you trust the other factor, are comfortable with his due diligence and method of operating, get regular reports of the account and stay in touch. If you don't do the record keeping and control the cash flow, you have little or no control over the account so you must only work with participants you completely trust. To lessen your risk, you may want to participate only as the "recording" factor (see the chapter "Participation").

As time goes by and your business grows, you may certainly choose to increase your client base and expand your geographical reach to a bigger region or go national. But starting locally is often a good idea.

Legal Assistance

Small factors frequently need the services of a skilled, competent business attorney. While legal expenses can be steep for any new business, failure to obtain professional legal advice can be far more costly in the long run. To find one in your area, contact the nearest State Bar referral service or ask other business owners who their business attorney is. Contact a few of the lawyers to learn their fields of expertise, with which issues they can and cannot help you, and their rates. You'll need to feel confident that your hard-earned money is being spent on competent, valuable legal advice and assistance, so choose your lawyer carefully. Members of the International Factoring Association (IFA) have access to a list of attorneys who specialize in factoring.

Remember that attorneys charge by the hour, and once you have retained an attorney, the clock starts ticking the minute he or she picks up the phone, starts writing a letter, or begins legal research for you. In addition to hourly fees, attorneys charge for faxes, long distance calls, copies, and every little item they can track. Depending on your area and the demand for the lawyer's services, expect to pay at least $175 to $300 per hour. If your attorney charges $200 an hour, your bill for a 15-minute phone call will be $50. If you have frequent or extensive legal work done, this professional cost can be one of your larger budget expenses.

An attorney who specializes in factoring law, and law for smaller factors in particular, is Mr. David Jencks of Jencks & Jencks, P.C., of Madison, South Dakota. He has created legal contracts and other documents written especially with small factors and their clients in mind, which are available through www.DashPointPublishing.com. Mr. Jencks will be happy to assist you with legal questions you have as you establish and continue your factoring business. His website is www.jenckslaw.com.

Start Small and
Don't Take on Too Much

The first few months you factor, you are vulnerable to mistakes and losses by virtue of your inexperience. You will learn from every transaction and every client. Common sense says to learn from those smallest in volume. The first account I factored was a one-person carpet cleaning company that factored less than $2,000 a month and submitted around seven invoices per week – each worth from $60 to $80. This client was a big factor's nightmare: a jillion little invoices, piles of paperwork and mailing, lots of verification calls, and a small discount ($2,000 x 5%) of $100 a month. Then subtract the cost of money, phone calls, consultant commission, and I wasn't paid much for my efforts. But what experience!

However, I couldn't have asked for a better first client. He had factored with a large factor who nearly put him out of business (never gave him reports, didn't pay several rebates, didn't keep in touch with him, and eventually closed their local office). He was probably nothing but a headache for them and I was surprised they accepted him in the first place. He needed to factor for both cash flow and structure (his records were literally filed in a shoe box). But we were a good match. He knew how factoring worked and was patient as I learned the ropes. The dollar amounts weren't critical if either of us made mistakes...which we did. He factored several invoices to start for which he honestly didn't realize he had already received payment from the customer! Clearing that up was a learning experience for both of us.

Working with him gave me confidence to do other deals. Learning with small clients helps you streamline the factoring process and prepares you for the larger accounts as they arise. After a few months of factoring small clients, you are able to take on more and bigger ones because you've gotten some bugs worked out of your system – and you are able to present a more professional appearance.

To begin with, don't take on more clients than you can handle either in terms of dollar totals or paper work. If you take on clients that push your financial limits, having one go bad on you early can knock you out of business in a hurry. You will be learning from the first few clients you factor; and you are most vulnerable at this time to taking on a client and/or customer who is a bad risk. Better to lose small amounts on small accounts.

Further, there is a lot of paper work involved in factoring. This manual provides the record keeping that works for me and which should for you as well. However, no matter how simple a system is, you'll want to customize it to your own needs and preferences. It will take a while to get the hang of what you're doing, work out the kinks and streamline your records. Again, learning the ropes is best done with small accounts and small volumes. Feed yourself in small spoonfuls while you're learning to eat.

So start small, be willing to take clients too small for anyone else at first, and learn as you grow. It's better to goof on a client with $100 invoices than one with invoices of $10,000, or $100,000 – even if you can afford to factor the larger ones.

Don't Get Greedy

One of the first things you will realize when you start factoring is how much more money you can make factoring larger invoices. As we saw in Chart 3, with a 5% rate you will make $50 on a $1,000 invoice, $500 on a $10,000 invoice, and $1,000 on a $20,000 invoice. Those increasing numbers can make a rookie factor greedy. At this point you must be careful.

The second client I took on lived out of state, agreed to excellent rates and wanted to factor significantly more than my first client. Due to my inexperience, I did inadequate due diligence and the account turned ugly. To make a long story short, I spent many long, frustrating hours over several months trying to recoup what was, at the time, a large portion of my factoring money. Worse, I had to pay interest on money I no longer had, I lost the potential income the funds would have generated and I spent even more money trying to recover these funds. It was a sobering experience that could have killed my factoring business almost as soon as it was born.

The "make your early mistakes with small invoices" rule rings loud and clear here. Yes, you can certainly make more on bigger invoices; but you can also LOSE more – a lot more! Losing a large amount of money can be more than a painful lesson; it can knock you out of the game altogether, especially early in your factoring career. On the other hand, losing small amounts as you learn the ropes is likely to teach you a painful lesson as to whom to factor and whom not to factor, but it will not put you out of business.

Even if you can survive a large loss early, it may take a long time to recover your initial factoring pool of funds. Doing so can only be done by obtaining more funds while you're still paying for what you lost. However, now you have less to work with and will therefore make less in discounts. You can make a lot of money factoring, but a single big mistake can take it all away in one fell swoop.

The lessons are obvious: be careful whom you factor and don't get greedy – ever! Factor small amounts to start with and build up the numbers gradually. You may take a chance once or twice and profit; but taking a big chance once too often will sting you. Many small factors start off well and do fine for about 4 or 5 years, but then take a big hit and go out of business. Even experienced, successful factors suffer serious losses, and it can happen to rookies even more easily.

So run your business accordingly; spread your money around in small enough piles that if you lose any one or even two of them, the rest will keep you going and you will hardly feel a ripple. It's the old "don't put all your eggs in one basket" adage. That saying's been around a long time because the wisdom therein is true – especially for factors.

Part 2

The First Steps

5
Charting
Your Course

Form and Direction

Once you've determined becoming a factor is a good move for you and before you start getting your money on the street, there is one more important preliminary step: determine the form and direction your business will take. While you may not need to go to the effort of a full business plan (not a bad idea though especially if you have some serious funds to invest), you should at least jot down your goals and what you hope to accomplish before you spend a lot of time, money, and energy. Review these goals regularly (at least every quarter or so) and update them as conditions change.

The form and direction your business takes will depend on your life's circumstances and what you wish to do with your factoring service. These, in turn, determine the amount of money you need to earn and the capital you need to have. If you wish to use the money you make factoring as supplemental funds to enhance your present income, the amount needed may be different from what it would be if this is the sole means of support for a growing family.

To prepare a map that will guide you as you develop your factoring business, write down your answers to the questions that follow. Keep handy both your written answers and the copies for future use; and make a note in your tickler file to review and update this information at regular intervals.

The Plan for Your Factoring Business

1. What is the intended use of the income you will make from factoring?
   __ Investment income to build your portfolio and net worth.
   __ Supplement to pension/retirement/present income on which you live.
   __ Primary income from which you will support yourself and family.

2. On a monthly average, how much do you *need* to earn in order to meet the intended use of factoring income in Number 1?

   First year $_____   Yearly Total: $_____
   In 1 year $_____   Yearly Total: $_____
   In 2 years $_____   Yearly Total: $_____
   In 3 years $_____   Yearly Total: $_____
   In 5 years $_____   Yearly Total: $_____

3. On a monthly average, how much do you *want* to earn in order to meet the intended use of factoring income in Number 1?

   First year $_____   Yearly Total: $_____
   In 1 year $_____   Yearly Total: $_____
   In 2 years $_____   Yearly Total: $_____
   In 3 years $_____   Yearly Total: $_____
   In 5 years $_____   Yearly Total: $_____

4. In order to meet the amounts in Numbers 2 and 3, you need a specific amount of capital (factoring funds). Chart 6 (in the chapter "Money") indicates your income if your average gross discount on all your transactions is 5%. Remember you must subtract your cost of money, operating expenses and bad debts from your gross income. How much will you need to fund monthly advances in order to meet your needs and wants in Numbers 2 and 3 above? (Use Chart 6, columns 2, 3, and 6.)

   In 1 year $_____   In 3 years $_____
   In 2 years $_____   In 5 years $_____

5. List below the source and amount of funds you intend to use as working capital (factoring funds):

First year
Source _____   Amount $_____
Source _____   Amount $_____
Source _____   Amount $_____
Source _____   Amount $_____
                                     Total $_____

Second year
Source _____   Amount $_____
Source _____   Amount $_____
Source _____   Amount $_____
Source _____   Amount $_____
                                     Total $_____

Third year
Source _____   Amount $_____
Source _____   Amount $_____
Source _____   Amount $_____
Source _____   Amount $_____
                                     Total $_____

Fourth year
Source _____   Amount $_____
Source _____   Amount $_____
Source _____   Amount $_____
Source _____   Amount $_____
                                     Total $_____

Fifth year
Source _____   Amount $_____
Source _____   Amount $_____
Source _____   Amount $_____
Source _____   Amount $_____
                                     Total $_____

6. In order to meet the amounts in Numbers 2 and 3 above, which of the following do you intend to do?

__ Start small and remain small.

__ Start small and grow to a certain size.

__ Start small and grow as large as you can.

7 a. Do you wish to work alone throughout the course of your factoring service, or do you plan to have one or more people work the business with you?

__ Alone   __ 1 Other   __ More than 1 other

b. If you plan to have others work with you, how many do you plan to include?

_____

c. Approximately when will this person or persons begin?

_____

d. What roles will each of you play? _____

_____

e. Approximately how many hours per week will this person or persons work and how much will each be paid?

_____

_____

8 a. To start, do you plan to work from your home or an outside office?

_____

b. Do you intend to keep working from this location or eventually work elsewhere?

_____

9. List the office equipment you will use to provide your factoring service.

Equipment	Have	Need	*If Needed:* Approx. Cost	When to Obtain
_____	__	__	$_____	_____
_____	__	__	$_____	_____
_____	__	__	$_____	_____
_____	__	__	$_____	_____
_____	__	__	$_____	_____
_____	__	__	$_____	_____
_____	__	__	$_____	_____
_____	__	__	$_____	_____

Total $_____

10. What measurable means (e.g. number of active clients, monthly/yearly volume, monthly/yearly net or gross business income, personal income, etc.) will enable you to say "My factoring service is presently succeeding" at these intervals:

First year _____

_____

_____

In 1 year _____

_____

_____

In 2 years _____

_____

_____

In 3 years _____

_____

_____

In 5 years _____

_____

_____

6

Learning to Be a Factor

Since the original edition of this book was published in 1995, I have observed a steady and consistent presence of people who are interested in becoming factors. The fact that this book has been selling steadily since that year speaks to this interest.

A very common question has been and continues to be, "Where can I go to learn how to be a factor?" I am asked, "Are there college courses, online classes or training workshops I can attend?" As far as I know, a university degree in factoring is not offered anywhere, nor are classes on the subject offered in university or college curricula. However, numerous resources do exist that can teach you how to be a factor.

Since finding these resources can take a bit of sleuthing, this chapter provides those of which I am aware. Like other resources in this book, those listed here will no doubt change considerably over time – some may disappear, new ones emerge, and existing ones evolve from the information provided below. But at the very least this gives you a starting point if you're looking for training in how to become a factor.

Get a Job

Ok, I know this will rub the wrong way with those of you having a strong entrepreneurial spirit. After all, the whole point of being a factor is that you're working for yourself, not someone else. But one way to learn the business is to go to work for a factoring company, at least for a while.

It's worth pointing out if you get a job with a factoring company with the intent of learning all you can and then leaving as soon as is expedient, you can expect most factors who know your plans won't be too eager to hire you. After all, from their point of view, they're simply training you to compete with them in the future. Would you want to hire someone if you knew that was their intent? Therefore let your integrity guide you as you consider and perhaps choose this route.

If you want to work for a factoring company, it helps to know that companies of all sizes have pretty much the same organizational structure to run the business. While large companies have multiple staff with each filling a specific task, and small companies have one or two people with multiple tasks, the tasks are the same.

Factoring companies need to have a **marketing** arm to bring in new business, an **underwriting** arm to perform due diligence and determine which prospects to accept or decline and which clients and customers to keep, and an **operations** arm to manage the daily flow of purchasing, tracking, and following up on invoices.

If you work for a larger factoring company, you are likely to work in one of these three divisions. You will learn the ins and outs of your particular job and division, but you'll only have general exposure to what the other divisions do.

For example, if you work as a Business Development Officer in marketing, you'll hone your marketing skills, learn which types of marketing work and which don't, establish contacts among referral sources, and in general learn how to bring in new business. But once that new business is booked, your job is to move on and find other new business; you'll see little of what the Underwriter and Account Executive do with the clients you have booked. You will learn if an account is accepted by underwriting, and how good the account turns out to be from operations, but you won't have nitty-gritty experiences or develop skill sets beyond your marketing job.

If you work as an Underwriter, you'll become familiar with the various credit reporting tools, and how to read and interpret credit reports on clients, their owners, and their customers. You'll learn to recognize red flags and warning signs of potential problem accounts, and identify signals that indicate accounts appear attractive and desirable. You'll learn how to find whether

UCCs have been filed on a prospective client, what to look for in others' filings, and how to file them yourself. In general, you'll learn to glean the wheat from the chaff in prospective clients found by the marketing people. Your job as Underwriter is to approve or decline prospective clients; but you won't learn how to find clients (marketing) or how to manage their accounts after they're approved (operations).

If you work as an Account Executive in operations, you'll learn how to verify and approve invoices, check the credit of new customers, and follow up on unpaid invoices. However, you'll learn little about marketing and the initial underwriting tasks of reviewing, then approving or declining new clients. These were done prior to the clients being added to the part of the portfolio you manage.

If you work for a small factoring company, you're more likely to get a first-hand look at everything that goes on in the business. However, what you in fact may work on is the part of the business the owner doesn't enjoy (pick one or two of the above three – marketing, underwriting, and operations) and/or with which he needs help.

At any rate, how can you find factors looking to hire? Well, there's the traditional route of going to a website like Monster.com and sifting through the multitude of finance jobs there, looking specifically for a factoring company. You may find a few leads, but it's searching for the proverbial needle in a haystack. There are better ways to get right to what you're looking for.

1.   The International Factoring Association has a job board on its website, www.factoring.org. After opening this site and clicking the Jobs menu, you'll see a link to Company and Candidate. After you register, you can see who's hiring, the types of jobs they have, and apply from there.

2.   You can go to a recruiting company ("headhunter") that specializes in placing factoring candidates. A company named Commercial Finance Consultants has been doing this since 2002 and is well regarded in the industry. This company's focus is on placing candidates in larger factoring companies; specifically they are looking for people to fill jobs as Business Development

Officers (marketing), Underwriters (due diligence), and Portfolio Managers or Account Executives (operations). They also place Presidents, CFOs, and VPs, but of course those folks know the business well already. You can learn more about Commercial Finance Consultants from their website, www.searchcf.com.

3. LinkedIn (www.LinkedIn.com) has numerous factoring groups you can join, and many of them have members who post job openings from time to time. If you don't already have a LinkedIn account (and you should if you have a business or are starting one), register for an account then join the various factoring groups. You'll receive regular postings via email from the groups and the job notices will be there.

Read

This book and the Small Factor Series, of which this book is a part, are probably the simplest and most economical way to learn the basics of being a factor and running a small factoring business. Because its focus is on factoring small receivables, this book doesn't provide some of the depth needed for those with the inclination and wherewithal to factor much larger portfolios that run into many millions of dollars. However, if you're a small entrepreneur who has more modest portfolio aspirations and financial abilities, this book, series, and other related ebooks are written especially for you.

Likewise, my website www.DashPointPublishing.com has many other books and resources for small factors to learn how to run the business. Poke around that site and you'll find pretty much everything a small factor needs to get the business up and running.

The Small Factor Academy

Several years ago I developed a two-day live training workshop to teach people how to become small factors. This material has been updated and converted into an online course called the Small Factor Academy.

This is a completely web-based instructional course. You register and complete each lesson at your own pace, using online videos and resources presented to go through the material. When all sessions are complete you will know what you need to run a small factoring operation. While this academy does not provide any formal college or institutional credit, the material will provide a solid foundation for you to begin your small factoring business.

You'll find everything you'll want to know about this training resource at www.SmallFactorAcademy.com.

If You Want to Be Bigger Than a Small Factor

As mentioned earlier, my material and other information available from Dash Point Publishing is geared to smaller factoring operations. If you are looking for more in depth material to run a larger factoring operation with more capital involved, a resource called **FactorHelp** is something you should investigate.

FactorHelp's material focuses on three stages of larger factoring operations: startup, growth, and exit. The website states the material will help in the startup stage with the following:

• Formulate your business plan and budgets
• Provide and customize a policy and operations manual
• Locate Start-up Capital and Funding
• Set up your operation
• Build your website
• Identify the best vendors to fit your company goals
• Purchase a portfolio or platform

In the growth phase, FactorHelp assists with:

• Portfolio/operations reviews
• Additional capital to grow your business
• Participations (buy or sell)
• Portfolio purchases

In devising an exit strategy, FactorHelp will assist to:

- Conduct an operation review in preparation for sale
- Complete a portfolio valuation
- Represent you to companies who have the ability to close the transaction

FactorHelp provides the above as either written material available on DVDs or as services provided. Their written material and pricing (plus shipping), as of this writing, is as follows for those who are not members of the International Factoring Association. Each item below is sold separately:

Factoring Operations Manual, by Debra Wilson	$3,950.00
Factoring Business Plan	$1,195.00
Projection and Budget Sheets	$1,595.00
Combo: Business Plan/Projection & Budget Sheets	$2,495.00
Factoring Accounting Manual, by Darla Auchinachie	$395.00
Factoring A/R Audit Forms	$99.95
Factoring Employee Handbook	$99.95

IFA members receive a 5% discount on most of the above items. The prices (plus shipping) for IFA members as of this writing are:

Factoring Operations Manual, by Debra Wilson	$3,752.00
Factoring Business Plan	$1,135.25
Projection and Budget Sheets	$1,515.25
Combo: Business Plan/Projection & Budget Sheets	$2,495.00
Factoring Accounting Manual, by Darla Auchinachie	$375.25
Factoring A/R Audit Forms	$94.95
Factoring Employee Handbook	$94.95

Learn the details of the above products and FactorHelp's services at www.FactorHelp.com. They are a Preferred Vendor of the IFA and the above products can be purchased from IFA's website, www.factoring.org; click on the Store menu, then the Products submenu.

The International Factoring Association

The IFA (www.factoring.org) is an organization made up of factoring companies, asset based lenders, and banks which purchase accounts receivable. It puts on an excellent annual conference in a different city every year, which always includes numerous workshops, an exhibit hall for vendors selling products and services to factoring companies, and discussion forums about various topics of interest to factors. Included is a round table discussion for small factors.

IFA also hosts numerous one- or two-day workshops throughout the year in various locations that each address a specific topic related to the business of factoring. Again, a Small Factors Roundtable Discussion is offered each fall in Las Vegas, which is of great benefit to smaller factors. For more information about IFA see the chapter "Additional Resources." Their website is www.factoring.org.

As you can see, learning to be a factor isn't so hard if you know where to look. And there's one other way to learn the factoring business that many people consider. The next chapter tells all about it.

7

Factoring Franchises

Another way to learn the factoring business is to buy a factoring franchise. In this chapter we will first look at the pros and cons of owning both an independent factoring company and owning a factoring franchise, then provide information on the four factoring franchises of which I am aware.

If you are considering purchasing a franchise, you should not only look at the advantages and disadvantages of having a franchise verses an independent company, but consider which suits your personality, skills and business goals best.

Independent Company Pros & Cons

Advantages

1. **You're the one and only boss.** You establish your own rules and procedures and decide everything. You'll choose and carry out your marketing methods and learn what works as you go. You'll do your own underwriting, deciding what due diligence tools to use and which accounts to accept and decline. You'll decide what your advance and discount rates will be, how you will conduct your daily operations, and then do the operations work yourself (or hire someone to do it). There is no one to tell you what you can and can't do, what you have to do, or what you should do. You decide everything.

In short, the buck starts and stops with you. You're the captain of the ship, and either you sail it into exotic ports of call and gradually build up your flotilla, or you go down with your ship in ignominy. If this is the kind of business you want to have, you'll be happier working in your own private company than buying a franchise. If all these responsibilities are more than you want, then a franchise may be better suited to you.

2. Having your own private company means you have **no franchise fees** as you get started. Sure, you'll have your basic startup costs of getting a business license, incorporating, obtaining office equipment you don't have, and the like. But generally these costs are low. The much larger expense of paying a franchise is spared and can be put instead into your first clients' invoices, which in turn starts making money for you right away.

3. Having your own independent company means once your business is established and making income, you make **no monthly royalty payments** as do franchisees. You keep all your profits and don't need to report them to anyone (except IRS of course). Everything you make is your business and in your bank account.

Disadvantages

1. **You learn everything by the seat of your pants**, and this can sometimes lead to an empty feeling of "I have no clue what I'm doing here." The learning curve can be intimidating as you do things the first time and wonder if you're doing them "right." No doubt you will ask yourself questions like, "Will this marketing method work?" "What is this credit report telling me?" "How do I make these invoice entries into my software and what reports tell me what I want to know?" While you are probably following the training materials mentioned in the last chapter, you may still experience the unsettling fear that you'll make a major mistake without knowing it. That fear can give you an uncomfortable and somewhat nauseous feeling very similar to weightlessness.

2. If you don't know anyone with experience in the industry, you have **no one to ask what to do or how to do it**. Clearly a wise idea is to have a trusted colleague mentor you in these situations, but finding such a person may take some time if you're starting absolutely cold with no industry contacts. Both of the above issues can lead to a feeling of isolation at first, until contacts are made.

3. You will almost certainly make **rookie mistakes** that will cost you money. If you make the classic mistake of being over concentrated in a client, customer, or invoice and a deal goes

south, you can lose a tidy sum of money. Therefore pay attention to other parts of this book that warn you about such mistakes.

Franchise Pros & Cons

Advantages

1. The hallmark of any franchise, from selling hamburgers to doing taxes to buying invoices, is that you are buying a **successful business model**. The reason people pay good money for franchises is that the model works, and has worked over and over again for many people, often for many years. The "seat of your pants" learning method of owning an independent company is absent here and for many people that is worth what they pay to be a franchisee.

2. In a franchise, you **learn how to factor from an established system**. There is a franchise manual that tells you how to do pretty much everything. If you run into a situation that you're not sure how to handle, the answer is probably in the book. Just look it up.

3. If it's not in the book, the franchise's administrative staff has experience in the factoring world, has probably run across this situation before, and is there to answer your questions. In short, you have human **expertise at your fingertips.**

4. As a franchisee you have an **immediate network of colleagues** doing the same thing you do. There is a sense of camaraderie, a feeling of being "in the trenches" with your fellow franchisees, that can overcome the sense of isolation some new independent factors experience.

5. **Franchisees can easily share deals among themselves** (called "syndicating"), especially if they run across a deal that's too big to handle alone. While independent factors can participate with others in much the same way, franchisees have a built-in network of colleagues who have been vetted by the franchise and are both experienced and presumably honest and trustworthy. If they prove otherwise the franchise will no doubt take appropriate action. Taking part in a syndicated deal can be an easy and quick way for a franchise factor, especially a new one, to get money on the street and gain a taste for the business.

6. One of the selling points franchises often plug is the advantage of using the franchise's name to provide **branding recognition**. In other words, you enjoy the benefit of using a name that is established and far better known than your new independent business name would be.

While the brand recognition of names such as McDonald's or KFC is certainly a huge benefit, factoring franchises don't enjoy anything close to such widespread awareness (at least yet). To put it another way: have your neighbor, your cousin or your plumber ever heard of any of the factoring franchises below? Have they all heard of McDonald's and KFC? You get the point. If the factoring franchise names are not familiar to people you know, they're probably not familiar to anyone else either, and the brand isn't worth that much, at least as far as name recognition.

However, you *can* use the franchise brand to indicate to prospective clients that you are part of an organization much larger than yourself. That can give them confidence that their receivables are in the hands of a company that knows what it's doing (even if you don't yet) and they're dealing with a well-capitalized company which has been and will be around for a long time.

Disadvantages

1. The first disadvantage that greets you early is the **upfront costs** required. While prices for franchise licenses vary, you will pay tens of thousands of dollars for any of them. As mentioned earlier, those independently-inclined factors typically would rather put that money to use funding their first few clients. The question becomes this: is spending that kind of money for the benefits a franchise affords worth the investment? The only person who can answer that for you is you.

2. Once you're a franchisee you are required to make monthly **royalty payments** for as long as you have your franchise. Again, royalty amounts vary but are typically in the 6-8% range of what you make each month. You may feel this is worthwhile during the early stages while you're learning the business and need all the help you can get. But after a couple years when you have the business pretty well mastered, how will you feel about

74

continuing to have this expense every month, especially as your business grows and your income increases? And that's forever.

3. Understandably, all franchises want people who bring a high probability of success to the table and who will represent their company well. Thus you must meet requirements as to your own personal net worth, available cash on hand, and business experience; and you need to be **vetted and approved** before you're admitted into the fold. While this is probably not an issue for most people wanting a franchise, it is a step you can simply skip and not even think about if you start an independent company.

4. Franchisees are required to **do things the franchise's way**. They will typically have specific requirements as to the industries and size of prospective clients you can accept and how they are managed. Some require that the underwriting be done by the folks back at HQ, which is a significant part of the business. If that's the case and underwriting doesn't approve a prospect you find, you have no choice but to accept their decision and decline the prospect. That can feel a lot like being an independent broker, or sales person for a larger factor, with no power to decide which clients you will factor and which ones you won't. You certainly don't have the complete control over your business that you would as an independent.

5. Franchise contracts require a **commitment of several years**, and if you find after a while that you'd like to leave the organization, doing so can be extremely difficult if not impossible, and/or very expensive.

After taking all the above into serious consideration and weighing all the pros and cons carefully, if you decide a franchise is the way to go for you, the next step is to compare the franchises themselves. The rest of this chapter provides information on four franchises.

While these companies are all involved in factoring invoices, each has a unique model. For example, some want their franchisees to actively purchase receivables from their clients and be involved in the daily operations of the business. Others want their franchisees to work in a marketing capacity, and leave the back office operations to headquarters. Some specialize in a particular industry, and some have multiple niches they fund. Again, carefully determine what kind of work you want to do and which model best fits what *you* want, before signing on the dotted line.

Below are the franchises with their contact information.

Compound Profit
www.cprofit.com
877 386 3716

Liquid Capital
www.lcfranchise.com
866 272 3704

Interface Financial Group
www.ifgnetwork.com
877 210 9748 USA
877 598 9851 Canada

Commission Express
www.commissionexpress.com
888 560 5501

Questions to Ask

When speaking to the franchises, the following questions may be asked as a means of fairly comparing the companies.

1. What is the history of your company?
2. What is your business focus?
3. How are you different from other factoring franchises?
4. What is the primary task or tasks of franchisees?
5. Do you have protected territories?
6. How does your company support its franchisees?
7. What is the cost of the franchisee license?
8. What is the amount of the monthly royalty fees?
9. Why should I choose your company over another franchise, or over being an independent factor?

As you visit the websites and talk to these organizations directly, you can use the chart that follows to record their answers.

	Compound Profit		877 386 3716
1	Company History	1	
2	Business Focus	2	
3	How are you different	3	
4	Primary task/s of franchisees	4	
5	Protected territories	5	
6	Support	6	
7	License costs	7	
8	Royalty fees	8	
9	Why should I choose you	9	

	Liquid Capital		866 272 3704
1	Company History	1	
2	Business Focus	2	
3	How are you different	3	
4	Primary task/s of franchisees	4	
5	Protected territories	5	
6	Support	6	
7	License costs	7	
8	Royalty fees	8	
9	Why should I choose you	9	

	Interface Financial Group		877 210 9748 USA
			877 598 9851 Canada
1	Company History	1	
2	Business Focus	2	
3	How are you different	3	
4	Primary task/s of franchisees	4	
5	Protected territories	5	
6	Support	6	
7	License costs	7	
8	Royalty fees	8	
9	Why should I choose you	9	

	Commission Express		888 560 5501
1	Company History	1	
2	Business Focus	2	
3	How are you different	3	
4	Primary task/s of franchisees	4	
5	Protected territories	5	
6	Support	6	
7	License costs	7	
8	Royalty fees	8	
9	Why should I choose you	9	

8

Marketing: How to Find Clients

Prospective clients are very close to the new small factor yet the neophyte often doesn't realize it. Locating, recognizing, and then closing prospective clients can take a while to learn. Once your business is established, your name is in circulation and referrals are coming from clients and even strangers, marketing becomes easy. But surviving until you get to that point, which sometimes take as long a year or two, is the hard part.

To help with this key aspect of your business, www.DashPointPublishing.com provides various books and resources that specifically address the subject of marketing for factors. Once you're on the site, click the Marketing menu and you'll find them.

The Internet

Website. You need to have a website to be considered legitimate, or at least serious about your business. Most factors have websites and after reading several, many look somewhat alike. Those that stand out – with unique innovations or services, a special look of professionalism and confidence, even humor done tastefully – will have more appeal to prospective clients and be more likely to generate a response.

If your website looks and reads like others, it may generate some inquiries from prospects shopping for the best deal or who don't meet your parameters. Therefore be sure to state very clearly and specifically the kind of clients you fund, i.e. size, location, industry, etc. The more specific your niche and the better you get that across, the less time you waste with those not meeting your requirements; they weed themselves out, saving you the trouble. Be careful to pre-qualify responses from your website because you can squander a lot of time answering inquiries from people who turn out to be non-prospects.

Shop around for a web designer if you need one. In general prices can vary widely and it's easy to drop a couple thousand dollars for web design and end up with very little for it. Be sure your site looks professional and is well done, or your site will leave the impression that you're not very good at what you do.

If you want to create and host your site yourself, you have a couple options. First, you can use an online site-building wizard and hosting service. These are point-and-click sites for creating your site, pages, and text, with step by step instructions, as well as hosting. They create very professional looking sites. If you want a shopping cart (though you probably won't need one) most of these provide them.

To find these sites Google "website templates," "website wizard," "website creator," or something similar and you'll find plenty from which to choose. These templates are a good place for novices to start building their first site.

Second, if you're so inclined, you can buy and learn to use a website creation program. Search "website creation software" or something similar, and again you'll find many. You need to be at least fairly proficient with a computer to use these programs and if you've never used them before there will be a learning curve. But once you know what you're doing, you're not dependent on someone else to make changes to your site, nor are you limited by the restrictions of the template sites.

Social Networking. Social networking sites (SNS) are online communities where friends, colleagues, and people with similar interests connect. Although there are some differences in how they are organized, they all function pretty much the same. They allow you to create an online profile, link with individuals or groups, and allow those individuals to post comments, create discussions, and give feedback on what you have written. You can search an SNS's database of users to connect with people or groups related to your interests or business field.

Social Networking provides a way to directly market to specific groups without the expense of print or other forms of media. For a beginning factor with a very limited marketing budget, this can be a godsend. Rather than investing money to market your company, with SNS you invest your time.

There are numerous social media channels and you probably have not heard of most of them. The best known at the time of this writing are LinkedIn, Facebook, Google+, and Twitter. The IFA launched its social media network community in September, 2011, in which any member can participate.

In social networking for businesses, your goal is to gain new leads or clients as well as to keep in regular contact with the clients you have. A client's word-of-mouth praise of your company is the most effective form of marketing, and social networking provides this unlike any previous medium could.

Begin by posting comments or starting discussions on your LinkedIn, Google+, etc. sites. Once posted, people in your network can give you feedback on your posts and recommend them to any or all of their own contacts, who in turn can do the same. This starts a chain reaction that is the inherent   strength and genius of SNS. Your contacts can "share," "recommend", "re-tweet," "+1", or "like" the post, which in turn gives you exposure to their network, and so on. This exposure from "going viral" can help you expand your network and make a *huge* number of people aware of your services and how you can be of benefit to them. This helps you gain followers and can definitely take on a life of its own.

To take it a step further, you can create social plugin buttons to add to your website that directly link to your social networking sites. For instance, you may have noticed as you search various sites a "Follow" or "Tweet" button for Twitter. Perhaps you noticed a "+1" for Google+, or a "Like" button that links to Facebook. LinkedIn has a "Recommend," "Profile," and a few other buttons, which allows people to share and direct traffic to your website. You can create these buttons by going to the "Development Pages" of each social networking site you join. If someone else created and updates your website they can do this for you quite easily.

LinkedIn is said to be the social networking site for companies, business people and entrepreneurs. Your profile is almost like a resume; in fact you can upload your resume to create the profile if you want. LinkedIn gives you a platform to exchange ideas, opportunities, and information pertinent to the business world.

LinkedIn makes it easy to connect with the contacts you already have. If you use Microsoft Outlook, Apple Mail or any other email application, you can import those contacts quite easily. You can invite these contacts to join your network. Once they accept, you have the starting point from which you grow. You can also recommend your friends and colleagues and accept invitations from people in their network.

LinkedIn has an abundance of interest groups, including many directly involved with factoring including the IFA. You can search for and join any of these or other groups which gives you access to some great newsletters and contacts related to factoring or anything else of interest to you. You can choose to receive (or not receive) email updates from any groups you join, and you can join as many groups as you want.

The benefits are indeed worth the effort you put in to your social networking experience; however there are some negative things you will want to consider. You can potentially get a lot of emails that you find of no interest, so manage your privacy settings to minimize this. Be sure to proactively respond to any questions, comments or even complaints people post about you and your company.

Social networking can be a fun but at the same time daunting task. As people invite you to join their network, try to limit your acceptance to people who will actually make a difference to your company. Will connecting to someone who sells real estate in Yazoo City lead to potential factoring business for you? If her network has people who need factoring, or can refer someone to you who does, then perhaps it will. If not, when you get requests to link with someone that seems to have no potential benefit or worthwhile connections for you, you can simply ignore the request. You are in charge of how much time you will allocate to your network. Try not to let it become overwhelming – after all, you have plenty of other things to do.

As you can see, the benefit of SNS is that without much effort and literally no cost, you can reach a multitude of people with your service and its benefits, recommendations from others, and even your opinions. It takes marketing to a completely new level, unknown ever before.

Search Engines. Try to get on as many search engines as you can but be careful of spending a lot of money doing so. Many will give you a free listing, while others can be quite expensive. You can also pay services to submit for you, but you may not know how effective this is. Hiring an SEO (Search Engine Optimization) expert can be money well spent if he's good.

Unfortunately, you'll find many, many large factoring companies with very deep pockets competing in the search engine wars for keywords like "factoring" and "accounts receivable financing." Therefore you need to consider first and foremost the purpose of your website. Is it a) to find and reel in new clients (which can lead to spending a bundle for search engine placement) or more simply, b) to be a sophisticated online brochure and resource for prospects and clients?

Quite frankly, if you try to win the search engine wars against the big guys by throwing a lot of money into search engine listings, you'll lose...and go broke in the process. This is where Social Networking becomes a key marketing tool. A website for a small factor is a superb medium for showing people whom you are, where you're located, and what you do. A well done website will make you look professional, tell people all about your company, and provide a means of easy distribution for your application and other forms. SEO and Social Networking are what drive a *lot* of people to your site, so you want to do all three extremely well.

Other Marketing Methods

Other methods of marketing a small factoring business fall into two broad categories, and within each category are numerous strategies. The two categories are **One-to-One Contact** and **One-to-Many Contact**. One-to-One Contact is telling an individual or a small number of people, either eye to eye or on the phone, what your business offers and its benefits. Conversely, One-to-Many Contact is telling a large number of people at once the same thing – what you do and its value to your audience.

One-to-One Contact is more effective but takes longer to reach a significant number of potential clients. One-to-Many Contact reaches many people quite quickly, but provides a far lower percentage of prospects and costs more. An effective marketing campaign will combine elements of both. No matter which method you use, always remember to address how factoring can help your listeners' business. People – especially business owners – want to know immediately the answer to WIIFM (pronounced "Whiff 'em"): "What's In It For Me?" If factoring doesn't solve their problem, don't waste their time or yours with your pitch.

It's very important to always keep in mind the target of your marketing efforts. First focus on businesses which are most factorable. Pursuing retail stores in a mall who sell only to consumers won't get you factoring clients. Isolate a specific industry in which you have knowledge or background, or ones in a specific geographical area. From there, narrow your mark: prospects with a certain yearly volume, those who have been in business for less than five years, with a specific number of employees, in specific zip codes, and so on.

Don't try to use every method described; it simply can't be done. Instead, select four or five that fit your personality, style and resources. Then draft an overall marketing plan that outlines your target group, the methods you will use, in what combination, in what order. Map out a definite time line on a weekly and monthly basis. Also plan ahead financially by determining how much each method will cost and how you will pay for it. Barging ahead with great excitement – yet without a well-conceived and executed plan – can end up an expensive, frustrating waste of energy and time, seriously draining your resources and enthusiasm. This is a separate plan from the one done in the chapter "Charting Your Course," but it is just as important.

Some say you must use a certain marketing method to be successful – often a particular social networking strategy, or perhaps cold calling, direct mail, or email campaigns. (Oddly enough, what they say you must use is just what they're selling.) However, if you're not comfortable with these, you'll probably do a poor job and hate every minute of it. Social networking for the complete novice or internet doofus is bewildering. Cold calling for people who are very shy or uneasy with strangers is absolute torture. Direct mail done without knowing what you're doing can be very costly and ineffective. Email marketing done wrong can get you blacklisted as a spammer.

For example, take the person who tried his hand at direct mail for the first time. He sent thousands of letters without receiving a single reply, and couldn't understand why. Frustrated, he asked an experienced colleague to read what he'd sent. The colleague immediately saw the problem: he had neglected to put his phone number anywhere in the mailing.

You're more likely to be successful with methods you enjoy, and that are an extension of your personality and skills. Marketing is very much a "one person's tea is another's poison" kind of thing. Pick the ones that taste best to you, learn how to use them effectively and carefully plan your course. Then go for it!

One-to-One Contact

Business Cards. One necessity if you do a lot of face-to-face marketing is a good business card. Collect as many as you can from all over (other financial professionals, trade shows, hardware store counters, grocery store bulletin boards, anywhere) and study them carefully. Some will be excellent, others worthless. What's your immediate impression when you look at a card? What catches your eye? Does it tell you what the business does? Does it give the person's name and how to reach him? Does anything confuse you? Does art work, logo, or lack of either add or detract? Does it fit the industry or type of work? Would you contact this business if you needed its service or product? You can learn a lot about what to include and exclude by studying other business cards.

While your card doesn't have to be expensive, it shouldn't look cheap or unprofessional. Consider putting a message on the reverse side, perhaps with a special offer such as finder's fees. Give your card out liberally, but don't print too many at once. You'll undoubtedly want to change the card's look or information two or three times the first year; making more than a few hundred at first will leave you with a lot of expensive bookmarks.

Elevator Speech. One of the first marketing skills to master is creating and delivering your "elevator speech," particularly for your one-to-one contacts. This is simply a 30-second (or less) description of your business you can present to anyone, anywhere (especially in an elevator!). It will succinctly tell them what you do, for whom, and what's in it for them (WIIFM…or WIIFT, in this case). A good elevator speech will generate quick interest from your listener/s if they need your service, or know someone who does.

Networking groups live by elevator speeches, which they often call "30-second commercials." Networking group members have an excellent elevator speech or two (at least) at the tip of their tongues, ready to present instantly to anyone. So should you. Here's are a few for small factors:

- *"I run a company that specializes in helping small businesses streamline their cash flow. We provide them advance funding on slow paying invoices so that they can meet obligations or expand."*

- *"Hello. My name is John Doe and company is John Doe Financial. We help people and businesses get **cash today** for **payments** they are **waiting** to get in the **future**."*

- *"Hi, my name is Jane Smith. I am the owner of ABC Funding. I buy receivables at a discount and advance most of the invoice amount as soon as the invoice is generated. That way, companies have the cash to pay payroll and payroll taxes, buy supplies at a discount, and do anything they need to do to maintain and grow their company while I wait for their check to come in."*

Here are four elevator speeches I've used:

- *"My company provides financing for very small business owners who are turned away by banks. Instead of providing loans, we purchase our clients' invoices for immediate cash which enables them to meet payroll, pay bills, accept larger customers, and many other business necessities."*

- *"My business supplies something every company needs: money! Our clients have invoices that take 30 days to pay, and we purchase their invoices with cash advances within 24 hours of the invoices being created. We've helped hundreds of businesses get started, grow quickly, and operate profitably."*

- *"I finance very small companies by buying their receivables at a small discount, as soon as their invoices are created. This enables my clients to increase their cash flow quickly, without generating debt. Our clients are small business owners who have been turned down for bank loans."*

- *"My name is Jeff Callender, my company is Dash Point Financial Services, and I get paid to wait! My clients are very small business owners who wait 30 days to receive payment from their business or government customers. I buy the rights to their payments, give them an up-front advance, and then wait for their customers to pay me. This enables my clients to give 30 day terms yet still get paid tomorrow.*

Get the idea? Generally your elevator speech is no longer than two to four sentences. You include three simple points:

1. Summarize what you do.
2. Summarize who your market is.
3. State the benefits of your service.

You'll probably want a slightly different elevator speech for various audiences.

Your elevator speech is something you will tinker with and perfect over time. Make yours your own and try various phrases and ideas. Practice saying it out loud and time how long the delivery takes. If it goes over 30 seconds, shorten it. Like your business card, it will change over time, so don't worry about getting it absolutely perfect as you start. It's a work in progress.

Having a couple good elevator speeches, and having them down cold, will increase both your confidence and the number of prospects interested in what you can do for them. And the best people on whom to practice your elevator speech are your...

Friends, Relatives and Acquaintances. Unless you're an orphaned, single hermit living alone in the hinterlands of Alaska or Siberia, you already have a built-in marketing network that can work wonders. You probably know or are in contact with a much larger circle of people than you realize who can be your very best source of referrals. The fact that these people already know you is your greatest advantage. They know first-hand your reputation, how you treat people and your trustworthiness. These are major issues you must address when working with strangers. But with people who already know you, this hurdle is nonexistent...unless they know you to be a dishonest, greedy, egocentric louse!

Review in your mind all the people in your life's circle, then make a list of people to contact. You might want to look over email address books, holiday card lists, people in your neighborhood, directories of your place of worship, civic groups, children's activities, and so on. You can meet or phone them and tell about your new adventure, send an email, or simply mention it in conversation the next time you're together.

Tell them what you're doing and how it can help business owners. Let your enthusiasm show, and chances are good they might know someone right off who could benefit. If not, ask them to give it some thought and get back to you.

ALWAYS say you give finder's fees, but be sure you've worked out how much that will be before you mention it! 10% to 15% of your gross discount for a year or for the life of the account, for all successful transactions referred, is a common payment for professional brokers. Some factors pay 50% of their first discount, others a flat $50 or $100, and nothing after that for referrals from nonprofessional brokers. You may want to pay a friend, relative, or acquaintance up to those amounts if a name they furnish turns into a client. Alternately, you could offer to make a donation to the persona's favorite charity rather than pay a commission.

People who "sniff out" leads, sometimes called "Bird Dogs" or "Scouts," can be invaluable. The idea of getting money for simply giving you a name will not only silence most skeptics (usually relatives) but motivate some to actually beat the bushes for you. I've had people make phone calls on the spot, even before I told them I'll pay them a fee, simply because they wanted to help a friend – me.

Don't underestimate the potential in this network of people. When I first started factoring, I described what I was doing to a friend, not remembering he owned a small distributing business. He immediately saw the potential benefit to his company (WIIFM) and a few days later called wanting to know more. After nailing down the details of his customers, factoring rates and advances, he soon became one of my first clients. He ended up factoring over $100,000 worth of receivables his first year.

Brokers, Larger Factors. When you use brokers you need to have some policies established as to the commission you pay, their role working with you, what information you need about prospective clients, businesses you will and won't fund and your minimum and maximum monthly volume. If they bring you very small receivables (less than $2,500 per month), the amount they'll make in commissions is pretty puny and it may not be worth the trouble. However, broker consultants can bring you a lot of business, so treat them well and with integrity. Word gets around brokers' circles very quickly when a factor is especially good or bad to work with.

Larger factors, especially those in your area, can be excellent sources of referrals. If you've referred potential clients that were too big for you, it is only natural for that factor to return the favor when prospects are too small for him. This relationship is mutually beneficial and can make both of you good money.

Make a point of introducing yourself to local larger factors and learn their parameters. If they turn away what you're looking for, say so. If you come off as a professional, there's a good chance they'll give you prospects they turn down. When a factor must turn down someone, it helps enormously if he can refer the prospect an alternative factor who's likely to help. Be that alternative and you'll have a steady stream of new clients.

Banks. What was just said about larger factors is equally true for banks. Bankers turn down loan requests every day. If someone can't get a loan but is a good factoring prospect, you can make the banker's job easier by being an alternative for the bank's rejected client: "We can't help you, but this person might be able to. Give him a call."

In addition to easing the banker's burden when turning someone down, you can be a source of new accounts where your factoring bank account resides. Getting referrals from your bank can be a triple-win: you get new clients, the client gets needed cash, and the bank is a good guy for making it happen, and perhaps, adds a new account to boot.

A few factors and broker consultants focus exclusively on contacting banks for leads. Certain bankers are more receptive than others. Many will be unfamiliar with factoring or not clearly understand it. Some view factors as competitors, others see us as scavengers, but some see factors as allies. Some banks have their own factoring division. Deal with them as you would a larger factor: find their minimums and maximums, industries served and avoided, marketing persons and so on – and then tell them how you can help with clients too small to fit their requirements.

The key is to find the right person – corporate lending officer, branch manager, and/or factoring division contact. Then establish a good relationship, make sure she understands how you can help her (WIIFM) and stay in contact. Sooner or later, this can pay off.

Accountants, Bookkeepers and Attorneys. Anyone who has his nose in a business' financial records is keenly aware, usually better than the business owner, when there is a cash flow problem. Accountants, bookkeepers, and attorneys are these very people and the more of them who know what you offer their clients, the more business you can get.

Like bankers, these folks will have varying attitudes about factors, and some will dismiss you out of hand. Many will have only a vague understanding of how factoring works and not appreciate the benefits. Some see factors as loan sharks; and, even if they recommend it, may want their client in and out of factoring as fast as possible because they think it is too expensive or a measure of last resort. Generally such professionals tend to be conservative with financial referrals and may be fearful that recommending factoring could leave them open to lawsuits if the roof later caves in. Getting referrals from people with such an attitude is difficult if not impossible. However, especially if you take time to educate them, some will realize factoring can be exactly what certain clients need and will be happy to refer you.

Having a solid reputation with a handful of "bean counters" and "legal beagles" can have similar win-win-win results as with bankers. You get a new client, the client has her cash flow problem solved, and the accountant or lawyer looks good and now has two people who are glad to give her new referrals. (WIIFM. See how this works?!)

Networking Groups. Networking groups take various shapes, from established national leads organizations with a consistent weekly schedule, to Chamber of Commerce mixers that meet monthly over a meal with no structured agenda, to informal local groups that do their own thing. Finding a networking group with the right combination of members and good chemistry can be a bonanza. But if it is full of people who can't help you because their sphere of influence doesn't mesh with companies needing a factor, or it's a closed shop/good old boy network, joining or working with this type of group is a waste of time.

If you use this method, find a group that has a good mix of finance-related members and people who know a lot of people. Look for a friendly accountant, attorney, banker, financial planner, insurance agent, etc. who will be able to give you more leads naturally than people who just service the real estate or housing market.

When I first started factoring I joined an established networking group called LeTip. Let me describe briefly how it works so you get an idea of what such groups are about. LeTip is a national organization with local chapters throughout the United States. In each local chapter, only one type of business can be represented: one lawyer, one dentist, one real estate agent, one plumber, one whatever. If you're a chiropractor and want to join a group with a chiropractor already in it, you must find another chapter. There are yearly national dues, quarterly dues to cover local chapter expenses and your weekly breakfast, and quarter to dollar "fines" for such things as not having a tip, not bringing a guest, not wearing your name badge, and so on. The whole purpose of the group is for members to give and receive qualified leads every week. A qualified lead is someone who needs a product or service and is awaiting a call from the tip receiver.

A good group can become a powerful marketing force that eliminates the need for cold calls. Each week one or two members from the group give a ten-minute talk pertaining to some aspect of their business. The business meeting is conducted during the mealtime, business cards are passed (and accumulated for all members to hand out to potential leads for other members during the week) and the tip bucket is circulated. Each member gives a 30-second commercial and drops his or her written tips into the bucket, giving a copy to the tip recipient. The person receiving the tip then follows up by calling the prospect.

While such a group works especially well for people with small ticket items (florists, carpet cleaners, gift baskets, service businesses, etc.), there are many advantages to groups like this for factors. You're one-on-one with business people with a wide variety of local contacts, and you gain high visibility and the trust of people who can bring you leads. Further, there are regional get-togethers involving several local chapters that will further expand your circle of contacts. Though dues may be somewhat high, one good client can pay for many years' worth of dues. While some professions won't be able to give you leads, good tips can come from unexpected places. The hairdresser in my group referred one of my best clients.

Attend a few groups as a guest and see if any can provide what you need. There are other organizations similar to LeTip such as

BNI (Business Networking International). Look for them on the web or ask around. To find a local LeTip or BNI group go to their websites at www.letip.com and www.bni.com. You can also Google "networking groups" and include your city or region in the search to see what is in your area. Perhaps you have an independent group nearby in addition to or instead of a nationwide group.

Purchasing Agents. Purchasing agents for school districts, city or county government, utility companies, large corporations, and the like have access to a gold mine of information: vendors to whom these entities pay their bills. Remember, the most creditworthy customers that clients can have are business or government agencies that will not go bankrupt or otherwise disappear, and who might take thirty or more days to pay. Finding clients who have this type of customer will make your due diligence a snap and let you sleep at night without wondering if you'll get paid. Marketing to vendor lists used by purchasing agents of school districts, utility companies, large corporations, and government agencies is a back-door way to getting the job done, and if you can pull it off, prospecting becomes easy.

Two things to consider: 1) these vendor lists can be voluminous, containing literally thousands of names; and 2) the purchasing agents probably won't be very willing to release the vendor information and may be downright uncooperative. They may say the information is not for the public or they're prohibited from releasing it. In some cases this will be true; in others, it's just too much trouble for an overworked clerk to give you the information. They might be prohibited from accepting a commission and there's no benefit to them for helping you, a stranger (their WIIFM answer is "zero"). Also, refer back to the "Friends, Relatives, and Acquaintances" section above. If you personally know someone who works in an office with this information, she may be more willing and able to help you than she would some stranger. A good, current, huge vendor list like this provides all the marketing leads you can use, and then some.

Seminars and Webinars. If you don't mind speaking in front of a group, conducting a morning or afternoon seminar or webinar can be another way of obtaining new clients. You'll need to have your ducks in a row, however. Use a well-organized marketing plan to advertise the seminar adequately. Well-placed radio or TV ads may do this best. You'll also need to have your room arrangements or webinar preparations, presentation, handouts and other requirements well-organized to conduct a successful program. Done well, you can easily pick up some good clients; done poorly, you can run yourself ragged getting ready or make a fool of yourself to prospective clients. The more seminars you do, the better you'll get. Make your presentation focus on WIIFM primarily, and don't get too caught up in explaining the detailed, specific "ins and outs" of factoring.

Free or nominal fee seminars, at a convenient and known location, are popular today for getting the word out about all kinds of businesses. Free admission will attract larger numbers, while prepayment of a small admission charge ($10 or $20) will assure a higher percentage turnout of interested attendees plus cover some of your costs. If there is another small factor in your area who has an interest in doing this, or perhaps an accountant or business attorney who would like to advertise her business with you, consider splitting preparation duties, expenses, fees presentation time, and topics. The best times of year to put on seminars are in early fall and the months of January or February. The idea of getting a fresh start with the new year can be an inspiration for people to attend such a meeting.

Trade Shows, Conventions. Keep your eye open for business trade shows and conventions that come to the city nearest you. You can pick up leads from these simply by walking the floor and visiting with other attendees and people in booths of companies that might be good factoring candidates or by getting a booth of your own. Having your own booth requires a fair amount of preparation and expense; but if you know how to do it, a good trade show can bring you enough leads to keep you busy for a long time.

Chambers of Commerce usually sponsor annual trade shows which are a bit smaller. These can be good for learning the ropes of both walking the floor and having your own booth. These are also good places to pick up business cards to inspire your own and for prospects to follow up later.

Cold Calls. If you enjoy the challenge of walking into an office or calling someone stone cold, and if you don't mind hearing nine "no's" for every one "yes," you can get all the clients you'll ever want by cold calling. Find a list of small businesses in your area and do your thing. If you have an industrial business park nearby or business buildings with one to five-person offices inside, you're all set.

Where can you get lists of prospective clients? Several places. Large and small companies (check the web) sell commercial data bases which provide carefully targeted lists. Credit reporting agencies like Dun & Bradstreet and infoUSA are examples. Chambers of Commerce can be a helpful resource for prospective lists, as can new business listings that are about a year old, from the newspaper or local business journal. These should be in your library and on their website archives. Also contact home-based business associations.

Telemarketing. It can be an expensive alternative to go with a professional telemarketing outfit, but a good telemarketer can keep you very busy with new prospects. You may be able to find an independent who works from home and won't cost an arm and a leg. You may need to provide the list of businesses the person will call.

A telemarketer can do your cold calling for you if you think that's the way to get new clients and can't face the 90% rejection rate that goes with the territory. Have a contract in writing describing the duties and payment for your telemarketer so there are no misunderstandings or surprises once they start finding you clients.

Client Referrals. Hands down this is the best, cheapest, and most effective advertising you can get. The only problem is, you have to get those first few clients before they can refer people to you! In time, this will probably be the only marketing you'll need to do; meanwhile, work hard at the other ways you've chosen to get to this point. Again, remind your clients every so often that you give finder's fees. Chances are, they'll have a neighboring business, vendor or customer (especially their slower payers, who might have a cash flow problem of their own) who might make good prospects.

One-to-Many Contact

Press Releases. One effective way to get your company noticed is to write a press release. Wikipedia defines a press release as "A written or recorded communication directed at members of the news media for the purpose of announcing something ostensibly newsworthy."

The goal of your press release is to generate interest in your topic; it should be targeted to a specific audience and have a strong news angle. For example, if your factoring company is launching a new service for a particular business segment such as government contractors, write about the benefits your service will be providing government contractors and how it will help those within that specific audience.

For those who have never written a press release or may not be familiar with the format, start by reading a few actual releases online from some of the larger press release distribution companies such as PR Newswire (www.PRNewswire.com) or Business Wire (www.BusinessWire.com). You can read a variety of press releases by subject, industry, company name, date, etc.

So how exactly do you write a press release? First, make sure the information in your release is newsworthy. Examples of newsworthy events can be the announcement of a new business startup, the launch of a new product or website, new events at your company or some philanthropic work your company has performed. Second, keep the reader's attention by focusing on how your company is providing a benefit to the targeted audience. Give specific examples of what benefits your company can provide readers. Share your success with readers and explain how you have achieved the growth and success you are writing about.

Do not craft your release to sound like a cheap advertisement for your company. Remember, you are trying to get your release picked up by media outlets and nothing turns off an audience more than fluffy self-promotion. It's also important to avoid technical jargon that will confuse and lose the attention of the average reader. A general rule of thumb is to keep the length to be somewhere around 500 words or less.

Once you have written your release it's time to share your information with the rest of the world. The easiest way to accomplish this is to utilize a distribution service which can do this at a reasonable cost. Search "press release distribution services" and you will find an abundance of companies willing to help you with this service. Most PR distribution service providers allow you to target specific media circuits based on geographical region and industry. The cost will vary depending on the length of your release and reach of the distribution. Your budget will dictate these decisions. For example, the cost of a release to local media outlets will be less expensive than one sent to a national circuit. Typically, a local press release of 500 words or less should cost less than $500 on average.

Ask yourself: "Is my company doing something newsworthy others may find interesting?" A well written press release can be a great marketing tool that draws attention to your company and increases sales.

Written Articles. Different from a press release, a written article is about a specific topic for particular publications like magazines, newspapers, journals, and various electronic media. Unlike a press release which describes a special service your company is providing or something noteworthy it has accomplished, a written article addresses a specific topic of interest to the publication's readership. For example, a press release might announce you have opened a new branch office to serve a particular region, or approved a $100,000 factoring facility for a new client in a specific industry, or sponsored a golf tournament to raise funds for a certain charity. A written article could describe how factoring benefits business owners in a specific industry in ten specific ways, and then describes the ten ways in detail.

If you have a knack for writing, submitting articles to various publications can be a free and relatively easy way to introduce factoring and yourself to a large number of people. While there's no guarantee what you write will get published, county business journals and smaller newspapers are often quite willing to accept well-written articles by a local writer on the subject of factoring, especially if they don't come off as self-serving. If you don't write well, consider contacting a reporter of a business journal or smaller city newspaper for an interview to describe factoring. You take your chances on what will be written, but the exposure can quickly lead to new business.

One of my first clients read an article I wrote in a local business journal. She had never heard of factoring before, called the paper to get my phone number (I foolishly omitted it at the end of the article[2]) and soon became a good client. Conveniently, she lived only a couple miles away which made working with her even easier.

If you have the time and stamina, writing a regular column for a small newspaper or business journal is among the best free publicity you can get. The consistent visibility is what stays with people and a regular column provides this. Again, direct your words to how factoring can help the readers' businesses, not to what you do. Remember WIIFM.

Providing similar articles for business-oriented blogs and e-zines can also be effective. Even if your words are printed only once, it's remarkable how long people keep articles before waiting to contact you. The same article above was uploaded to America Online and available there. About two years later, I received a call from a business journal publisher in New York asking for permission to reprint it. Both electronic and printed articles have a wonderful advantage of being easily saved by readers for a long time, as well as being picked up by other media and republished.

Newsletters. Once you have even a few people in your contact list, consider putting out a monthly or quarterly newsletter. Like blogs, coming up with fresh content after a while can be a challenge, but these are a great way to keep your name in front

---

[2] *Always* include your phone number, website and email address at the end of such articles. How many prospects did I lose in this instance who were too busy to take the trouble to find me?

of people you know, have met, or want to remember you. Through many electronic channels, you can distribute it to prospects, clients, colleagues, brokers, larger factors, friends and relatives, people whose business cards you've collected, and others who could bring business.

Many online newsletter companies provide templates that are easy to use and make distribution a snap. Do a web search for "email newsletters," "newsletter service," and the like and you'll find them. Some as of this writing include Constant Contact, iContact, MailChimp, CoolerEmail, MyEmma, Campaigner, and LetterPop. There are many more.

Set a regular time to publish, put those dates on your calendar, and follow the plan. Especially to start with, keep your newsletter simple. Even a one-pager can be enough to begin. Include information that will benefit your recipients, updates on your company's services, add a note of humor, and perhaps spotlight a client or other business with whom you deal. Always keep it upbeat. Remember, the best way to get new business is to remind people what you do and how you can help them and others. The purpose of your newsletter is to make the recipient think of YOU when she becomes aware of a need for factoring.

Classified Ads. Printed classified ads are going the way of the buggy whip and have been replaced with sites like Craigslist. If you go this route, posting classified ads on Craigslist should be done at least weekly if not almost daily, and can take some time. However the number of people who use Craigslist is gigantic, and you never know who might be looking not just for firewood, appliances, or a gig, but actually be a small business owner trying to find money for working capital.

If you advertise here (free of course, so the price is right) expect to get inquiries from people who are not factorable. You'll be sorting through a good deal of chaff to find the kernels of wheat.

You might also put classifieds in various trade publications of industries that are factorable, or home business publications. These can also be good places to submit articles you've written. A strategically placed ad after an article can further induce someone to call.

Street Signs. Relatively small street signs located near busy intersections with a stop sign or light are another idea. You must keep the number of words to a minimum and the lettering large. For example, "CASH FOR INVOICES, (253) 555-5555," is enough to fit onto a two-by-three foot sign, so that most passing motorists will be able to read it. You'll want to check your city or county sign ordinances so you're not breaking any law; breaking sign codes that are enforced may result in a nasty fine or having the signs removed and thrown away.

Make your sign look professional. Go to a quick sign shop and ask their advice on materials, color, lettering, etc. before having it made. If there are no legal problems putting them up, a few good-looking signs in strategic locations can be a relatively inexpensive and a very effective avenue to new business.

Magnetic Car Signs. Using a vehicle to advertise your factoring business is a natural. Magnetic signs can be made inexpensively by your neighborhood sign shop, and cost more if you want a digital graphic[3] or reflective lettering or graphics which stand out nicely after dark when a headlight shines on them.

Magnetic signs can be put on or taken off your car any time you want. Test your car door first with a small refrigerator magnet to make sure it sticks; some cars have metal alloys that won't hold a magnet. Also, be aware that you must keep the car surface clean where the magnet attaches. Dust, accumulating between the magnet and the car, will weaken the grip and the sign can fall off as you drive along.

Your sign should include a catchy phrase, your company name, phone number, and website URL if it's brief. The phrase might be something like "CA$H for Invoices in 24 hours," "Alternative Financing for Business," "Improve Business Cash Flow," or something similar to grab motorists' attention. Keep the wording simple and the lettering easy to read: motorists will

---

[3] Digital graphics are a blended mix of colors printed on a sign, as opposed to one color vinyl letters or designs. Digital technology is used to print graphics and logos with color gradients, very intricate designs, and photographs.

have to rely on memory or a hastily scribbled note to record your information. Make it as easy for them as possible; too much information is unreadable.

Magnetic car signs are an excellent way to advertise to local prospects, as that's who will read your sign every day as you make your commute, do your errands, or even drive to leisure activities.

Use a magnetic sign on a pretty normal-looking vehicle; don't put it on your Lamborghini, nor on your heap with plastic taped over a missing window and dented fenders rusting through. Your vehicle is a statement of your business practices and success. The only down-side of this marketing method: you need to keep your car clean.

Vinyl Vehicle Lettering. Tasteful lettering and graphics on your vehicle's windows, sides, and/or back have the same advantages of magnetics. The only difference is it costs a bit more and once it's on, it stays there – unlike a magnetic that can go on and off any time.

Vinyl can be removed from a vehicle without permanent markings. Yet you need to think of this as a more permanent look on your vehicle; therefore think this through more carefully than magnetic signs.

Vinyl lettering makes your vehicle a full-time "company car." It's easy to leave it on (compared to the magnetic surface you need to keep clean) but you need to consider this: are there ever times or places you want to drive without identifying who you are or what you do?

For example, if you're factoring on the side and have a full-time job where your co-workers see you come and go, advertising your side business this way may not set well with your boss.

If such issues don't matter however, vinyl lettering can give your business a look of permanence, show you're serious about it, and set well with prospective clients. Prices will depend on how elaborate the design, square footage of surface coverage, and your use of digital graphics or reflective vinyl – which may be worth the extra cost. Tell the sign shop your budget and they'll give you an idea of what's available for your price range.

Just like a magnetic sign, keep the design simple and the wording sparse. Avoid intricate logos that will be time-consuming for the sign shop to reproduce or install, as this will increase your cost. Again, this is good "bang for the buck" advertising with the exposure it gives you, especially if you drive a lot. I was once asked how many trucks I had in my fleet because this person saw my vehicles with their signage so often. I had a "fleet" of one and just drove around town a lot.

Public Speaking. If a sea of faces staring at you while you talk doesn't intimidate you, public speaking can be another free and highly effective means of finding business. Civic and business groups which meet monthly usually have a speaker at each meeting. Invariably, the person in charge of arranging speakers is looking for someone to fill a slot. Find out who this person is for your local Lions Club, Rotary, Chamber, home-based business association, and the like, and offer your services. Just as with putting on seminars, you must be prepared and appear as a knowledgeable, professional person, or your public speaking event can be more damaging than beneficial.

Here's an idea to use if you're invited to speak before a group. Bring many business cards with one specially marked on the back. Pass them out as you begin your talk. When you finish, give a door prize (perhaps a certificate for a meal for two at a nice local restaurant) to the person who ends up with the marked card. Done effectively, you may have interested prospects call the next day or two; you'll also have a good chance of getting invitations to speak to other groups.

Direct Mail Postcards. Gurus of marketing often say direct mail is the only way to go. However, as mentioned in an earlier chapter, this can be very expensive. Good, attractive designs, mailing lists, postage, printing, and paper costs add up fast. Then too, it takes a lot of time to get the mailing ready. Much direct mail (considered "junk" by recipients) that comes in an envelope doesn't even get opened, so use a mailing that nearly always is read: postcards. They cost less to mail, less to produce, and are far more likely to be read than the nicest letter on fancy stationery with an expensive brochure included.

More importantly, use some eye-catching graphics, cartoons, fonts, and/or colored paper so that your mailer grabs the reader's attention immediately. You have approximately three seconds for the reader to decide if what you've sent is worth reading. Something that tickles the funny bone or clearly speaks to his need (WIIFM) will greatly increase your chances of winning that three-second decision.

Postcards are most effective if they are mailed in a series, about one to three weeks apart over a one- to three-month time span, to the same recipients. Develop a plan, carefully target those who will receive your mailing, and follow through completely. Be sure to budget adequately. Timing your mailings can be important. Events requiring cash flow–first of the year (fresh start), spring (tax time), other months quarterly taxes are due, and seasonal needs for your target businesses–should be considered.

Response rates are generally low for direct mail (2-3% is considered good), so don't send out 10 postcards and expect your phone to ring. Get your list ready, mail out maybe 25 cards per week, be systematic in your coverage, and follow up each card with a phone call.

Radio/Cable TV Ads. These can be powerful media. Ads designed and placed on radio and TV may not be as expensive as you think. Call various radio and cable stations to get an idea of how much 30- and 60-second spots are. Prices will vary widely with the size and audience of the station, hours of the day, time of year and number of times you advertise. After the year-end holidays (the good time for advertising a seminar you're putting on), rates are often lower because most advertisers have exhausted their marketing budget in the December blitz and the media company needs revenue.

Radio and TV personnel are usually available to help you in making your ad or presentation come off professionally. While you may not want to use this media as your very first marketing method, once you know what you're doing in the factoring world they can be an effective means of reaching new clients.

Business/Trade Journal Ads. Printed advertising can be costly and needs to run many times before it's even noticed. Consider what publications your target audience reads and price how much printed ads are in these. Generally, printed advertising is one of the more expensive means of reaching prospects for the number of responses you get. But because it's fairly easy and people like to see their company's ad in print, many neophytes do this early in the game, spend a lot of money...and then try other methods more successfully. However, trade and business journals with online publications can be a better alternative here though prices can vary. Ask what they provide and costs.

Radio or Webinar Guest Spots. Acting as a radio or webinar guest is another method to try once you're established and confident in the factoring world. You can get tremendous exposure as a guest. A few inquiries will lead you to the people, stations, or companies you should be calling, and this wide exposure costs nothing more than the calls. Start with a web search looking up "radio guide" or similar keywords to point you in the right direction. As you learn the ropes, you'll improve your presentation and can use the experience to tout your expertise as a "frequently interviewed media guest." Pretty impressive.

Part 3

Handling Funds

9

Banking and Funds Transfers

Choose Your Bank Carefully

Deciding which bank you'll use may not consume much thought; but if you are in an area where you have several banking choices, choose your bank carefully.

First, shop the banks for checking account charges (try to get free checking), minimum balances, understandable and complete monthly statements, and internet banking services that are easy to use and provide the features you require. Even more, get to know the branch manager well. Take him out to lunch once you set up your account. Not only can this person be a great source of referrals, he also can be a handy problem solver if there is ever a problem with your account.

Also, be sure the manager understands what you're doing as a factor and will accommodate any special banking needs you have. Most banks will not let you deposit checks made out only to your client. Be sure the banker understands why you may need to do this. Even if customers are instructed to make checks out to the factor, some will make checks out to the client anyway and you need to be able to deposit these checks. Therefore, make sure your bank has on file a copy of your contract with each of your clients. The contract must specifically give you power of attorney to endorse and deposit their checks into your account. If a bank won't cooperate with you on this critical matter, find one that will. If you can't (which is quite possible) you probably need a lockbox, assuming the lockbox will accept third party checks.

Since 9/11, finding a bank that will cooperate in this regard has become much more difficult than it once was. Banks are especially concerned over the appearance of money laundering

107

activity, and some bankers use this as the reason for not allowing you to deposit checks made out to another party. However, the same bankers who use this excuse usually do not really understand factoring and are more concerned with a superior or bank regulator who is always looking over their shoulder, waiting for them to make a mistake. It is safer and easier for a banker to simply say your request "cannot be done," rather than to really learn about what you're trying to do, or stick his neck out just a little to accommodate this banking need of your business.

If you have had a close banking relationship for many years with a local bank, you *may* find them receptive to this request...but don't count on it. If you find resistance, simply go up the ladder and keep asking to speak with someone further up until you find someone who understands what you're requesting. If and when you finally find that person, their simple say-so is enough to immediately make this service available to you. If you never find such a person, you'll have to try another bank or have customers make all payment checks out to your company (more on this later).

One of the biggest considerations in choosing your bank is obvious: convenience. Because you will make frequent runs to the bank (unless you use a lockbox or check reading machine – ask if your bank provides this tool), find a bank that is close to your home or office and is open hours most convenient to your schedule. Some banks have branches located in or beside large grocery stores that are open more hours than regular bank branches.

Sending Funds

Getting money into your client's hands (or bank accounts) is a central part of your business. There are several ways to do this, and we will look at each of them. The two most commonly known means of transferring funds are writing checks and sending bank wires. However, there are others, some of which you may find preferable. I certainly do.

Checks. The advantages of checks are that they are familiar, inexpensive to create, and universally accepted. The disadvantages of checks is that they're a bit cumbersome to complete, sign, and get into the hands (or bank accounts) of your clients. Also, if you have a client in a different state, her bank may, as a matter of policy, put a hold on making funds available from your check for anywhere from a few days to a couple weeks. This can be a great aggravation for you and your client, and there's nothing you can do about it. It is a common occurrence if your client regularly maintains a low balance or has any history of NSF checks with the bank, either of which are likely with very small clients.

Checks take more of your time to prepare than any other means of transferring funds, and if you have to overnight a check to a client who's out of town or out of state, this can be fairly expensive. You can deposit a check into a local branch of your client's bank if there is one near you, but if there isn't that's not an option. If there is a nearby branch, you end up spending a fair amount of time driving around and waiting in line at the bank. If you're doing that for several clients, this is not a good use of your time. If you want to write a check, it's best to have the client pick it up at your office if they're not too far away. You can also just mail it to them, if they're not in a hurry to receive the money (which usually is not the case).

Bank wires. Wires are sent by your bank, and funds are pulled directly out of your account and sent to your client's bank, where they are deposited into your client's account the same day they are sent (usually). Though wires are familiar to most people, the process of how money is actually transferred through a bank wire is something of a mystery to many. Here's how they work.

You notify your bank, usually by phone or online, that you want to withdraw x dollars from your account and wire it to your client's account. Your bank will require the receiver's bank routing number (also called the ABA number), which is an identification number each bank has, as well as the client's bank account number. Some larger banks have different routing numbers when wires are sent than the number printed on the client's checks, so check with the receiving bank before sending the first wire. Wires may also require you to provide the name of the bank, the name on the account, the address of the account, and the amount to transfer. At minimum you'll need the bank name, routing number, account number, and amount. There is a deadline each afternoon, usually around 1:00 to 3:00 or so, depending on the bank, by which time wires must be submitted to be sent that day.

If you give your wire information to a teller or someone in your local bank branch, they must send the instructions to their wire department. Once the wire department has the needed information, they send it electronically to the receiving bank and the funds are deducted from your account. Someone in the wire department of your client's bank must receive the wire and then transfer the funds into the account designated. The money isn't automatically deposited into your client's account all by itself. A person has to do that.

Bank wires are usually same-day transfers, but you can't always assume they will be. As you can see, human hands at both banks are needed to move the funds from your account to your client's. If you're sending a wire from the west coast to the east coast, keep in mind the three hour time difference. If the wire is not sent in the morning, it may not land in the client's account until the next business day, especially if the receiving bank's people are busy.

However, even if you're sending the wire to a bank in the same time zone, if the receiving bank's people don't deposit the wire in a timely fashion, the funds may not land that day. Receiving banks are good at blowing smoke on this, saying it wasn't received on time or giving a variety of excuses. The simple fact of the matter is, once your bank sent it, the receiving bank's people may not have deposited it in your client's account in a timely manner. It's common for them to lay blame elsewhere.

Be aware that a few smaller rural banks and credit unions are not set up to send or receive wires directly and must go through a larger bank to do so. This makes sending and receiving wires through such institutions slower and sometimes a bit of a hassle.

Because bank employees' time at both ends is required to make wires happen, the sending bank charges you to send a wire, and the receiving bank charges your client to receive a wire. If you have extremely high wire volume, you may negotiate with your bank for free wires, but your volume and bank balance need to be significant. Typically banks charge from about $8 (if you're lucky) to $40 to send a wire (and more for international wires), and about $5 to $20 to receive a wire. This makes bank wires one of the more expensive ways to send money, though they are fairly convenient and fast, as long as both sending and receiving banks handle the wires without the use of another bank. When that's the case, wires are not very fast.

ACH. ACH stands for Automated Clearing House and is also known as EFT, for Electronic Funds Transfer, and direct deposit. You can send ACH's through your bank (if it provides them; once again some smaller banks and credit unions do not) or through an ACH service.

ACH payments are a very handy way of making deposits to your clients. Instead of writing a check and depositing it into your client's account, mailing or sending it by overnight courier, or wiring funds, you simply sit at your computer and make a transfer of funds via the internet in a matter of seconds. Again, you need your client's bank account number as well as the bank's ABA number to send the funds. Once you're set up to send an ACH, you simply enter the client's banking numbers, the amount you want to transfer, and send. There is also a daily deadline for sending an ACH, though it is usually later in the afternoon than the deadline for wires.

ACH's are cheaper and easier than other methods of transferring funds to your clients, and definitely one of the more convenient ways to run this part of your business. These transfers are made through the Federal Reserve Bank, and involve an electronic transfer of your bank's funds to your client's bank. That is, you're transferring your *bank's* money with no float and an immediate transfer of funds – which the bank looks upon as a loan. Funds are not withdrawn from your account until after the bank has sent the funds on your behalf. If your balance is less than what you sent, you've essentially send funds you don't have. Not surprisingly, this doesn't make the bank happy.

Therefore in order to qualify for ACH payments from your bank, you must apply for the privilege just like you would for a bank loan, with your business financials, tax returns, personal credit report, the whole bit. If you can't qualify for a loan, you may not be approved for ACH. While you may look upon this simply as a substitute for writing a check, the bank doesn't, so be prepared. However, if you can qualify for this service, it is well worth the effort. It will save you many hours of preparing and mailing or depositing checks. To learn of my first experience applying for ACH payments, see the story in the chapter "Additional Resources" called "A True Story about ACH Transfers and Bankers." What an education, both about ACHs specifically and how banks think and operate in general. Read it.

As mentioned, ACH services exist that provide ACH transfers, which are a bit different from your bank. Typically they will provide you with a higher daily limit and their requirements for approval aren't usually as stringent. However, many take longer to actually transfer funds. While a bank will usually transfer ACH funds in one or two days, meaning money you send today lands in your client's account the next business day or the day after, ACH services often will wait for funds to clear from your account before sending them. That can mean a wait of three to five business days before your client receives the money.

The ACH services and banks also usually have a monthly charge of perhaps $5 to $25, plus a per transaction charge. My bank charges a monthly service fee plus a daily rate. The daily fee is $1 per batch of ACHs sent together, plus 25 cents per transaction for next day ACHs or 20 cents for second day ACHs. Thus, when I send next day ACHs to 10 different clients in a single batch, I pay $1 + (10 x .25) for a total of $3.50 for the day. My monthly ACH charges are consistently around $100 or less, which is reasonable considering the number of ACHs I send.

While some factors charge their clients to send ACHs, since my bank's ACH cost is so low I don't charge my clients to send them; thus most choose ACHs over wires. That's because wires cost them $15 for me to send, plus their bank's charge (typically another $15 or $20) to receive. So most of my clients prefer to wait a day to get their money for free, rather than pay about $30 to get it today. In their shoes I would too.

Before using my present bank, I considered an ACH service that charged $10 per month plus $1 per transaction. The service gave a much higher daily limit than my former bank did at the time, which sometimes was not enough for my daily transfers. Remember: the daily limit may include transfers *into* your account in addition to transfers out. Unfortunately, the lag time for the money to arrive in my clients' accounts was much slower than the next day option I have with my present bank, which I (and my clients) clearly prefer. If you can get a sufficient daily limit with your bank and increase it as needed, sending ACHs through your bank is probably the best option.

The amount of your ACH charges will depend on how much the provider wants your business and how much your volume is; the more transactions you do, the less each transaction costs. When looking for an ACH provider, either through your bank or an ACH service, do your best to negotiate costs. This is a fairly competitive market and you may be able to talk them down from what is originally proposed. Also get a demo of their online software to see what it takes to make an ACH transfer. Some interfaces are much more intuitive and easy to use than others. To find ACH providers, Google "ACH processing." You'll be surprised at the variety of what you'll find.

Intrabank transfers. If your bank provides them, intrabank transfers can be another way to transfer funds, though they can be quite limited. An intrabank transfer is a transfer of funds between two accounts that use the same bank. If both you and your client have an account in the same bank, this may be an option.

Some online banking allows you to transfer funds this way, but severely limit the amount of funds you can transfer per transaction. For example, my present bank allows intrabank transfers that cost $1 each and land in my client's account right away. However, there is a limit of $1000 per transfer which is often not enough for an advance or rebate I'm paying. Thus I find it easier and faster to just send most clients ACHs or wires, as they prefer.

Bill Pay/Direct Pay. Most banks provide a bill paying service which allows you to pay routine and recurring bills quickly and efficiently, either electronically or with a check sent by the bank. Many also provide a service allowing you to pay companies or individuals directly online without sending a check. Different from an ACH, you must register with your bank for these services and it might take a few days to set up. Typically funds arrive the date you specify they are due (when prepared in advance) for bill pay. For direct pay they usually arrive right away or the next day, and the charges are somewhat more than ACH costs, making ACHs the preferred method of sending money for most factors. However if you are not able to send ACHs, this can be an alternative.

Receiving Funds

Receiving money from your clients' customers can be done several ways: depositing checks at a branch, depositing checks using a check processing machine in your office, receiving wires, receiving direct deposits, and a lockbox. Let's look at each.

Check Deposits at a Bank Branch. This is the old fashioned way used by people for decades long before electronic banking came along, and certainly still works. However there are a few issues with making deposits this way that make it less convenient than other alternatives available.

First, you need to receive the checks in your mailbox or have them overnighted or hand-delivered to you. This method also means you need to make a trip to the bank to deposit the checks. If you don't mind that, fine…as long as the checks are made out to your company's name and not the client's.

Unfortunately, despite often Herculean efforts on your part to provide a Notice of Assignment (see the chapter "Record Keeping") and make follow-up calls to be sure they will pay you and not the client, followed by assurances they will, guess what? Many customers *still* make their checks to your clients anyway. This leads you to wonder about the intelligence of a great many accounts payable departments across the country, as well as being one of the most effective means of rapidly turning your hair gray.

Banks balk at depositing checks made out to a third party (your client), and most flat out refuse. That means if a customer makes the check in your client's name without your company name anywhere on the check, you must either

1. Have the customer re-issue the check, properly made out to your company. Not surprisingly, this never earns you brownie points with the customer.

2. Have the client endorse the check over to you. That of course also causes delays and may incline a client to just deposit the customer's check in his own account and write his own check to cover it. This is a *very* bad idea because most small factoring clients rarely have a healthy balance in their bank accounts (and in fact are often overdrawn), and the check they write to cover the customer's check will very often bounce. Trust me on this one.

3. Have a Power of Attorney in your contract that allows you to endorse customer checks this way. This sounds good in theory but is anything but fool proof. Almost always a teller will see it's a third party check and refuse to deposit it; that's what they're trained to do. You can explain you have a Power of Attorney and blah, blah, blah; but if the manager isn't there or someone above the teller won't give the ok, you're going to leave with only a heavy black cloud of frustration swirling around your entire body, and the check still in your hand – not in your bank account.

Hopefully you have some kind of process with your bank to accept third party checks because, guaranteed, you're going to receive them. Unfortunately with many banks this is tough. Obviously the first thing you need to ask a bank before you open your factoring account is this: can they accommodate your depositing third party checks in some way?

So depositing checks in a local bank branch is fine as long as you enjoy driving to the bank every day, and every check is made out to your company, and/or your bank is unusually cooperative with third party checks.

Check Processing Machines. This device is a small contraption you've probably seen on a bank teller's desk. When you hand her a check and deposit slip, the teller places the paper in the machine and *zip!* The paper zooms through the machine in a U-shaped slot and the transaction is recorded. The teller gives you a receipt with a cheerful smile and you're on your way.

Many banks provide these devices to business customers to make deposits electronically without having to come to the bank. You get your machine, plug it in a handy place in your home or office, and make your check deposits this way. While you're still processing paper checks (getting the mail, opening it, and preparing the deposits), you're also saving yourself a trip to the bank, standing in line, and driving back. Your deposits are recorded immediately, the cost is considerably less than a lockbox, and many small factors like using this method. Talk with your banker about what it takes to set this up and costs, and consider whether it will work for you.

Receiving Wires. Rarely you'll come across a customer who wants to pay you with a wire. While this kind of payment is quite unusual, the customer might suggest it if they are way overdue paying an invoice and actually feel guilty about it. (Yes, that does happen every now and then; it gives me hope for the human race.)

Also, if you're working with a participant in a factoring deal who needs to send you money immediately (often the case when a client is awaiting his advance today), this is usually the best way to do it. The sender will need the same information about your account as you need when sending a wire – bank name, account name, routing number for wires, account number, etc.

Because your bank charges you for receiving a wire (typically $15 to $30 or so), this is not a method you want to use every day for routine deposits. But it can be useful when you want the funds in a hurry or want to be sure the money won't bounce if it's coming from a client or customer whose bank balance you have reason to question. A bank wire won't bounce because the bank won't send it if the sender doesn't have adequate funds.

ACH Deposits. Just as many factors prefer sending funds via ACH because they are easier, faster, and less expensive than checks, many companies pay their bills this way as well.

The advantages to you and your client of this method are:

1. Funds arrive faster than checks, usually arriving first thing in the morning the next day or two after they are sent. It's nice to greet a new day by seeing these deposits sitting in your bank account when the day begins.

2. Funds go directly into your account without your having to do anything. Nothing to enter, nothing to save or file; the funds are just there, happily ready for you to use. Nice.

3. You'll quickly appreciate customers who pay this way AND provide information via email or online, showing which invoices are being paid and the amount paid for each one. This gives you a record of what you received and the invoices paid, much like a completed check stub. If customers provide this information, you can make a PDF of the payment explanation and save it in your Deposits folder, providing an electronic paper trail of every deposit you receive.

Unfortunately not all customers provide such helpful information. Many just send the funds and that's it – no explanation, nothing. If they don't provide data as to what's being paid, receiving payments this way can be one of its disadvantages. Read on.

Disadvantages of ACH deposits:

1. If you don't know who sent the funds and the amount doesn't match any outstanding invoices, figuring out what it is paying can be a challenge. If the client's name is included in the transaction, it's easy. If it's not, and an entry like "MMB ACH AP000215597" for $3,247.56 is all you have to work with, good luck. Sometimes these codes are easier to decipher than others, and they are usually consistent with deposits from the same customer. So when you know who sent the first one, you can usually figure out the next.

2. If you know who it's from but don't know what it's paying and the amount doesn't match any open invoices, you are wise to call to confirm exactly which invoices are being paid and the amount for each. Especially when numerous invoices are being paid at once, you have no idea which invoices are included and if the amounts are correct or overpaid or underpaid. All you can do is guess what the deposit covers if you don't ask.

This can be a risky proposition if you are batching many small invoices from a client (i.e. advancing on many little invoices on a statement as if they are one invoice, and not itemizing each small invoice on the schedule). When you're paid an amount with no explanation for what it's paying, you have no clue if the customer has skipped or short paid any invoices you haven't tracked individually. If you just apply the payment to the oldest advances in your system, over time you can end up not getting paid for invoices you show as due. However because the customer (in their system) already paid or declined to pay those invoices, and you were never informed, you are going to be out the money unless you have enough in the client's reserves to cover it or the client can otherwise make it up. That can get dicey and the chances of your ending up with the short end of the stick are quite good.

So if you are paid with ACH deposits, be sure you are very clear exactly what invoices are being paid on *each* deposit. Don't assume anything or you may eventually live to regret it. Been there, done that – one of my worst factoring losses occurred this way.

Lockbox. Another way to receive funds is a lockbox. This is a post office box that is owned and managed by a bank or a lockbox company. You direct all your check payments to this box number, where the bank retrieves the mail, opens the envelopes, deposits the checks into your account, and provides you a daily report of payments received.

If your bank will not allow you to deposit checks made out to your client in your local branch, this may be an alternative (though many banks still require checks be made out to you or to the bank). Make sure of your bank's policy as to whom the checks must be made if you want to use a lockbox. With my bank, receiving third party checks in my lockbox is just fine.

Lockboxes are often used by factors as this service performs the task of an employee for a much lower cost. A small factor needs to determine if his operation is large enough to justify this expense, which will usually run around a couple to several hundred dollars a month, depending on the services provided and the volume of checks arriving. For those whose time is tight or who don't want to make a regular trek to the post office and/or bank, lockboxes can be wonderful. For part-time or very small operations, however, they may be too expensive.

Now that my factoring business is well established, I consider a lockbox to be one of the most critical and important tools needed to run my business as efficiently as possible. To learn more, see my ebook *How I Run My One-Person Factoring Business*, available from www.DashPointPublishing.com.

Clearly, there are many reasons for choosing your bank carefully, so do your homework before making a final selection. Determine what banking services and funds transfer methods you need and see who will provide them. However, be aware that some banks consider factoring to be a high-risk business and may not be willing to provide the services you want; a few may even be unwilling to open an account for you.

Spending enough time choosing the financial institution best suited to your needs will provide great savings to you in time, convenience, service to your clients, and even money...which brings us to our next chapter.

10

Money

The Cardinal Rule of Money

Before taking another step, you must memorize The Cardinal Rule of Money. This Rule is the same whether you're factoring, gambling in Vegas, or playing the stock market. Each has a certain kinship with the other: risk. The Cardinal Rule of Money is, **"Don't risk more than you can afford to lose."** Don't bet the farm. Don't ante up everything you have. When going into a casino, you must decide your limit, how much you're going to play with, the most you're going to play in a given hand and the total amount you can stand to lose. Do this even before you walk in the door. Then stick to your limits...and have fun!

When you factor an account, you are taking a calculated gamble that runs something like this. Assume an 80% advance and 5% discount: on a $100 invoice, you are betting $80 that the invoice will be paid and you'll make $5. On a $1,000 invoice, you're betting $800 that you'll make $50; on a $10,000 invoice, it's $8,000 and $500, and so on. Viewed this way, you may think the risk isn't worth the return, which may be true. However, with good due diligence, analysis of the businesses involved and enough transactions, you can make the odds of losing as small as possible. While risking $80 to make $5 may not sound like a good proposition, when you make enough $50's and $500's and $5,000's on deals that you know are as safe as possible, you spread your risk well and make income that adds up.

Another parallel is an auction. The only way to come out ahead in an auction is to decide, before the bidding begins, the maximum amount you will bid for an item. Otherwise, in the excitement of bidding, you can get carried away and end up spending lots more than something is worth. Factoring is the same: in the excitement of making larger and larger discounts, you may find yourself with an account that's not worth what you're putting into it in terms of time, hassles or possible losses.

The players who are most successful in the long run are the most patient, careful and methodical – not the highest rollers. While factoring is not for the faint of heart, neither is it for the reckless.

How Much Money You Need to Factor

In an earlier section entitled "Small Numbers Add Up," we spoke of grossing $5,000 or $10,000 by factoring 10 or 20 clients a month. Naturally, it takes some seed money to be able to factor just one client for any amount. Without money to start with, you can only refer deals in the factoring business.

As a factor, you use a pool of funds that is regularly recycled. If you have $20,000 available, you could factor five clients monthly for $4,000 each (assuming their customers pay every 30 days). If you have $100,000, you could factor ten clients for $10,000 each or some other combination. However, in reality, it's not quite that clean. You'll have some accounts pay in 15 days, others in 60. The juggling act you continually play as a factor is keeping your money on the street every day possible so that it's working for you, making sure it all comes back, while taking care to not run out of funds when a client comes to you to factor another batch of invoices. If your pool runs dry, you'll either need to obtain more funds, bring in a participant, or (heaven forbid) turn your client down. Hence it behooves you to know approximately when an invoice will be paid, when new invoices will be arriving, and how much you will have available at a given time. Good software will help enormously here.

How much money you have to factor will determine how much you make before overhead expenses. Determine how much your money costs you (from loans and other sources) and use Chart 6 to estimate your factoring income. Remember, the numbers assume all your money is on the street and doesn't include bad debt losses.

Chart 6: Amounts Needed to Factor

Amt of Invcs	Amt in Advncs 80%	Amt in Advncs 70%	5% Avg Factor Discnt	0% Cost of Money	Income Before Overhd	Annlzd ROI w/ 80% adv	Annlzd ROI w/ 70% adv
10,000	8,000	7,000	500	0	500	75%	86%
25,000	20,000	17,500	1,250	0	1,250	75%	86%
50,000	40,000	35,000	2,500	0	2,500	75%	86%
100,000	80,000	70,000	5,000	0	5,000	75%	86%
250,000	200,000	175,000	12,500	0	12,500	75%	86%
500,000	400,000	350,000	25,000	0	25,000	75%	86%

(=12% APR)

Amt of Invcs	Amt in Advncs 80%	Amt in Advncs 70%	5% Avg Factor Discnt	1% Cost of Money	Income Before Overhd	Annlzd ROI w/ 80% adv	Annlzd ROI w/ 70% adv
10,000	8,000	7,000	500	70	430	65%	74%
25,000	20,000	17,500	1,250	175	1,075	65%	74%
50,000	40,000	35,000	2,500	350	2,150	65%	74%
100,000	80,000	70,000	5,000	700	4,300	65%	74%
250,000	200,000	175,000	12,500	1,750	10,750	65%	74%
500,000	400,000	350,000	25,000	3,500	21,500	65%	74%

(=18% APR)

Amt of Invcs	Amt in Advncs 80%	Amt in Advncs 70%	5% Avg Factor Discnt	1.50% Cost of Money	Income Before Overhd	Annlzd ROI w/ 80% adv	Annlzd ROI w/ 70% adv
10,000	8,000	7,000	500	105	395	59%	68%
25,000	20,000	17,500	1,250	263	988	59%	68%
50,000	40,000	35,000	2,500	525	1,975	59%	68%
100,000	80,000	70,000	5,000	1,050	3,950	59%	68%
250,000	200,000	175,000	12,500	2,625	9,875	59%	68%
500,000	400,000	350,000	25,000	5,250	19,750	59%	68%

How Much You'll Make

However you accumulate your factoring pool of funds, you can calculate how much you will earn, broadly speaking, by multiplying the total amount you have on the street by the average discount you charge, then subtracting the cost of your money and overhead. In other words, say you have $40,000 with which to factor and you keep these funds in regular circulation.

With an 80% advance, you can factor $50,000 worth of invoices ($50,000 x 80% = $40,000). Multiply $50,000 times 5% (average discount you receive) and you'll make $2,500 gross. Subtract from this the cost of your money (say, an average of 12% APR or 1% per month on the amount you advance) and what you have left, after overhead expenses, is your profit. Given this scenario, with $40,000 on the street, which costs you $400 monthly (1% of $40,000), you'd make $2,100 ($2,500 – $400) monthly, minus overhead. This assumes the money is always on the street, turns regularly, and is not lost to bad debt.

Obviously, you are not going to get rich overnight factoring with numbers like this if this is your full time job. Remember, you're only learning how to swim in the shallow end of the pool – you don't begin by taking on the English Channel on day one. However, if you are working with $40,000 of your own investment money as a part time investor/factor, $2,500 is a great monthly return on $40,000.

Be patient as your factoring clientele and transaction amounts increase, and don't try to grow too fast. Just like a baby, allow yourself a good year to learn how to walk in this business.

The key strategies are to:

1. Have as large a pool of money available to you as you can; the more you have, the more you can make (yet realize that the more clients you factor, the more record keeping you'll have...and eventually that may mean employees).

2. Keep as much of your money on the street as you can. If you're paying to use someone else's funds, you're losing money if you don't keep it in circulation; if it's your own money, you don't make as much.

3. Pay back loans/lines of credit you're not using as soon as you know you don't or won't need the cash. Don't pay for money you're not using to make money.

4. If possible, use money you don't pay to use (your own or from interest-free sources).

5. Keep your overhead as low as possible.

6. Don't factor accounts that take too long to pay (they tie up your money and may never pay).

7. Be careful which clients and customers you take on, and don't get lazy with your due diligence. One hit not only can wipe out principal and profits, but it can take many months from which to recover.

How Much to Charge

This is your call, depending on how much you want to make and what the market will bear. One small factor charges 6 to 8% for the first 30 days and goes up from there, which is a tidy profit. Another charges a flat 9% for the first 90 days. Since around 2% to 4% for 30 days is fairly normal for larger invoices, these may not be out of line. However, realize that those numbers can sound astronomical to potential clients – 8% translates to 96% APR in their minds (even though such reasoning is faulty) – and could scare them off.

You will get more business if your charges are in the 5% range for very small accounts; the question is, can you make enough with rates like that? It's up to you. You may or may not want to adjust your rates and advances according to the stability of your clients and their customers; but remember, we're dealing with small potatoes and you may talk your way out of a deal if your rates sound too high.

I've found a straight forward approach to work well: "My advances usually start at 75% to 80% and my discount rate is 1% per week up to 90 days. If an invoice is out 3 weeks you pay 3%; if it's out 5 weeks you pay 5%, and so on. At 90 days, recourse kicks in. If conditions warrant, the rates may be slightly higher or lower, but that doesn't happen very often."

I've seen some new factors come up with very complicated, convoluted discount rates: x% for the first x days, y% for each of the next y days, then z% if it goes past so many more days, plus a fee for this and a charge for that. Personally I find such complicated rates unnecessary, and often only confuse clients. When a client is confused by your rates, he may begin to wonder if you're overcharging him (when in fact you're not) because he simply doesn't understand how his charges are calculated, and they may seem higher than he expected. Such suspicion is very bad for your business and you want to avoid it completely.

Simple, round rates don't make anybody's head hurt, including mine. As long as you make enough to help clients, run your own business, and get ahead, that's what it's all about. Plus your clients will look upon you as a people person interested in helping them, rather than a number cruncher who makes decisions hunched over a calculator. In their position, which kind of person would you rather deal with?

Where to Get the Money You Need

Your original pool of funds can originate from several sources.

Your Own Resources. These may be the easiest or the most difficult to obtain, depending on how much you have or are willing to use. Your own resources can include savings, inheritances, insurance policies, retirement funds, stocks, bonds, mutual funds, the sale of property, valuables, a business, or whatever you may have available. Just remember the Cardinal Rule of Money: Don't risk more than you can afford to lose.

There are two schools of thought on whose money is best to use, your own or OPM (Other People's Money). The advantages of using someone else's resources are:

1. You can make money even if you don't have any of your own, and/or

2. You can build up profits without risking your own money.

The disadvantages of using someone else's are:

1. It's harder to get

2. You have to pay it back (whether you make money with it or lose it), and

3. You have to pay it back with interest.

My personal feeling is that it's better to use as much of your own money as possible, but use only money you can afford to lose. If you've got $50,000 or $100,000 available, you can turn quicker profits than if you have to pay interest back from the profits you make factoring. Further, if you take a hit, you won't have to pay interest on money you no longer have. If you have $10,000 and want to have a pool of $100,000, use your own $10,000 and get the rest from the sources below. Over time, pay them back to the point where you're using as much of your own money as you can: you'll then make more because the cost of your money is less.

A strategy for using your own money is this: assuming your company is incorporated, lend your business your own money at 12% interest APR (or whatever amount you choose) on an interest-only payment basis. In other words, lend the company $10,000 at 12%, and make interest-only payments each month of $100 back to yourself. Alternately, make it an amortized loan for a lower interest rate for a longer period, again making monthly payments. Write a promissory note with the terms of the loan, just as you would for any private lender (see below). Check with your accountant or attorney for the most advantageous way to do this.

Relatives/Friends. After using your own resources, these may be the next best source of funds, as long as you're on good terms and these people trust your judgment. You can offer relatives and friends a far better return on their money than they can get at banks with money markets or CD's. However, they need to realize that investing in you poses a greater risk and if you go out of business their money is gone. Be up front about that, but also instill in them the confidence that this will not happen. You also need to consider the repercussions if their money were to be lost.

What kind of arrangements can you make with relatives and friends? That's up to you. What may be most beneficial to you is to draw up a promissory note (see below), in which they loan you a specified amount of money for a specified length of time (for example, $10,000 for nine months) or with some other specified date of maturity. You will pay them a certain interest percentage – 10%, 12%, 14%, 16% – you decide what you can handle based on your factoring rates (or figure your factoring rates based on how much the money costs you) but keep it as close to 12% as you can. These rates must be attractive to them and still be profitable for you. You can make payments monthly, quarterly, or roll it over and pay the total interest when the note matures. The terms of the loan will dictate its payback. Monthly payments are easier on your cash flow than quarterly or less frequent times.

Put your note or loan in writing even with a relative, and stipulate a definite maturity date. The payment schedule, interest rate, and amortization schedule should also be documented and included. All this paperwork protects you by proving this money is being loaned to your corporation, not given to you personally. This makes it clear that this is NOT a personal arrangement on which you might be taxed. Also, make it clear the persons giving you the loan are not "investors," as Securities laws don't permit you to take on "investors" unless you meet rather stringent requirements. The penalties for noncompliance can be severe. Give regular reports of how much interest they have made (see the sample Lender Report below). This reminds them not only that they are helping your business and you appreciate it, but that they're making money with you.

Lender Report

from
ABC Financial Services
to
John Q. Lender

Amount of Note: $10,000
Interest: 12% APR

Pmt #	APR Interest	Monthly Payments Amt.	Date Payment Due	Date Payment Sent	Amt. Paid to Date
1	12%	$100.00	6/1	6/1	$100.00
2	12%	$100.00	7/1	7/1	$100.00
3	12%	$100.00	8/1	8/1	$100.00
4	12%	$100.00	9/1	9/1	$100.00
5	12%	$100.00	10/1	10/1	$100.00
6	12%	$100.00	11/1		
7	12%	$100.00	12/1		
8	12%	$100.00	1/1		
9	12%	$100.00	2/1		
10	12%	$100.00	3/1		
11	12%	$100.00	4/1		
12	12%	$100.00	5/1		
Totals		$1,200.00			$500.00

You may also find people who prefer to supply funds for specific transactions, clients, or customers. This works much like a participation agreement and often offers a higher rate of return to your lender. Just be sure you keep careful track of which lender has funds with which client, schedule, or invoice/s; and pay them in a manner agreeable to both of you. Good factoring software provides this.

Self-Directed IRAs. Utilizing funds in self-directed IRAs from Equity Trust Company, PENSCO Trust Company, or Entrust Administration, Inc. can be a great way to obtain working capital from others and provide them with high yielding tax-deferred income. Here's how it works.

Your lender establishes a new IRA with one of these companies with either newly invested IRA funds and/or by transferring money from an existing IRA. The holding company then becomes the custodian of these funds. They do not make recommendations as to where to invest the money, they simply do as directed by the IRA owner; hence the term "self-directed" IRA.

The owner of the IRA instructs Equity Trust, PENSCO or Entrust where to invest the funds, who then sends a check as directed. The company receiving the funds makes interest payments to the custodian on behalf of the IRA holder.

How do you get started? First, when you have a lender who wants to place IRA funds in your company, contact either Equity Trust (www.trustetc.com), PENSCO (www.PENSCO.com), or Entrust (www.entrustadmin.com) and let them know you own a factoring company and have a private lender with IRA funds. Your lender wishes to invest this IRA with your firm through their company. You will need to fill out paperwork which indicates yours is a legitimate factoring business that meets their criteria to be a recipient of IRA funds, though these three companies have somewhat different requirements here.

Meanwhile your lender contacts Equity Trust, PENSCO or Entrust and fills out forms as well. These documents include a transfer form, by which funds from an existing IRA fund are transferred to Equity Trust, PENSCO or Entrust, who then becomes the manager of the fund. The lender can transfer all or just a portion of another IRA when creating the new IRA. The lender also fills out a Direction of Investment form, which indicates the amount and where the individual wishes to place the IRA – in this case, with your company.

You then provide a promissory note or whatever documents you use to securitize the funds and give this to the custodial company. Once all the paperwork is in place (expect it to take about a month when setting this up for the first time) and the custodian has received funds from the investor, the management company sends you a check or wire. And there's your working capital.

You then make interest payments to the management company on behalf of your lender according to the terms of your Promissory Note. These checks are made out, as an example, to "PENSCO Trust Company DBA (IRA holder's name)." You do not send interest payments to the lender, but to the custodial company. They place these payments in an interest-bearing account on behalf of the IRA holder, who can then further direct the use of these funds. When enough funds have built up from your interest payments, the lender may want to re-invest them with you as well. This way you can increase the pool of funds available, slowly but steadily.

The custodial companies charge fees which are comparable to each other, though calculated somewhat differently. The fee rates depend on the size of the investment and include charges for various management services. At least $10,000 is a reasonable minimum amount for one of these investments, as the fees for smaller sums will take too much of the interest they'll earn.

The benefit of this arrangement is that you pay the same interest you would to lenders providing traditional (yet taxed) funds, while your lender receives the interest tax-deferred in her self-directed IRA. With traditional IRAs, she is not taxed on the interest until her IRA is cashed in when the investor reaches her 70's. For Roth IRAs, the interest is not taxed when the IRA is cashed in.

Potential lenders probably have IRA funds in relatively low-yield investments. Placing just a portion of these IRA funds in your factoring company at 12% APR (or whatever you pay) is certainly more attractive than low single-digit yields investors are accustomed to receiving – and it's tax-deferred, to boot.

With specific restrictions, you can invest your own IRA funds in your company by using a self-directed IRA managed by any of these trust companies. The main constraint is this: to invest your IRA in your company, you must be a minority (no more than 49%) owner of your business, and the other owner(s) cannot be close relatives (spouse, parents, children, siblings). These restrictions are dictated by federal law, and Equity Trust, PENSCO, or Entrust can give more details. Generally speaking, you probably don't want to invest your own IRA in your company. If you own more than 49% of your company, you can't.

Be aware that IRA funds managed by banks and traditional investment firms will usually tell you that IRA funds cannot be invested in a factoring company. The truth is, IRA funds cannot be invested in a factoring company *with them*. But you absolutely can invest IRA funds with one of the self-directed IRA custodial companies mentioned above. The bank or other investment firm may not know about the existence of self-directed accounts. But if they do know about self-directed IRAs and you have your IRA with them, they probably don't want *you* to know about self-directed IRA accounts.

Self-Employed 401(k) Plan. These are also known as a Solo 401(k), Individual 401(k), and Roth 401(k). If you want to retain majority or 100% ownership of your company and still utilize your own IRA funds, an alternative is to establish a Self-Employed 401(k) plan.

Small business owners with no employees or only a spouse as an employee can establish a Self-Employed 401(k) plan and take a loan from that plan. Individuals can borrow up to the lesser of $50,000 or 50% of the balance in their Self-Employed 401(k). If you need access to capital and want to tap into your retirement accounts, establishing a Self-Employed 401(k) plan allows you to borrow from your retirement funds.

The loan from your Self-Employed 401(k) is not treated as a withdrawal. As such it is not subject to tax nor the 10% penalty for early withdrawal as long as you repay the loan on time. There is no limit on the amount of money that you can transfer to a Self-Employed 401(k) plan. The transfer can be from a 401(k) you had with a previous employer, from a qualified plan that you currently have in your business, or from your existing IRAs. Once you have money in your Self-Employed 401(k) you can request a loan. A Self-Employed 401(k) loan can be used for any purpose.

Repayment of your loan balance is subject to government guidelines, but generally you have five years to repay the loan. The interest rate on the loan is usually close to the prime rate. Your loan payments and interest payments go into your 401(k) account, so in essence you pay the loan back to yourself. Expect to pay a small administrative fee to process your Self-Employed 401(k) plan loan. Also, you may be subject to mutual fund contingent deferred sales charges or other sales charges when you transfer money into and out of your Self-Employed 401(k) plan.

The Self-Employed 401(k) is for small business owners only. You must be the only employee in your business, or if you have employees all of them must be co-owners in the business or spouses of the owners.

Other plans exist and more appear as time goes by. The three IRA management companies mentioned earlier can provide information on a Self-Employed 401(k) program as well as the others; spending some time learning about these can be a sound investment of both your time and retirement funds.

Investors. Generally, these are best to keep within your circle of friends and relatives. Be careful about advertising for funds, as you can get in hot water with Securities and Exchange laws if you solicit funds for investment. Consult with your lawyer about using someone else's money in your pool of factoring funds to avoid problems with the SEC – both when you start taking on lenders, and when the number of lenders you have becomes more than a few.

Banks/Institutions. Banks, credit unions, and lending institutions are extremely careful and often prove impossible for many small business people to use as a source of funds. Trying to get a bank loan for factoring funds can teach you volumes about the frustrations your clients experience when attempting to do the very same thing: trying to get money to start or grow their business. (See "A True Story about ACH Transfers and Bankers" in the chapter "Additional Resources.") It is likely why they turn to you in the first place.

Banks require at least two or three years' business financials. If your factoring company is new you're probably out of luck getting a business loan or line of credit. Most banks don't want to loan to factoring companies anyway. Why? Pretty simple, really. As one bank officer said to me, "Why would I lend money to a factor who is funding businesses banks turn down?" Point taken.

Your best bet may be to get a bank or mortgage company financing through a personal line of credit that is based on your regular job (if you still have it), your spouse's job, and/or the equity you have in your home or other property. If you have a fair amount of equity in your home, this may be the easiest source of fairly large amounts of factoring money, as long as you don't mind having a second mortgage. If your business is the least bit successful, and you haven't taken any bad hits, factoring will easily pay this as you go. However, if you have a major loss, you could lose your home. If you're married, is that something that would make your spouse happy?

Credit Cards. If you have good credit, you may get frequent invitations in the mail to accept new credit cards. If you decide to use credit cards to pay for receivables you'll buy – and let me be blunt…it's not a good idea – you must make an unbreakable agreement with yourself that funds you obtain this way will be used only for factoring, and not for paying your regular business (or personal) bills.

The reason is simple: credit cards' finance charges can eat you alive if you're not making money from the credit they provide. Put differently: if you're paying 18% (not unusual) for credit card money, and you use it to pay a $200 utility bill, that bill actually costs you $200 plus the finance charge every month. Worse, it's not generating income to help you pay the debt.

However, if you use credit card money with which to factor, that 18% works out to 1.5% monthly; if you're charging 5% monthly factoring fees, you're still coming out 3.5% ahead (or 42% APR – not a bad investment from any angle). Most credit cards charge an "advance fee" of about 3%, so in reality the cost of cash is 3% (first month) + interest rate. What's more, credit card interest compounds on unpaid balances making it even more expensive than other traditional loans.

The danger of losing advances made from cash borrowed with credit cards makes this type of financing very risky and I discourage you from using it. Bad debt losses with credit card-borrowed money can be horribly expensive, possibly taking years to repay. If you don't repay it your good credit rating will be ruined. In general, credit cards are not the way you should finance your factoring company. Remember the Cardinal Rule of Money.

Factor Funding Sources. Companies who specialize in funding factors of various sizes do exist. You can find them through the IFA website www.factoring.org, reading IFA's magazine *The Commercial Factor,* attending IFA's annual conference, and asking other factors. If they've been around for a while, they'll know of these sources.

FactorFox Software. Those using FactorFox to track their receivables have a built-in connection to companies and individuals who are interested in participations and/or providing loans or lines of credit to smaller factors. Subscribing factors can post requests for participants, loans and lines which are accessible only to registered funders. Likewise funders can enter their own posts as well, indicating the types of transactions they are willing to fund. No other software platforms provide such a service, and it is included with a factor's regular subscription to FactorFox.

Other Factors. When used in conjunction with one or more of the above, other factors' resources can be an excellent way to stretch your factoring funds. Become familiar with other factors open to this idea, and make arrangements with them to participate with you. If you split expenses and income 50-50, the record keeping is pretty straight forward. You may even find larger factors willing to allow you to appear as the sole factor to your clients, while they supply most or even all the funds for your transactions, and pay you a greater amount for doing the record keeping than if you were only the broker. Using other factors' resources allows you to take on more clients you otherwise would have had to broker, refer to someone else, or turn away.

Be aware, however, that most experienced factors who are interested in participations will require that they be the recording factor – i.e. the one providing the back office work. Understandably, they trust their own procedures more than someone else's. Such a requirement may not be the case, however, with funders found through the FactorFox network.

If you must use other people's money and not your own (or you own credit), it may be best to simply borrow it. If you do, the best arrangement for you is to have an unsecured loan based on a Loan Agreement with each lender, and a Promissory Note for each loan. Promissory Note "A" below can be used for loans unattached to specific transactions; Promissory Note "B" is used for loans made for particular factoring Schedules or invoices.

Generally, operate your business as a corporation or LLC, and if possible, do not personally guarantee business obligations including the loan obligation provided in the Lender Agreement. However, if the only way to obtain funds is through a personal guaranty, consider using a form similar to the one below. If possible, include a limitation on the guarantee by time, amount, or otherwise. For example, here is a limitation based on time:

"Limitation. This guaranty shall automatically terminate on the 180th calendar day following the first date shown above, and shall not apply to any loans, notes or arrangements by Lender made after that date, nor to any loans, notes or arrangements which are not in default as of that date. However, it shall not terminate as to any loans, notes or arrangements made by Lender in which there is a default as of the termination date, provided that guarantor has received written notice of default prior to the termination date."

Some guaranty forms don't provide for attorney fees and collection costs; you're better off using a form without these when you're the guarantor. The worst form of guaranty to use when you are the guarantor is that used by larger regional banks for commercial loans. Often two or three pages in length with very fine print, it includes waivers for every possible claim or defense a guarantor might have, lasts forever, and covers all forms of debt or obligation the borrower might have to the lender. You will do well to avoid such an extensive guaranty in any circumstance.

Sample Loan Agreement and Promissory Note documents are on the following pages. These documents will vary in form from state to state; there may be state laws and regulations concerning loans of this type. In every important business transaction – including these – you should consult your attorney and accountant about the proper wording of agreements so your interests are protected, and the accounting and tax results can be understood. Word to the wise: consult these professionals before your transactions are consummated.

Lender Agreement

This agreement, dated _____, 201__, is by and between _____ ("Borrower"), whose address is _____ and _____ ("Lender"), whose address is _____.

Recitals

1. Borrower is engaged in the business of purchasing accounts receivable from various clients at a discount below face value; and

2. Lender desires to loan money to Borrower for the purposes, and upon the terms, as set forth herein.

IN CONSIDERATION OF THE FOREGOING, the parties hereto agree as follows:

1. <u>Sums</u>. Lender agrees to loan to Borrower the initial sum of $ _____. Upon the Agreement of the parties, Lender may loan additional sums to Borrower under the terms and conditions provided herein.

2. <u>Sole use</u>. The amounts loaned by Lender under this Agreement are to be used by Borrower solely to purchase accounts receivable from clients of Borrower.

3. <u>Deposits and rate</u>. The amounts loaned under this Agreement will be deposited by Borrower in its working capital account at _____ Bank until such time as funds are withdrawn to purchase accounts of various clients. Borrower will pay Lender simple interest on amounts advanced under this Agreement at the rate of and on a timely basis according to a Promissory Note for each loan the Lender provides.

4. <u>Terms of repayment</u>. Each loan advanced by Lender shall be evidenced by a signed promissory note from Borrower, providing among other items, the terms of repayment.

5. <u>Not a security</u>, business purpose. The parties agree that Lender is making loans to Borrower for a business purpose, that Borrower will use these funds solely in its factoring business, that this is not a personal, family or consumer transaction by either Lender or Borrower, that it is a business

loan arrangement not an investment contract, and that repayment by Borrower is due regardless of the operation or profitability of Borrower's business.

6. *(Optional – use only if Lender requires collateral):* <u>Security interest</u>. Borrower hereby grants Lender a security interest in the following personal property ("collateral"), which security interest shall last so long as there is a balance of more than $_____ (the "Floor") owing by Borrower to Lender. The collateral is (a) Borrower's contract rights with, and (b) accounts receivable which are owed to or factored by, the following clients of Borrower: _____.

Lender agrees there is no security interest in contract rights, receivables or other assets related to any other client of Borrower, or of any other assets or property of Borrower, and (upon request by Borrower) Lender shall so certify in writing. To perfect the security interest, upon request Borrower shall execute and deliver to Seller a form of financing statement which describes the collateral in the same way, and which is appropriate in form under all the circumstances. When the total balance of all loans is below the Floor shown above, upon request Lender shall acknowledge the security interest no longer exists and shall terminate any UCC Financing Statements.

7. <u>Obligation</u>. The obligation of Lender to make future loans may be terminated by Borrower at any time, or by Lender on not less than 120 days notice; but that termination shall not affect the then-outstanding obligations to make payments under Notes to Lender. For all loans and notes, the parties agree that there shall be no penalty or fee for any partial or complete prepayment.

Lender	**Borrower**
Dated: _____	Dated: _____
By: _____	By: _____
Print Name: _____	Company Name
By: _____	By: _____
Print Name: _____	Print Name: _____

Promissory Note "A"

$_____   _____
                                (City) (State)

                                _____
                                        (Date)

FOR VALUE RECEIVED the undersigned promise(s) to pay to the order of
_____ the principal sum of _____
dollars ($ _____) together with interest thereon from date at the rate of
_____ percent (____%) per annum until maturity, said interest being
payable monthly on the _____ day of each and every month in lawful money
of the United States beginning on the _____ day of _____,
201___, in monthly installments of _____ dollars ($_____),
and continuing thereafter until _____.

The maker and endorser severally waives demand, protest and notice of
maturity, non-payment or protest and all requirements necessary to him/her
liable as maker and endorser and, should litigation be necessary to enforce this
note, the maker and endorser waives trial by jury and consents to the personal
jurisdiction and venue of a court of subject matter jurisdiction located in the
State of _____ and County of _____.

The maker and endorser further agrees to pay all costs of collection, including a
reasonable attorney's fee in case the principal of this note or any payment on
the principal or any interest thereon is not paid at the respective maturity
thereof, or in case it becomes necessary to protect the security hereof, whether
suit be brought or not.

This note is to be construed and enforced according to the laws of the State of
_____; upon default in the payment of interest when due, the whole
sum of principal remaining shall, at the option of the holder, become
immediately due and payable and it shall accrue interest at _____ (____%)
percent, from the date of default.

Default shall include but not be limited to non-payment of any respective
installment within ten (10) days from the due date set out herein after ten (10)
days written notice to the undersigned, or nonpayment on three different
occasions of any installments within five (5) days subsequent to the due date
therefor set out herein.

                        (Your Company Name)_____
                        Corporation

        By: _____
                Its President

        Attest: _____
                Its Secretary

Promissory Note "B"

$_____   _____
                                    (City) (State)

                                    _____
                                    (Date)

FOR VALUE RECEIVED the undersigned promise(s) to pay to the order of
_____the   principal   sum   of
_____ dollars ($ _____) together with
_____ percent (_____ %) of fees earned thereon from purchase of
Accounts Receivable effected by the funds provided for this note, to wit:

_____

_____

_____

The maker and endorser waives demand, protest and notice of maturity, non-payment or protest and all requirements necessary to hold him/her liable as maker and endorser and, should litigation be necessary to enforce this note, the maker and endorser waives trial by jury and consents to the personal jurisdiction and venue of a court of subject matter jurisdiction located in the State of _____ and County of _____.

The maker and endorser further agrees to pay all costs of collection, including a reasonable attorney's fee in case the principal of this note or any payment on the principal or any interest thereon is not paid at the respective maturity thereof, or in case it becomes necessary to protect the security hereof, whether suit be brought or not.

This note is to be construed and enforced according to the laws of the State of _____; upon default in the payment of interest when due, the whole sum of principal remaining shall, at the option of the holder, become immediately due and payable and it shall accrue interest at _____ (____%) percent, from the date of default.

Default shall include but not be limited to non-payment of any respective installment within ten (10) days from the due date set out herein after ten (10) days written notice to the undersigned, or nonpayment on three different occasions of any installments within five (5) days subsequent to the due date therefor set out herein.

                        (Your Company Name)_____
                        Corporation

        By: _____
                Its President

        Attest: _____
                Its Secretary

11

Participation

As mentioned earlier, participation is a tool that can help inexperienced factors feel comfortable with their first few deals, as well as provide extra resources if under-capitalized. But participation assumes both factors hold each other in absolute trust as to honesty and integrity. Both also need to agree about what each looks for in clients, how to screen them, and how to determine advances, rates, and other considerations.

Factors who want to participate with you need to understand and have confidence in how you operate and expect you to keep in close contact. The rewards of such a relationship can be great for both of you. You make higher discounts than you would referring and have the funds to handle more and/or larger accounts than you could with only your own resources. The other factor gains new accounts that would be unavailable otherwise, which are serviced by a knowledgeable person right in the field, at a cost less than in-house staff. A win-win proposition all the way around!

If you supply funds to another factor, you must be absolutely confident in his honesty, integrity, due diligence and professionalism with which he handles clients and customers. It's best to personally know factors to whom you are providing funds. If you don't, at least a background check on them is wise. Use a written agreement in all cases. I strongly recommend you know and trust the other factor quite well before you begin doing business, as the potential for incompetence (if not outright fraud) is quite real, and you must protect yourself. On the other hand, remember that factoring is a risky business no matter how skilled and honest you and other factors may be. You can lose money even when you're both above board and everything looks safe. The Cardinal Rule of Money again applies when you participate.

Using the most appropriate legal documents for participations, especially with someone you don't know well, is something of a legal quagmire, as you'll see below. Consult your attorney as to what is best for your situation. I appreciate attorney Stewart Martin's extensive input into the rest of this chapter.

Because participation offers such great potential for two or more beginning small factors, I asked Mr. Martin to provide a form which could be readily used by two factors in this case – one acting remotely and one acting locally. However, such a business relationship is neither simple nor capable of a single form which would apply in very many circumstances. What follows is his response.

There are several phases in a participation relationship: initial discussion, sharing due diligence forms and methods, drafting an agreement, implementing the new relationship, and monitoring for changes that will improve the arrangement. Let's look at each.

The Discussion Phase

When you begin talking with a prospective participant, explore the normal business practices you each use. Be sure you both see "eye-to-eye" on most if not all critical issues before you do any business together. First consider the limits that you would place on clients and/or customers. List and discuss the due diligence procedures you each use and the comfort level you both need. Also consider how you obtain your clients, what steps you use to qualify them, and other business operations you each find important. This will let you both understand the similarities, and more importantly, the differences between your present business operations. Some folks are more "loose" than others would be comfortable with, or take less time and effort in qualifying a client or customer. By discussing issues like these in advance, you will know whether you can cooperate and feel comfortable working with each other; and, if you can establish that all-important relationship of trust. Also discuss what risks you are willing to take and not willing to take; and which kinds of business owners you trust and do not trust.

We'll use the term "Funding factor" to describe the person who primarily provides funds and "Local factor" for the person who primarily does the operations and due diligence.

An important aspect for the Local factor is how much cash, on a regular basis, the Funding factor can provide. The Local factor wants to establish long-term consistent relationships with his clients, and to do that, needs a regular source of funds. Both must understand what will be provided by each: advances, due diligence, bookkeeping etc. The forms to be used for each aspect of the business should be exchanged and approved. You may need to compromise in making one or another choice but just be sure that you each agree to use the same documents for your formal agreements.

The Drafting Phase

As you enter the phase of drafting a written agreement between the Funding and Local factor, you should list all the duties of each person. Here are some sample duties that you might consider:

The Local Factor might be responsible for:

- Performing the due diligence (application form, UCC-1, credit checks, etc.)
- Maintaining regular personal contact with the client
- Record keeping and the reception and disbursement of client/customer funds
- Providing regular reports to the client and participant.

The Funding Factor might be responsible for:

- Supplying the Local factor with funds for advances
- Reviewing due diligence and reports
- Making observations, suggestions, and raising questions to best serve the client, customers, and both participants.

You should carefully define the standards for acceptable clients and customers. Also define the specific steps that the Local factor will go through in the due diligence process.

Now comes the difficult part: what type of relationship will you have? There are a variety of relationships that might provide the same end result: money from the Funding to the Local factor, and service by the Local factor to assure quality. But each of these different approaches has different legal rights and responsibilities, and they fall into patterns based on the evolution of the law in other areas of business and finance. Consider which one may suit your needs, and which one may suit the needs of your participant.

Types of Participation Relationships

The Lender and Business Factor. In this arrangement, the Funding factor would simply act as a lender and provide either fixed amounts of money with a pre-agreed repayment schedule, or meet the "requirements" of the local factor. Requirements financing gives the local factor more of what he or she wants, but can make the funding factor nervous. Under an unlimited requirements arrangement, the local factor might notify the funding factor that by next Tuesday $20,000 needs to be deposited to the Local's account. Therefore, most requirements agreements will have a ceiling on the amount that is available in a single request, the total amount that is outstanding, and a minimum number of days notice before any request for funds. You will want to think carefully about who has the right to end the relationship, and how the wind-up will occur, etc. This is essential so that the local factor will have enough lead time to replace the funds or let his clients know there is a limit on the factoring available.

Normally, there is a loan agreement establishing the arrangement overall, and separate promissory notes for each advance or "loan." To secure each loan, there is usually a blanket security agreement, but I use the word "blanket" with caution. A local factor normally will not want to have only one lender, and may have arrangements with a bank, other lenders, or participants. So it is important to segregate the lien interests (security interests) which each lender has. If the local factor already has a blanket lien with a bank, he may need a subordination agreement between the funding factor and the bank, providing that the funding factor's new lien will have priority over the blanket lien of the bank, at least as to certain collateral. So, in segregating the collateral, consider whether you want to do it by client, by each Schedule of Accounts which are purchased, or some other method. Refer to the preceding chapter on lending arrangements, and the sample Lender Agreement and Promissory Note "B."

Partnership or Joint Venture Agreements. It is not very likely that either of you will be so comfortable that you are prepared to be partners for all purposes. However, there is a special kind of business form called a "joint venture." A joint venture seems similar to a partnership but is limited in the scope of the business, or is limited in how long it lasts. So you might be joint venturers with a particular client for a period of one year, for that client indefinitely, or for a group of clients for nine months. These arrangements are very flexible, and you should each discuss what makes the other feel comfortable and what might be profitable. Besides, in defining how long the relationship could last, you might consider whether it will automatically renew or if it requires a notice from one party or the other to renew. In any partnership or venture agreement, you will want to carefully spell out the duties of each party: to loan funds or contribute them as capital, to do due diligence, to use forms (it is good to attach these as exhibits), to notify each other on a regular basis, to provide certain reports every so many days, etc. Keep in mind that in a partnership or joint venture, to the extent it exists, each person is personally liable for the entire business operation. And, if the public is misled or thinks the authority of a joint venturer is broader than you have provided in your contract, it may have "apparent authority" which could bind you to an even larger scope of responsibility than you thought. So, it is important to discuss which materials will be given to clients, how advertising, telephone listings, and other details which the public will notice are to be conducted.

Agent for Disclosed Factor. Since your prospect or existing client is already used to factoring, another approach is for the local factor to act as an agent for the funding factor. In this situation, the ultimate responsibility and power rests with the funding factor; and, the local factor is their dutiful agent. By "dutiful" I mean that traditional fiduciary duties of loyalty, care, skill, and business opportunity would normally bind the Local factor to the Funding factor. If there is any variation from that general rule, it should be spelled out in the agency agreement between the two factors. For instance, since the agent is already in a factoring business it may mean only certain selected opportunities (over $50,000 or in a certain industry) are given to the funding factor; the rest can be kept with the local factor and not shared. This agency relationship should be disclosed, normally, to the client who is being serviced. If it is not disclosed, the local factor will be personally liable and on the hook in every respect.

A Separate Participation Company. The last approach, the most involved, and yet perhaps most powerful in the long run, is to consider setting up a participation company. We know there is strength in numbers, and the combined financial strength of two or more factors, along with their personal guarantees, might allow not only their spare cash to be used, but to obtain reasonable interest rates on bank or private money which can be leveraged by the individual factoring businesses. I suggest that such a separate company be formed as either a corporation or limited liability company (LLC), and I would imagine the individual factors would be shareholders or members of that company. Obviously rules of governance (who has votes, whether there is a single manager or president in charge), percentage interests of ownership, voting, capital contributions, the ability to be "redeemed" out of the company upon demand, who will receive funds (whether in rotation or pro rata availability) and a number of other matters would need to be discussed and agreed in writing. Such a sophisticated arrangement is beyond the scope of this book, but hopefully some of these points will get you thinking if you believe a long-term permanent company is the answer.

Implementing the New Relationship

Selecting which of these methods of participation is most appropriate is difficult, and very important. You should involve your business attorney early to obtain her suggestions about structure and key points to consider in the negotiations. If you don't have one, by all means run to the nearest State Bar referral service and get an experienced attorney by your side. Participation is too risky to try it "alone."

By the way, there are different types and personalities of attorneys. Not all of them are sharks or those who see everything through the eyes of a jury-trial advocate. Some attorneys are entrepreneurial in nature, or more cooperative. You might consider having your attorney read sections of this book. Although you may have to pay for the time reading, ask if she'll volunteer it as background work in preparing to do legal work for you. Remember, you probably know far more about factoring now than your attorney will initially. Having a better understanding of factoring and your business will help your attorney give you better advice and more productive suggestions for how to negotiate a participation arrangement.

Monitoring for Changes

Finally, realize that no new venture (including a participation arrangement) starts off perfectly. When the Apollo missions to the moon were launched in the general direction that would lead them to a lunar orbit, hundreds if not thousands of course corrections were required in order to land successfully. Likewise, in your relationship with a participant, you should each monitor the other's behavior, live up to the agreement that you carefully drafted, and fine-tune the procedures as well as the whole arrangement as you go along. Probably every week or two you should call your participant on the phone and touch bases on shared clients. This way, your relationship will strengthen, the quality of each business will improve, and ultimately the profitability of each participant will increase. Participation is a complex arrangement, both legally and logistically, so be sure to go into it with your eyes open.

The more time you spend planning, the less likely you will have risks of upset, misunderstanding or losses.

Part 4

Risk Management

12
Reducing Your Risk

Fundamentals for Factors, book 2 of this series, contains a section with three chapters which discusses the risks factors face and how to minimize these risks. Rather than repeat that information here, let's expand on some of these points and add a few more.

Protect Yourself

You can take several measures which will provide protective shields. Remember, however, the potential for loss remains an ever-present aspect of factoring. As the name of this chapter makes clear, your aim is to *reduce* risk; you cannot *eliminate* it. If zero risk is what you're after, factoring is the not business for you.

Avoid Over Concentrations

Without question, this is by far the most important safeguard you can implement, and harks back to the Cardinal Rule of Money. If you religiously follow all other risk management practices but overlook this one, you can still lose big time and be out of business in a heartbeat.

The goal and policy of many factors is to never invest more than 10% of their funds in any one client, customer, or invoice; they constantly monitor their concentrations to be sure this proportion isn't exceeded. Maintaining low concentrations is a critical method of limiting risk; in fact, in my opinion it is the single most important risk management tool any factor can use...and it's free! Monitoring your concentrations doesn't cost a penny and can save you a fortune, but you must do it regularly.

Charts12-1 through 12-5 show various client concentrations. As you study these pie charts, ask yourself: "What will happen to this factor if any one or two of these accounts (pie wedges) go bad? Will the loss seriously harm or even kill the factor's business?

Chart 12-1 is a fairly common example of a new factor's client concentrations. Having a very small number of clients makes spreading risk around somewhat difficult. If the client with 54% of the factor's funds were to defraud the factor, not make good on large invoices, or otherwise not repay the factor, the loss would be significant. However, the same misfortune happening with the client holding 13% would not be as harmful to the factor. Therefore, assuming you have enough capital when you start, a fair amount of it will not be used.

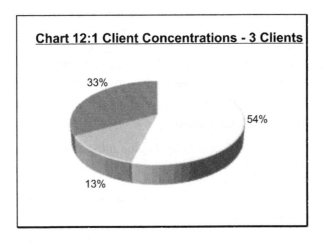

In Chart 12-2, the small factor has added two clients and has spread her concentrations safely.

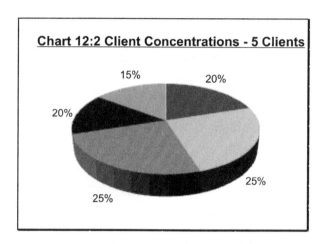

In Chart 12-3, a risky imbalance has occurred. If the client representing 60% of the business were to have problems, 60% of the factor's money would be in jeopardy. Don't let yourself get into a position such as this.

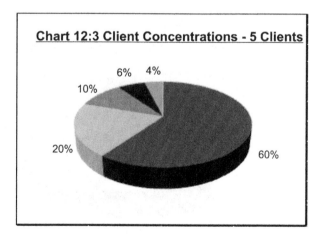

Chart 12-4 may represent a typical small factor's distribution of funds. The factor's resources are overly concentrated in the client holding 35%; otherwise, the risk is fairly well distributed.

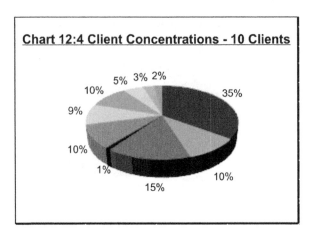

In Chart 12-5, the factor has grown considerably and now has 25 clients. This chart shows an excellent distribution of funds, keeping risk to a minimum in all accounts. This represents safe concentrations among all clients.

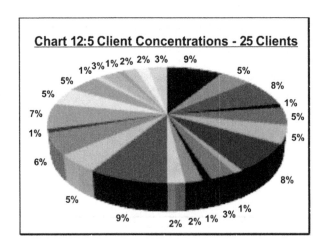

Set Credit Limits

The logical way to avoid over concentrations is to set limits on the credit you extend to clients. Likewise, set a limit on the total money invested in the invoices of any customer, and establish the dollar amount of the largest invoice you will buy. This protects you from having too many eggs in any of these baskets, as mentioned earlier.

Most medium-sized factors will not accept clients factoring less than $10,000 per month. In my own business, I have turned this rule upside down. To limit my exposure, especially with new clients (where a factor's risk is often greatest), I set initial client credit limits at $10,000 and accept only clients who start factoring with monthly volumes *less* than $10,000.

This goes against traditional factors' thinking but I have found this practice to be not only one of the best safety valves I've ever used as a small factor, but leads to referrals from larger factors when they must turn away deals that are too small for them. What's more, when a client reaches a certain level of factoring volume (in my case, I set it at $60,000 to $75,000 on a consistent factoring basis), I either bring in another small factor to participate with me, or simply hand the client to a larger factor (the same one who referred the client earlier, if that's where he came from). This limits my total exposure with any client to $75,000, and keeps me from risking what is, to me, more than I can afford (or just choose) to lose. For further thoughts about this subject, read the first of three stories in the chapter "Additional Resources" entitled "A Small Factor's Thoughts about Big Factors' Concerns."

Once a client has been incubated with me, finding another factor willing to take the account is not difficult. If the client was not originally referred to me by a broker, I receive a nice commission from the larger factor. If the client was referred by a broker, I make sure the new factor will continue to pay the broker. I no longer make income from the client, but have kept the broker happy and know he'll refer future small clients to me.

If a broker brings you a client who in time outgrows you, do your best to protect that broker's interest when referring the client elsewhere. This is simply a matter of fairness to the broker and also good business for you: the broker will appreciate what you're doing and be inclined to continue referring new business to you.

Set Aging Limits

Set aging limits (the amount of time you wait for an invoice to pay) that you consider prudent. The longer they take to pay, the less are your chances of collecting. When you're waiting for checks to come in – especially when clients have new invoices coming up they want you to fund – even 40 or 50 days can drag on and seem like a very long time for money you're waiting to receive.

Following up on overdue payments is easy to let slide, but not following up is a very big mistake to make. In fact, good follow up is important enough to deserve its own chapter in this book. Take the words in the chapter "Preventive Maintenance" to heart! They will seriously reduce your risk.

Factor on a Recourse Basis

Recourse factoring means if a client's customer does not pay an invoice for *any* reason, the client is responsible to cover this nonpayment. Non-recourse factoring means if a customer does not pay for reason of insolvency or inability to pay, the factor will take the loss. However, with non-recourse factoring, if an invoice is disputed by the customer, the client is still responsible to the factor.

Because of the obligation of the client to repay factors under a recourse relationship, the argument can be made that recourse factors are lending money to their clients. After all, if a customer doesn't pay an invoice, the client must pay the factor back in the form of cash, a new invoice, deductions from advances. rebates, reserves, or a combination of these. This repayment raises the issue of usury, with which you must be familiar.

Usury is the maximum interest than can be charged by law on a loan. and each state has its own usury laws. In many states these laws are different for business and consumer loans. Some states are very general about what they consider usurious business rates, while others are very restrictive. For example, in Washington state a lender can charge anything a business borrower agrees to in writing. A usurious rate can be claimed only if there is no written and signed business contract agreement as to interest or discounts. In other states business usury is a fixed percentage, as low or as high as 10%, 24%, or 36% APR, depending on the state.

Some argue that factoring should be considered exempt from usury because no loans are being made – the factor is buying receivables at a discount, not charging interest on a loan. However, when recourse occurs, the client must make up the advance and discount earned: is this "paying back a loan" and therefore subject to usury laws?

In some places this is not an issue as long as you meet the state's usury requirements. For example, say one state's laws require there to be a signed contract between two businesses, but any interest amount is allowable. If a factor does business with a private individual on a recourse basis, that factor could be in violation of usury because the contract is between a business (the factor) and a private party (the client). But if both parties are businesses, the factor can charge any amount ("interest") which the client agrees to in writing.

However, in states with more strict usury laws, the discount becomes an issue because usurious interest amounts are usually a lot less than the APR of a factor's discount (a 30-day 5% discount per month with an 80% advance equals 76% APR). If a factor operates in a state where usurious interest is above 18% APR, that factor could be considered to be charging usurious rates. If that factor were to end up in court with a client, a judge could level severe penalties against the factor.

The location in which the factor or client operates determines which usury laws are to be applied, and you're in luck if your state's laws are friendly. Obviously you need to learn your state's business usury laws. To find these, do an internet search looking up "usury" and the name of your state. Look for the actual laws in the state's constitution if you can find it. If you can't find specific information, contact a knowledgeable business lawyer and ask what the laws are. If he doesn't know, ask where you can find out.

If your state's usury laws make recourse difficult or impossible you should provide non-recourse factoring. As long as your state allows it, you're safer to factor on a recourse basis. Non-recourse can cost you some advances and discounts unless all your clients' customers are rock-solid – and some of them may not be. If your client gets large enough that you need to refer him, providing non-recourse through a larger factor can be a selling point for handing him off to one. Again, you're looking out for his welfare and he'll appreciate that.

Because your client will bear the loss of a bad invoice, recourse factoring provides you the following safety nets:

1. Clients are less likely to dump bad customers on you.

2. Clients are even more interested in collecting, besides wanting to keep their discounts lower.

3. You'll get your discount and advance back even if the customer doesn't pay, assuming the client has the means to make good on the unpaid invoice. Be sure your contract specifically states the recourse nature of your factoring relationship, unless this is precluded by the usury laws in your state.

With recourse factoring you need to do a thorough job of due diligence with your clients as well as their customers. If the customer isn't good for the invoice and your client can't make it good either, you still end up eating the loss. Recourse to the client is only as good as that client's ability to pay. Obviously doing your homework before you begin is the name of the game with recourse factoring – and even more so with non-recourse.

Make it clear to your client that he should never factor customers about whom he has the slightest doubts about their ability or inclination to pay. Neither of you want to factor poor-paying or exceptionally slow-paying customers. Making up unpaid invoices hurts his cash flow badly (which is why he's factoring in the first place) and can dig him into a deep hole with you.

Establish Reserves Beyond the Advance Holdback

When you advance 75%, you have a built in holdback reserve of 25%, from which your discount is taken. However, if the invoice doesn't pay you're still out the 75% you advanced. What do you do if this isn't paid by the customer and the client can't cover it?

Exchanging for a new invoice, deducting from advances, rebates, outright cash payments from the client, or a combination of these are the common answer. Yet each can create a cash flow problem – a problem he knows too well already, and the reason he started factoring in the first place.

A simple solution is to establish a separate reserve account. Make very clear to the client why and how you do this. When a customer short pays or doesn't pay, tapping the reserve will often take care of the shortfall. If there is still more owed than is in the reserve, taking the remainder from advances, rebates, cash, or new invoices doesn't have quite the bite as before.

When I finish explaining this reserve (which I call an Escrow Reserve), many prospective clients say, "That's a good idea," and are happy to cooperate. This is what I tell them:

"Establishing a separate reserve account will protect both of us if your customer short pays or doesn't pay at all. To safeguard against this risk, we will temporarily set aside a very small portion of your advances to create an Escrow Reserve account, which acts as a 'rainy day' fund. Here's how it works.

"I'll give you a 80% advance, and temporarily put 5 of the 80 into your Escrow Reserve. We'll establish an Escrow cap of 10% of your credit limit, and build up the reserve to that cap. For example, let's say you factor a $1,000 invoice. You'll get 75% or $750 cash for your advance, and I'll put 5% or $50 into your Escrow Reserve. In 30 days when your customer pays $1,000, I'll keep $750 for the advance, $50 for the Escrow Reserve, plus 5% or $50 for the discount. I'll owe you the remaining $150 as a rebate, which I will provide right away. Once your Escrow Reserve reaches that

$1,000 cap, you receive your full 80% advance from there on.

"Setting aside a little from each advance will provide $1,000 to cover unpaid or short paid invoices, and we'll draw from this fund first before requiring you to trade a new invoice, or deduct the money from a new advance or rebates.

"If we need to use the Escrow Reserve or if we raise your credit limit, we'll build up the Escrow again from future advances. When you are finished factoring, the reserve is yours and will be paid to you in full."

Clients who have factored before or who are astute business people usually see the wisdom of this procedure. Potential clients who see how it protects their cash flow appreciate the prudence behind it. Accountants or attorneys with very sharp pencils might suggest to the clients they're paying the equivalent of somewhat higher discounts because they don't receive their full advance until a later date. However, these people in particular will also see the wisdom of an added cushion against short payments and non-payments. This added protection benefits both you and the client.

Due Diligence

Proper due diligence, public records searches and filings, and credit searches on appropriate parties are critical for limiting your risk. The next three chapters are dedicated to these subjects.

Incorporate or Become an LLC

While this is another expense, it's a good idea to do when you move from brokering to factoring and/or have some serious money on the street. The reason is simple: as a sole proprietor, if you go bankrupt or lose a lawsuit, all your personal property can be used to make the debt payments or restitution due. If you are incorporated or an LLC (Limited Liability Company), your personal property is better protected. Also, as you make more income from factoring, tax laws will benefit you more this way. LLC's provide better flexibility and protection than partnerships and are often recommended by attorneys. Finally, having "Corporation," "Inc.," or "LLC" at the end of your business name gives you more credibility. Check with your attorney and accountant to determine which entity best fits your situation.

Credit Insurance

This is insurance larger factors sometimes purchase to protect themselves from a catastrophic loss. I say "larger factors" because the minimum factoring volume to make this insurance cost effective is around $1 million. If your volume is less, your best insurance as a small factor is to religiously follow the risk management methods in this series, particularly avoiding concentrations in any client, customer, and invoice, and keeping a fairly low cap on the total volume you will allow for these.

If your volume is large enough, credit insurance provides your business with protection against customer nonpayment because of insolvency, slow payment, or inability to pay. Most credit insurance carriers require coverage on your entire portfolio, rather than just those customers you're most concerned about.

Premiums are calculated as a percentage of your sales, and the rates vary depending on the history and historical debt loss of your company and customer base. Typically the cost is less than 1% of sales. The level of indemnity usually ranges from 80% to 100%, depending on the policy you select, your experience, your portfolio, and your premium target. Like any other insurance, deductibles are in place so there is little point in filing a claim on smaller accounts which fall under the deductible amount. In general, credit insurance is used against catastrophic losses, not smaller, routine losses most small factors are likely to experience.

Be aware that using this type of insurance usually means your credit insurance company must approve all your clients' customers. In turn that means your carrier will become your underwriter for determining which customers you can and cannot factor. Some factors will be glad to give this responsibility to the carrier; others may not want to lose control of this important part of their business. Choosing between the two becomes a management decision once your business reaches this level if and when it does.

The advantages of credit insurance are:

- Protection against large bad debt losses
- Pre-approved coverage for large accounts
- Ongoing account monitoring which provides early warning of potential credit risks
- Ability to secure better financing terms for working capital by offering your lender insured receivables as collateral.

EULER ACI is a carrier that covers factors' accounts receivable. Founded in 1893, this is a large company with branches across North America and around the world. Go www.eulergroup.com for information.

If you feel you need credit insurance and have a large enough portfolio, you might consider using a credit insurance broker. Accounts Receivable Insurance (*ARI* Global, Inc.), founded in 1996, is a broker specializing in credit insurance. Most of *ARI's* licensed brokers were former direct writing agents. This means they are formally trained on the products they are selling, as well as the entire industry's product line.

As with any broker, *ARI's* job is to locate a carrier with the most value for the premium paid. They have relationships with carriers all over the globe. Insurance carriers have multiple contracts and literally dozens of different types of endorsements. *ARI* selects and tailors these endorsements which provide your company the maximum coverage for your investment.

ARI has several offices nationwide, with headquarters in Tampa, Florida. Their website is www.ariglobal.com.

Trust Is the Name of the Game

With all of these risk management tools in mind, let me reiterate a key element of factoring. You must act in every way and at all times so that your clients hold you in complete and utter trust.

Your client must trust you as she would her banker, accountant, lawyer, doctor, pastor, rabbi, and anyone else in whom she entrusts the welfare of her life and business. If there is the slightest doubt about your character, integrity or business expertise, she will pull away and you won't keep her as a client very long (or get referrals).

If your motives are pure – if you are putting your client's needs above your own selfish interest (notice I did not say your need to be secure and profitable; be clear about the difference) – you will develop loyalty that will pay for itself ten times more than any advertising budget. Think about the professionals with whom you deal and those you completely trust with your important business and personal affairs. Why do you trust them? Go and do likewise.

13
Due Diligence

What Is "Adequate" Due Diligence?

Someone once asked me, "Why do due diligence costs vary so much among factors? Some charge nothing, while others require $100 to as much as $500 or more just to check out a prospective client. What does it take and how much does it really cost to do adequate due diligence?"

My answer: what constitutes "adequate" due diligence is in the eye of each factor. And I posed a counter-question: Why is due diligence even necessary? The answer is this. Factoring is a business that involves risk to operating capital. A factor's income is based on discounts received for factored invoices. These discounts pay for services the factor performs, plus the risk the factor assumes in advancing funds against a client's receivables. A factor's working capital – advances and earned discounts – can be quickly lost in just one bad debt.

Suppose a prospective client comes along and is interested in factoring with you. In order to decide if you want to invest your money in this prospect's business, you want to learn as much as you feel is necessary about this company, its history, its customers, and its management's skills. You perform due diligence to learn these things. The purpose of due diligence is to limit risk. While due diligence carries no guarantee that money will not be lost in the course of factoring, it provides indications as to which clients and customers will be less risky and have fewer complications, and thus be more desirable. When your due diligence is done, you decide if you want to take on this client's receivables – this risk – or pass. Just how much and what kind of due diligence you feel is "adequate" is up to you.

Due diligence is one of the more difficult aspects to learn when becoming a factor of small receivables. It is imprecise, subjective, and provides no guarantees you won't get burned. As mentioned previously, the purpose of due diligence is to *reduce* your risk, not *eliminate* it, and to help you determine which other precautions to take to further limit risk after factoring begins. (For those precautions, see the chapters "Reducing Your Risk" and "Common Mistakes.")

I consider due diligence to be analogous to putting together a jigsaw puzzle. When you first consider a prospective client, the space where the puzzle pieces will rest is blank. You know nothing about this prospect or his company because you have no puzzle pieces. Each part of your due diligence – information on your application and each item you learn in every step of your underwriting – provides a separate piece of the puzzle. Several pieces must be lying on the table before you have any idea of what the picture actually is, but as you add more and more pieces the picture gradually begins to make sense.

The more pieces of the puzzle you have fitting together the better you see the attractive and adverse attributes of this prospect. While your due diligence will never provide a complete picture with every single piece in place, you want to have enough puzzle pieces put together before you make a decision. The number of puzzle pieces to suggest your due diligence is "adequate" is up to you.

The purpose of this chapter is to point out the subjective nature of due diligence, present what is commonly done by other factors, and invite you to decide how extensive your due diligence will be. Will your process be carefully planned and carried out, very loose and easy-going, or somewhere in between? You decide. You're the boss.

Starting Your Due Diligence

Generally speaking, you want to learn all you can about the prospective client personally, as well as his honesty, business experience, debts, lien positions, and financial position. Then you want to find the financial health and stability of his customers.

Most factors start with an application form. By reviewing this information and asking questions for clarification, you'll determine whether or not the prospect fits your parameters. That is, are this prospect's monthly volume, invoice amounts, and quantity in your range, are you comfortable factoring receivables in this industry, is the geographical location acceptable, and so on.

The more new prospects you consider, the more you will have a sense for what due diligence needs to be performed on each. Some factors routinely run the same due diligence on all prospects; others do more in-depth searches with certain prospects than with others. What follows are the various due diligence tools available.

Often prospective clients are in a hurry to start factoring and understandably become impatient with delays caused by due diligence. While you need to respond to their need, you also need to protect your funds. One of the peculiarities I first noticed about larger factors when I began was how extremely careful and unwilling they are to be hurried. There is a good reason for this: when they were not careful and were hurried in the past, they got stung.

Begin with Free Searches

Before you spend money on UCC searches, credit reports, and the like, start with free searches available to anyone. From these you can gain information which can provide quite enlightening insights.

When I begin to underwrite a prospective client after reviewing the application, I look up the client's website, do a web search on the person's name and city, search his location on internet maps like Bing or Google Maps, and make a point of looking for him on such sites as LinkedIn, Facebook, and Google+.

While I don't get financial information here, I can certainly learn a lot about the individual not found in professional reports. For example, Google the person's name as well as city or state, especially if it's not a common name. What turns up? Multiple references or none? If you find something, does it mention his business? If it does, is a favorable picture painted, or at least not a negative one?

Search the prospect's website – does he have one? Is it appropriate to what he does? Does it appear to bring in business? Does it give you confidence in him as a prospective client?

Looking further, is the prospect or her business listed on LinkedIn? If so, this gives an indication that she is probably serious about what she does and may have at least some internet savvy. What does her LinkedIn profile tell you? Does she have recommendations from others? Is she well positioned to compete in her market?

Can you find the prospect's home and/or office on the maps? What does it tell you about the area in which he lives and/or works? Do these locations legitimize the business or make you wonder? Does it give you confidence that what he's told you is true, or raise questions or concerns?

What you find on sites like Facebook and Google+ may give information you'll never find anywhere else. Take for example the prospect I found on Facebook pictured in black clothing, an assault rifle in hand, and a menacing look on his face. Or another prospect who posted numerous photos of himself clearly inebriated at parties, and hanging out with people I would consider questionable at best.

When you see images like these and wonder about the person's judgment used in posting them, asking yourself the question "is this a quality investment?" makes your decision both quick and easy. If you do these simple, free internet searches before paying for professional reports, you may save yourself some time and money by not needing to look any further.

Learning More about the Prospect

When I first told a larger, experienced factor to whom I had referred some transactions that I was beginning to factor small deals myself, he congratulated me and then immediately asked me if I were doing recourse or non-recourse. When I said recourse only, he made a point of telling me to:

- get business financial statements
- get personal financial statements
- get personal guarantees
- continue to verify invoices.

You can choose to skip these if you want to close a deal quickly – you're the boss, remember – but you live with the consequences in any event. Let's look at each.

Business financials (balance sheets and income statements) for the last couple of years will tell you how much a client has coming in, going out, where his money is tied up, and overall how stable, and therefore how safe, this company will be to factor. If he is new and doesn't have these, your risk is increased. Not only do you know little about him financially, you may be dealing with someone inexperienced in business and/or with his product or service. He (like you learning to factor) will no doubt make costly mistakes as he learns. This is where your gut feeling about the person comes into play – does this business owner strike you as someone who has what it takes, or not?

Personal financials (a statement of net worth – total assets and total liabilities – and income taxes paid) will tell you how much personal income she makes and what she has to fall back on. You're also looking for assets you can grab if the sky falls in on her account. The reason you want to know all this is so you are assured she personally (apart from her business) has enough to cover whatever you may be owed. This also helps you determine a limit as to how much you want to factor her in a given period of time, as well as a limit to the total amount of credit you want to give (which is also based on how stable her customers are).

Personal guaranty (one of the signed documents which is part of your contract) states precisely this: regardless of what happens to his business, your client will personally make good on any money owed you. This gives you greater protection if his business flops, provided he has the personal resources to pay what you're owed. Occasionally a business owner will balk or even refuse to sign this, particularly if he is being advised by an attorney or accountant. You must decide if no signature here is a deal killer. If there are problems collecting in a recourse situation and the owner hasn't signed a personal guaranty, you may have great difficulty recovering the debt. Make sure, however, the business owner's personal resources are sufficient or a personal guaranty is worthless. Also be sure that they do not state the title of their position in the company on this document and that the company's name is not by the signature. This is important: it means they are guaranteeing personal funds, not business funds.

All principals of the business must sign this document for you to be fully protected. They need to be clear that this puts them on the hook personally to ensure you are paid, even if their company is incorporated. If the business is in a community property state, the principal's spouse or principals' spouses must also sign it. Check with your attorney regarding the laws in your state. If you must do non-recourse factoring, this document may not be necessary; but remember, you have less security if there are problems. Again, ask your attorney what to do for your particular situation.

Continue to verify invoices. This can be one of the more tiresome tasks of factoring, but it's frequently educational. When you receive an invoice to factor you verify it by calling, or getting in writing, to determine each of the following:

- the service has been rendered or the product received in good condition
- the customer is satisfied with the service or product
- the payment will be sent to you directly.

Verifications can save both you and the client a lot of hassles down the road when you learn (as does happen) that something went awry and the customer in fact *doesn't* intend to pay the bill. In fact, the customer probably wouldn't have told your client there was a problem until a month or two later, if at all. Thus you serve as a quality control agent – another benefit of factoring. Only after the invoice is verified (and if there is a problem, after it's resolved) do you provide the advance on an invoice. This is why it may take a day or two before the advance is forthcoming.

Verifying invoices by faxed letter can save a lot of time and offers documented proof of acceptance by the customer.

The document "Certificate of Acceptance" can be an excellent tool for routine verifications. A shipping receipt, bill of lading, or other proof of work done or product received (time cards for a temp agency, for instance) – properly signed by a responsible party at the customer's business – can also provide verification.

FactorFox includes both a phone verification page for every factored invoice, and a report that can be signed by the customer to provide proof of acceptance. Samples of these forms are provided in the chapter "Record Keeping."

Other Tools

There are other due diligence tools a small factor does well to employ: aging reports, UCC-1 filings, credit reports, and background searches.

Aging Reports

If your prospect can provide aging reports, get them. These are a gold mine of information concerning their customers and how long they take to pay. If the client uses a bookkeeping program like QuickBooks®, have her run a current Aging Report, which will show currently unpaid invoices, and a Customer History Report, which will show how long past invoices took to pay.

Information in both these reports is invaluable to you, and will help you enormously when deciding if you want to accept a prospect as a client, which of her customers you do and don't want to factor, and if you'll give her different advance or discount rates than usual. If these reports show nothing but extremely slow- or non-paying customers, and/or a huge number of very small invoices, you may simply decline her right away and save a lot of expense and time with further due diligence.

Not all small clients will be able to provide you with an aging or customer history report, but always ask for one. Most computer business accounting programs come with these reports.

These reports may be called various names, but are usually found under the Receivables and/or Customer reports menus.

Try to get a report that will give a year's history of paid invoices (sorted by customer and payment times) with the invoice amounts. If the customers maintain their past payment patterns, you'll see pretty easily which ones are best to factor and be able to predict future payment patterns for customers on a Current Outstanding Receivables report. In other words, if certain customers have histories of paying in a week, others in a month, and others in three months, the best ones to factor are those who pay in a month.

Aging reports can vary widely in how they are laid out on paper, but the basic information is pretty similar: name of customer, perhaps their address and phone number, invoice amounts, and length of time out. The length of time is usually divided into columns named "0 – 30 Days," "31 – 60 Days," "61 – 90 Days," and "Over 90 Days." Some aging reports will add a column for Current (within terms) before the "0 – 30 Days" column, and some will add a column of "90 – 120 Days" before the final column, "Over 120 Days."

Be aware that the Number of Days column may reflect either

a) the number of days from the invoice date, or
b) the number of days from the due date.

In the latter case, if a customer is given net 30 payment terms, the invoice has been out 30 days **plus** the number of days in the column. Obviously in this case, you want most invoices to be in or near the Current column. Ask the client which of these two aging methods is used in this report; you may not be able to tell just by looking.

On the following pages are a sample Current Outstanding Receivables aging report and a sample Closed Receivables aging report for the fictitious Acme Services Company, using number of days from the invoice date.

Try this exercise.

1. Review only the first report. Which customers are you likely to accept with only this information?

2. Now review the second report and compare the information here to that in the first report.

3. How does the second report further inform your decision?

4. Would you change your decision on any customers now?

Chart 13-1: Aging Report:
Current Outstanding Receivables

Acme Services Company

Customer	Inv. #	0 - 30	31 - 60	61 - 90	91 +	Total
AAA Business Svcs	1355			500		500
253 555-1443	1378		1,575			1,575
	1488	350				350
	1565	900				900
		1,250	1,575	500	0	3,325
Barry's Berry Farm	1285		2,500			2,500
360 555-9889	1556	3,000				3,000
	1766	1,000				1,000
	1790	4,000				4,000
		8,000	2,500	0	0	10,500
Delightful Deli	1200				225	225
206 555-1345	1256				295	295
		0	0	0	520	520
Never Never Land Sales	4562	2,500				2,500
509 555-PPAN	5661	4,500				4,500
	5862	7,000				7,000
	5955	3,000				3,000
		17,000	0	0	0	17,000
Pink Elephant Advertsg	2599			1,000		1,000
206 555-9873	3700	1,000				1,000
		1,000	0	1,000	0	2,000
Reverb Music Store	1014				25	25
206 55BLAST	1022				50	50
	1032				35	35
	1532				60	60
	1544			50		50
	2554		15			15
		0	15	50	180	235
Total Outstanding Rcvbls		**27,250**	**4,090**	**1,550**	**700**	**33,590**

Chart 13-2: Customer History Report:
Closed Invoices, Last 12 Months

Acme Services Company

Customer	Inv. #	0 - 30	31 - 60	61 - 90	91 +	Total
AAA Business Services	445	400				400
253 555-1443	586	595				595
	599	350	750			1,100
	701	500				500
		1,845	750	0	0	2,595
Barry's Berry Farm	253	1,000				1,000
360 555-9889	456		2,500			2,500
	625				1,500	1,500
	755		2,000			2,000
		1,000	4,500	0	1,500	7,000
Cascadia Clinic	654			500		500
253 555-0988	786		1,500			1,500
		0	1,500	500	0	2,000
Never Never Land Sales	452	1,500				1,500
509 555-PPAN	564	2,500				2,500
	753	6,000				6,000
	783	8,500				8,500
		18,500	0	0	0	18,500
Oscar's Cans & Liners	15	25				25
509 555-SCUM	35		75			75
	77	50				50
	105	100				100
	155		25			25
	236	35				35
	350	50				50
	369	60				60
		320	100	0	0	420

Chart 13-2, continued

Customer	Inv. #	0 - 30	31 - 60	61 - 90	91 +	Total
Pink Elephant Advertising	125		500			500
206 555-9873	159		1,000			1,000
	456		750			750
	756		500			500
	789		1,250			1,250
		0	4,000	0	0	4,000
Reverb Music Store	456	500				500
206 55BLAST	754		150			150
	788				50	50
		500	150	0	50	700
Samson's Gym & Hair Salon	156		250			250
206 555-SNIP	265			450		450
	354	100				100
	568		300			300
	686	100				100
	782			500		500
	793				750	750
	825		350			350
	835	75				75
		275	900	950	750	2,875
Ursula's Umbrellas	56	500				500
206-555-DRIP	156	500				500
	265	500				500
	387	500				500
	444	500				500
	489	500				500
	500	500				500
		3,500	0	0	0	3,500
Total Closed Recvbls.		25,940	11,900	1,450	2,300	41,590

UCC-1

The next tool is the UCC-1 (Uniform Commercial Code) form, which places a lien against a client's collateral. This is described in detail in the chapter, "UCCs."

Credit Reports

Another tool is a credit report on the client, customers, and/or their principal(s). There are several credit reporting companies out there, and the one(s) you use is up to you. Dun & Bradstreet is the best known and gives extremely thorough reports. However, there are some disadvantages to D&B for the beginning factor.

1. They're expensive. The larger the report you wish to retrieve (larger means more information), the higher the cost.

2. There are a lot of companies who are not listed in D&B. This is especially true of very small companies, many of whom you are likely to factor.

3. Much of the information in D&B reports is supplied by the companies themselves, which makes the very information you're looking for suspect in some people's minds.

For your purposes as a beginning small factor, carefully review the credit reporting resources in the next chapter. Compare prices and features offered such as small business and personal credit reports (you'll want both for clients), UCC-1 searches, other lien and judgment searches, etc. Get as much information from each as you can, and you should be able to find a service that best fits your needs. Look for a free sample report online to help you compare the information each service provides in its reports.

You may want to have your client share or absorb the cost of these when they apply. Just be sure you make it clear what their cost is and why you need the information. If you obtain credit information on a customer, the client will be more than happy to learn what you find.

If you're considering factoring a very young company, there probably won't be a business credit report available. Hence a personal credit report on the principal(s) can often tell you what you need to know. The assumption in this case is how they pay their business bills will be reflected in how they pay their personal bills. You need written permission to run a credit check on a private individual, so include wording on your application that provides this approval from your prospect when she submits the application. You don't need permission to run a credit check on a business.

You certainly want to run a credit check on customers they want to factor. This is the most basic due diligence. Remember the invoices are only as good as the customer's ability to pay. Charging back invoices because a customer doesn't pay could end up harming your client's cash flow or even result in a loss of money for you. Credit checks on customers may also confirm a client's word that someone is a good, regular payer. You may find in their credit report that "it ain't necessarily so."

I want to know as much as possible about a prospective client, and usually run a full credit report on the client's business and on the client personally. If I find a history of judgments, significant tax lien problems, problems indicating severe financial mismanagement, criminal history, write offs by collection agencies, or other significant red flags, I will turn the prospect away. However, don't expect small business clients coming to you to factor will have glowing credit. That's often a reason they can't get loans or funds from other sources.

What we are looking for is a pattern that suggests the business owner is honest, reasonably proficient at running a business, not likely to become a problem account, and of course has good paying customers. If the individual looks responsible, has customers who are creditworthy and pay in our preferred 2-week to 2-month window, chances are good we will accept them as factoring clients. However, before doing so, we want to be as sure as possible there are no stones left unturned. We want as many jigsaw puzzle pieces as possible.

Background Searches

Some factors utilize other means of looking further into a client's character, financial solvency, liens, and more. Numerous investigative companies offer a variety of background and lien search services that may be helpful to utilize.

These companies usually provide UCC and tax lien searches, judgment searches and pending litigation searches at county and federal levels, plus criminal background checks. There are many companies with websites that provide background searches and

other due diligence services for you; some are mentioned in the next chapters.

Tax Issues

A potential risk factors face, despite thorough due diligence, is funding a new client who is in arrears with tax obligations, yet this arrearage doesn't appear on UCC searches or credit reports. How can this happen?

UCC searches and credit reports find only tax liabilities with existing liens already in place. Because IRS can take a year or more to issue a lien, UCC searches may show a business has a clean record even though it could actually owe IRS many of thousands in tax liabilities or have missing tax returns. Such companies may be in the cross-hairs of IRS even though no lien yet exists.

A company named Tax Guard, Inc. is a tax compliance monitoring service which provides indicators of tax risk for U.S. asset-based lenders and factors. They provide a means for factors to obtain both prospective and current clients' tax risk profiles.

Their Tax Guard Liability Index is created from a monthly analysis of over 5,000 companies Tax Guard monitors for tax compliance. They identify all companies that have federal tax liabilities and the total amount of each. Tax Guard also identifies whether IRS has issued a tax lien against each liability; even if it has, the lien may not yet show up on UCC searches and credit reports. The aggregate data is compiled to show how much total tax risk exists for funders.

Tax Guard provides both one-time and on-going reports. The one-time report, the Tax Guard Due Diligence Report (DDR) allows you to evaluate the tax compliance status of a prospective client. The DDR provides a complete summary of the historical and current status of the prospect's federal tax returns and federal tax deposits and creates the Tax Risk Score (TRS).

The ongoing report, the Tax Guard Monthly Monitoring Report (MMR) is provided every month throughout the life of the account. The MMR monitors for tax compliance changes. Future tax risks are identified so you can manage the issue before a tax lien is filed. A monthly summary report, aggregated

MMR's for all monitored clients, provides an up-to-date assessment of portfolio tax risk.

Due Diligence Costs

Due diligence costs vary with the source from which the information is obtained. Financial statements and aging reports given from the client are free and thus a good place to start. Checking references is also a low-cost means of obtaining information. Cost of UCC searches and credit reports will depend on the size and type of information desired and the company from which it is retrieved. Also affecting costs are whether you supply information on your customers' payments histories to the agency.

With all the above considered, credit reports can cost anywhere from very little to well over $100 for a full-blown credit report (see the next chapter). One hopes the information in credit reports is accurate and up-to-date, but unfortunately this is not always the case. Tax Guard's one-time report is about $50 as of this writing; thus if you decide to use this service for all new prospects, your due diligence increases by that much in addition to other underwriting costs.

This is where due diligence costs escalate quickly, depending on the number of searches you need to feel your due diligence is "adequate." Thorough due diligence takes time and money. Some factors consider these expenses the cost of doing business and absorb all or a portion them. Others cannot afford to spend hundreds of dollars apiece on several new prospects each week, only to find they were "tire kickers" and not really serious about factoring.

However, charging a prospect – especially a very small business – all or even just a portion of these costs may push such clients to a competitor who doesn't have a due diligence charge, or discourage others from factoring altogether. On the other hand, charging at least some out-of-pocket reimbursements can quickly distinguish serious prospects from those who are "just looking."

Some factors consider in-depth searches undependable and no more predictive than a coin-toss, and therefore worth neither the trouble nor expense. I knew of one successful factor who simply ran a lien search on the client and checked D&B ratings on customers, period. Is that really enough? Probably not for most factors but it was for him. "Adequate" due diligence is in the eye of each individual factor.

When deciding how much due diligence to perform in your business, perhaps the best question is this: "What is adequate due diligence for *my* peace of mind with *this* particular client?" Remember, the purpose of due diligence is to *reduce* risk. Nothing can completely *eliminate* it.

Other Considerations

The thought of going through such a rigorous due diligence process may raise a question: "Will asking prospects for all this paperwork kill a deal?" In some cases it may – especially for very small accounts. If you're afraid it will, you need to judge if the account is worth the risk and how hungry you are for the business.

If a prospect acts like you're snooping or wonders why you need all this information, turn the tables and ask, "If you were going to be investing many thousands of dollars of your money into the business of someone you don't know, what would you want to know about this person?" I asked a hesitant prospect this very question and his immediate reply was, "Everything."

Understanding your perspective helps prospective clients see you're only trying to protect yourself – something any business owner appreciates. What's more, I have learned that when someone acts uneasy about your digging into their background, they usually have something to hide. Those with nothing to hide are happy to let you look all you want.

On the other hand, all this may be overkill for exceptionally small accounts. If you're going to factor someone for $5,000 a month and you know it'll never be much more than that, you need to consider whether losing this amount is worth the cost of all the underwriting. This is especially true if the person is previously known to you as being "as honest as the day is long."

In this case, you may choose to skip some of these precautions. If you do this, you can certainly close deals in a hurry and turn your money over quickly. However, if a client grows more than you expected and you then want the protection the background checks provides, going back and doing this later will be more difficult than if you had done it when you first considered the new account. The client may justifiably wonder why you didn't do it back then in the first place.

Also be very clear that even though you have known someone for a long time, or a person is honest through-and-through, you can still lose money with him or her. While fraud may not be a risk with such a person, there are a number of circumstances that can befall an honest client: past debts, investments or business deals gone bad, divorce, illness, injury…you name it.[4]

If your prospect needs the cash badly enough – and many do – he'll gladly sign any papers you put under his nose, especially if he believes doing so will supply the cash for his cash-starved business. Closing deals like this are a breeze and enjoyable. Just be sure you are comfortable with the findings of your due diligence, whatever it may be. You could be staring at the completed jigsaw puzzle picture for a long time.

---

[4] The author's ebook *Top 10 Illusions about Risk and Loss* discusses this in detail.

14

UCCs

Most people with little exposure to the world of finance, loans and factoring are quite ignorant of the Uniform Commercial Code (UCC). Yet once this door opens a crack they find a whole unexplored world there, and it can be somewhat daunting.

What Is the Uniform Commercial Code?

The Uniform Commercial Code is a branch of law that has to do with debts owed by one party to another. Any time one person or company provides money to another person or company, the one providing funds understandably wants assurances he will be paid back. The law makes provision for this in the Uniform Commercial Code.

Each Secretary of State's office in the country has a division that handles UCCs. When the party who provides money to another seeks greater security of repayment, the providing party will complete a UCC-1 form and is referred to as the "Secured Party." The person or company receiving the funds is called the "Debtor" on the UCC-1 form. When this form is completed and registered with the Secretary of State, a lien (pronounced "lean") is put in place which secures the collateral of the Secured Party. The collateral is whatever the Secured Party says it is on the form, which is authorized by the Debtor.

When this lien is filed, the information becomes public record. Think of it as a nationwide bulletin board, notifying everyone that the secured party has first rights to the collateral if there is ever a problem recovering the money. Why is this important?

When everything goes smoothly, a UCC filing is unnecessary. A borrower pays back her bank loan with regular payments, is never late, the bank gets its money back, and everybody is happy. Likewise, a factoring client's customers pay their invoices, the factor gets his money back, and everybody is happy. In such transactions a UCC filing has no significance.

However, such perfect transactions do not always occur in the real world. If a borrower defaults on a loan and declares bankruptcy, the bank stands to lose the remaining unpaid principal. If a factoring client has outstanding invoices that are uncollectible and the client's business declares bankruptcy, the factor stands to lose just like the bank. Having a UCC filed – and having it filed before anyone else – will provide some protection to these secured parties.

Let's use an example. When they started the factoring relationship, Factor A filed a UCC-1 form which secured the accounts receivable and assets of Client B. They factor for a period of time, when unfortunately Client B falls on difficult times and ends up with $200,000 worth of debts he cannot repay. His assets are only $100,000. Sadly, Client B feels the only way out of the problem is to declare bankruptcy, which he does.

However, Factor A has purchased $25,000 worth of Client B's receivables. Some of these invoices are paid by the customers, but $20,000 is determined to be uncollectible and Client B is of course unable to pay them. Without a UCC filed, Factor A loses the $20,000.

However, Factor A filed the UCC and did so before any other secured party, thereby placing himself in "first position." When the bankruptcy is complete, the determination is made that there is a total of $70,000 in remaining assets in Client B's company, which must be distributed to its debtors after court costs and attorneys fees. Being in first position, Factor A is first in line. He receives the $20,000 owed, and Lender C, who is in second position, is next in line to receive what she is owed. If Lender C is owed $75,000, she will only receive the remaining $50,000 in assets, and the rest must be written off as a loss. In this scenario, parties in third or lower positions are out of luck.

As you can see, debtors are paid back in the order of their UCC filing position, which is determined solely by filing date. The first to file is in first position. Bankruptcy disbursements are not made by simply determining the amount everyone is owed and splitting up the assets equally between them. The remaining goods go to those first in line (after the trustee and attorneys are paid, that is). If Client B's assets were determined to have been only $15,000, Factor A would have received $15,000 and lost the remaining $5,000. Lender C would have been completely left in the cold.

Also, holding a lien protects the lien holder from garnishment by other debtors, as long as the other debtor is not IRS. IRS liens trump all other liens no matter when they're filed.

Suppose you have a lien against a client's receivables. If that client owes someone else money and that person tries to garnish the client's receivables, you not only own the receivables in the first place, you are in first position and the receivables are protected.

I had a client who was a printer and who owed money to a paper company that did exactly this – the paper company tried to garnish his receivables which he had factored with me. It was nice to have my attorney deal with the situation, and he appreciated the proper paperwork I had done – my UCC-1 was properly filed and in hand, plus the signed factoring contract documents were in my files. The paper company had filed no liens and even though they had a judgment, they were out of luck in this case because my UCC protected my rights to the receivables. They belonged to me, not my client, and hence the paper company had no right to them.

Therefore, as you can well understand, any factor or bank will want to be in first position with every one of its clients. If a client wants to factor and already has a bank loan or line, the bank has no doubt filed a UCC already. If the bank can be persuaded to subordinate at least part of its position (the accounts receivable) to a factor, the factor will likely accept this client. If a bank will not subordinate, the factor will be required to take a second position and must decide whether to accept the deal anyway or decline.

Likewise, the presence of tax delinquencies, judgments, and the like usually involve liens which will put the parties involved in first position. Unless these situations can be worked out – and sometimes they can, particularly tax liens – the deal will probably not be doable for the factor. No first position usually means no deal.

UCC-1 forms are available from the websites of Secretaries of State and from the UCC filing and service companies described at the end of this chapter.

Revised Article 9

In July of 2001, the Uniform Commercial Code underwent significant revisions that affect factoring transactions. These changes are usually referred to as "Revised Article 9" or "RA9" of the Uniform Commercial Code. Generally speaking these changes made UCC procedures more uniform across the country, and much easier to file. However you must be careful to file correctly or the protection the Uniform Commercial Code is intended to provide will be lost.

You must be aware of the following points which are in effect under Revised Article 9.

1. **Company Name**. Using the correct, full name of your client's company is very important. In many states, a slight variation in the name can make a filing ineffective. Therefore you should obtain copies of a business' organizational documents, including a copy of their state registration certificate, to determine the client's correct legal name that is registered with the state. Trade names and DBA's are not effective. For Sole Proprietors, the full, complete name of the owner should be filed, such as "John Jacob Smith," rather than "Jack Smith" or "Smith Enterprises." You should verify the name with a driver's license or Social Security card and have a copy of this documentation on file.

2. **Signatures**. Obtaining the client's signature on the UCC-1 form is not necessary with RA9. You are only required that the client *authorize* you to file the UCC-1 Financing Statement as the Secured Party. Be sure your contract uses this language.

3. **Where to File**. Filing is done in the jurisdiction in which the client is located. Dual filings (state and local) have been eliminated except in the case of real estate fixtures, which

your factoring transactions won't include. How do you determine where the client is located? It's not quite as simple as you might think.

- Filings for **corporations, LLCs,** and **limited partnerships** are done in the state of their organization. That is, if a company is located in Missouri and incorporated in Delaware, the UCC is filed in Delaware. Therefore you need to see the first page of the articles of incorporation or equivalent to get both the exact name and the state of organization.

- Filings for **non-registered organizations** like general partnerships and joint ventures are filed either a) at its place of business if it has only one location, or b) in the state of the chief executive office if it has more than one place of business.

- Filings for **sole proprietorships** are done in the state in which the owner's principal residence is located. Therefore if a sole proprietor's office is located in Portland, Oregon, but the owner resides in Vancouver, Washington, the filing is done in Washington state.

If it is not clear which is the proper jurisdiction, you should file in each jurisdiction that might be the client's place of business or residence.

UCC Filings

Filing fees vary from one state to another and most are in the $15 to $50 range. Specific UCC requirements for each state are available from the website of its Secretary of State.

A helpful web page is provided by Capitol Services at www.capitolservices.com. On that site, click the Resources link, then the link named Links to State Websites. There you select any state from the dropdown field to go to that Secretary of State's website's UCC information.

Another site with direct links to all Secretary of State websites is that of Cl@s. This site is www.clasinfo.com and the page with the links is www.clasinfo.com/global/secretary_of_state.cfm. This page alphabetically lists all 50 states and the District of Columbia. Each state's name is a link to its Secretary of State's website.

The least expensive way to search for existing UCC-1 filings, and to file your own, is directly from the site of a specific Secretary of State. But each state's site is very different. Some are clear and easy to navigate, some are very confusing. Some allow you to run a search for free, many charge for searches, and some require you to register an account to search their data base and/or file online.

All should provide their costs and how to file, but finding that information is sometimes a bit tricky if the site's organization is confusing. Keep the information you've discovered on each state's requirements and costs for future reference; you'll be glad you did the next time you want to file for a new client in a state in which you've already filed.

The first due diligence you perform is to discover if there are tax liens filed by IRS or the state against the business, and any other liens filed by a bank, other factor, collection agency, private party, or anyone else. If there is a filing and a UCC-3 termination has not been filed, you will not be in first position. If the debts have been satisfied and a release or subordination (UCC-3) filed, this should show on the record. If a termination has not been filed but the client's debt has been satisfied, contact the client and/or the previous secured party and ask this be done. You won't be in first position until it is.

How do you know if a lien is on file? First ask the prospect, who may know. However, never rely solely on this as most have no clue. UCCs are a matter of public record and you can simply do the research yourself by using credit reports that display lien filings and/or public records searches. However, credit reports sometimes miss the presence of duly filed UCCs, and you're safest bet is to search the Secretary of State's site or use a UCC search and filing service company, some of which are listed at the end of this chapter.

When you are no longer factoring a client, and especially if they're factoring with another company or want a bank loan or line of credit, you need to file a termination of your lien. This is done by completing a UCC-3 form (available from the same places you obtain a UCC-1) and filing it with the same Secretary of State with which you filed the UCC-1. There is usually a charge for this of around $5 to $20. If you don't terminate your UCC-1 and a client presents you with a written demand to do so, you must comply within 20 days of their demand. If you don't, you can face a $500 penalty. So simply be in the habit of filing a termination when an account is paid in full and closed on your books.

There are many companies which offer UCC searching and/or filing services for a fee. Let's look at a few.

Public Records Search Companies

Accurint® (www.accurint.com) is an information management company owned by the corporate giant LexisNexis. You use Accurint® to find people and businesses, their assets, obtain background information, and uncover bankruptcies and criminal histories.

Accurint® is a web-based service that can be accessed with a User ID and Password. You need to apply and be accepted for an account. Accurint® has a monthly minimum charge that could be seen as fairly steep by some new small factors, so you'll need to be serious about factoring to get your money's worth here. The minimum charge provides a specific number of monthly searches; if you go over that number you are charged extra per report for the overage that month.

While there are many types of searches available with Accurint®, you will most likely just use the searches below to check out prospective client businesses and their owners.

The Comprehensive Report for an individual person (the business owner) includes many searches. You won't need all of them, but everything below is available as of this writing. I've put a checked box (☑) next to the ones I routinely run when checking out a new prospective client.

Summary Report including:
- ☑ Comprehensive Report Summary
- ☐ Address Summary
- ☐ Relative Summary

      ☐ Others Using Same SSN
      ☐ Date & Locations where SSN Issued
      ☐ Neighborhood Profile (Census data)
      ☐ Include Company Header
☑ Include Motor Vehicle(s) Registration
☑ Properties
☐ Florida Accidents
☐ Neighbors
☐ Associates
☑ UCC Filings
☑ Possible Criminal Records
☑ Bankruptcy
☑ Liens & Judgments
☑ Include Driver's Licenses Information
☐ Phones Plus
☐ People at Work
☐ Relatives

The Comprehensive Business Report finds information for any of the following searches on a business. Just like the individual person search above, you won't need all these so just choose those you want by checking their selection boxes, then searching all those checked with one click. Again, the ones I use for looking at a prospective client's business are checked below.

Base Report Features:
☑ Name, Address and Phone
☑ Parent Company, Id Numbers and Industry Information

Additional Report Options:
  Business Filings
    ☑ Bankruptcy
    ☑ Liens & Judgments
    ☑ Corporation Filings
    ☑ Business Registrations
    ☑ UCC Filings
☑ Associated Businesses
☑ Associated People

Assets
- ☑ Properties
- ☑ Motor Vehicles
- ☐ FAA Aircraft
- ☐ Watercraft
- ☑ Internet Domain Names
- ☑ Dun & Bradstreet Records
- ☑ IRS5500
- ☑ Liens & Judgments
- ☐ Include Driver's Licenses Information

Accurint® does not provide credit reports with numbered scores as do D&B, Experian, Ansonia, Cortera, and others. However Accurint® does provide easy public records searches for UCC filings, corporate records, bankruptcies, tax liens, judgments, criminal records (right down to parking and speeding tickets), and personal assets of your potential clients. Other information Accurint® provides makes this a great resource for locating people who owe you money and have skipped out.

While Accurint® provides a means of searching for UCC filings and other public record information, you are not able to submit UCC filings through Accurint®, which is limited to public records searches.

KnowX. Like Accurint®, www.KnowX provides quick access to comprehensive public records information, but again you cannot file here, only search. The searches for particular data are similar to Accurint® without the required minimum monthly charge. You can pay by individual search, a daily amount, or a monthly rate.

UCC Search and Filing Service Companies

If you don't want to search UCC filings or enter your own filings yourself from a Secretary of State website, several companies provide these services. While using such a company is more expensive that doing the searches and filings from a Secretary of State site – you pay the state's normal fees in addition to the company's charges – there are some advantages:

- You only have to learn the company's search and filing methods, not those for every single state.
- Your searches and filings are stored in one convenient location for easy reference.
- Staff are on hand to help if you have any questions.

You need to decide if paying the extra cost is worth the time and effort to search and file with the states directly. When you run across a state's site that is particularly confusing, it probably is.

Below is a list of some of these UCC search and filing companies as of this writing. To find a current list of providers, Google "UCC filing services" and "UCC search services."

CT Lien Solutions www.ctliensolutions.com
Capitol Services, Inc. www.capitolservices.com
Corporate Services Company (CSC) www.cscglobal.com
All-Search & Inspection, Inc. www.all-search.com
National Corporate Research, Ltd. www.nationalcorp.com
Parasec www.parasec.com

15
Credit Reports

Pulling credit reports on the internet is remarkably easy; the hard part is figuring out which ones suit the type of information you need, learning how to read them, and deciding which ones you can afford.

Because credit products and their prices change quite regularly with every provider, I have not provided samples of various reports or how much they cost; the information simply changes too quickly. Instead you'll find below website links and my own experiences with these companies so you can get the most up to date information yourself and then make your decision.

The services mentioned in this chapter are just some of the credit reporting services available; expect to put some time into your web research to determine which reports are best suited to your business, and realize there are more out there you can find without much digging.

Dun & Bradstreet (D&B)

Dun & Bradstreet is perhaps the best known of all business credit services. For many small factors much of what D&B provides may be more expensive and provide more information than you need. However, many larger factors use D&B and you hear its name often in discussions among them.

When I worked for a large factoring company several years ago, D&B was the company's primary source of credit information. However while working on my own as a small factor, most of D&B's reports' price tags have been beyond my budget despite D&B's efforts to provide products for small companies.

To decide for yourself, go to www.dnb.com and have a look around. Observe the names of their reports and the costs; if you can't find sample reports quickly on the site, Google the names of specific reports followed by the words "sample report" or "example." For instance, look up "paydex example" and you'll see some. This will give you the opportunity to see not only the various reports available from D&B but also the other providers below.

Experian

Experian is a well-known and often used source for credit reports. Because these reports are also on the higher end price-wise, I didn't use them for many years. However since I am able to get a discounted price (explained below), I now use these reports regularly and find them to be especially valuable. In fact I realized that had I been using Experian reports years earlier, I probably would have turned away some clients I funded who turned out to be less than stellar.

Why would I have declined some of them? The less expensive reports don't provide the depth of information Experian does. Experian's data provides many more of the jigsaw puzzle pieces mentioned in the last chapter the other reports lacked. After all, that is the purpose of your due diligence – to give you enough information to determine when saying "no" is the best decision.

Experian's official website is www.experian.com. However, this link is more for individuals seeking their own credit score and how to improve it. Click the link to Small Business and that puts you in the area suited for what you need.

You can sign up and receive reports from this site; however if you sign up here you pay full price. Members of IFA and FactorFox subscribers receive discounted prices off all Experian reports. When you join IFA, get all the information you can about how to take advantage of these discounts.

194

FactorFox subscribers have the choice of numerous annual and monthly report volumes and types of reports from which to choose. Again, ask about this when you start your subscription and are ready to run credit reports. You will be referred to an Experian sales executive who is familiar with the arrangement with FactorFox, can provide many sample reports, help you learn how to run and understand the reports, and answer your questions.

Cortera

Another credit provider is Cortera (www.cortera.com.) Prices for Cortera reports are considerably less than Experian, and not surprisingly the information is less in-depth. However the data is still worthwhile to small factors and the price of each report is quite affordable.

Cortera also provides an alert system for a reasonable monthly price, and subscribing to this service lowers the cost of each individual report you pull. You must provide monthly data to Cortera (as well as Experian, Ansonia, and others), but if you use most factoring software packages these reports are easily generated.

FactorFox has some credit companies' reports embedded within the software, so you can run their reports without leaving FactorFox. Monthly uploads to the providers are also automated with this software, so you don't need to spend time creating the reports, saving them as csv files, and emailing them. It's all done for you while you sleep.

Ansonia Credit Data

Ansonia Credit Data (www.ansoniacreditdata.com) is another provider of credit reports for factors. Their data base provides information for both transportation factors and non-transportation factors, though their long-time forte was trucking data. If you have an Ansonia subscription, you can run their credit reports from within FactorFox as the search feature and reporting are built right in.

Their staff is friendly and very willing to help. Like Cortera, prices per report are quite affordable and billed on a per-report basis. You're not required to submit your data, but receive a lower price per report if you do.

Smyyth Networks

Smyyth (pronounced with a long i, like "sigh") Networks is a very large company that provides many credit products to businesses. Their services of most interest to factors include credit reports, an in-house collection agency, credit insurance brokering, a complete credit management system, and credit groups (see below). Their array of services can be a bit overwhelming to a small factor and many of them are beyond the scope of our businesses, but this is a company you should know.

Smyyth provides several credit network groups for various industries, including a factors network to which factors contribute credit data for others in the network. Those who join this network can interact and see statistics on factors' reported data. Reports are quite thorough and provide good information. Pulling credit reports is done from their service named rational*i*, part of the company Bernard Sands, which is fully owned by Smyyth. Once you become familiar with these reports, you realize the information is quite in depth. Go to their website at www.smyyth.com for more information.

Credit.Net

Another player is Credit.Net (www.credit.net). This company is a division of Infogroup, Inc. (www.infogroup.com) whose primary business is providing marketing products to small and larger companies.

Infogroup has provided prospecting lists factors can use as a means of finding and marketing to potential clients for quite some time. These lists can be very specifically targeted and provide a method of finding exactly the kind of leads you're looking for. Infogroup's services allow you to market across numerous channels including email, the web, social media, and text messages, in addition to traditional direct mail. Their services can help you plan a campaign well-suited to your marketing plans and are worth considering.

Credit.net's data base contains basic information on some 15.5 million businesses, including business name, address, phone number, SIC code, number of employees, name of owner or manager, estimated sales volume, key executives, and a business credit score assigned by Credit.net.

The Sample Report link on Credit.net's home page opens the sample report, which is easy to read and understand. It includes the credit rating score, a recommended credit limit, and in many cases a small picture of the business' building. These are followed by the list of information above, a summary of business expenditures, legal filings, and UCCs.

If you've read credit reports from other providers, you notice Credit.net's information is comparatively brief and does not include payment histories – that is, there's no record of how long this company takes to pay, as is included in other providers' reports described above. Why?

Credit.net uses algorithms to arrive at its credit score, rather than data submitted from companies with trade experiences. Their model considers number of employees, years in the data base, industry stability and barriers to entry, census data, and other factors to arrive at the scores assigned – but not payment histories. Their site says the scores are "practical, statistically sound indicators of probable ability to pay."

This reflects the company's core business as a marketing database, rather than a credit reporting database. Since there are no trade experiences collected by Credit.net, you shouldn't rely solely on its data for decisions other than very small transactions, especially when searching customers' credit. In fact, the fine print at the bottom of the report gives this advice: "In no event should the information contained on this report be used as the sole source in making a credit decision." More on this shortly.

Credit Reporting Agencies for Trucking Factors

While transportation factoring is on my list of industries most new factors should avoid, those who have worked in trucking for many years can enter this arena far more safely than those without such experience. Credit reporting services are available whose data is specific to the trucking industry and are described below:

Ansonia Credit Data

As mentioned earlier, Ansonia has a data base for both trucking and general factoring. Transportation factors speak well of Ansonia's trucking data and reports. Take a look at Ansonia's reports at www.ansoniacreditdata.com.

Debtor411

Debtor411 (www.Debtor411.com) provides excellent online credit reports exclusively to transportation factoring companies of all sizes. Debtor411 collects credit data only about transportation brokers and shippers.

Contributing your company's data is not required, though of course encouraged. Its automated system collects, compiles and analyzes first-hand payment experiences directly from factoring companies. The data base is purged and updated weekly.

A sample transportation credit report is easy to find on the website. The information gives you multiple reports bundled into one report, along with individual credit scores and critical details. You only pay for what you use and you do not have to pre-pay for credit reports or run a minimum number each month.

With Debtor411's scoring, analytics and charting system you can identify historical trends. Its proprietary match-control technology enables you to isolate the most recent credit experiences and guides you in building custom reports that hone in on the debtor information you need.

Carrier411

Carrier411, a sister company of Debtor411, provides other data valuable to trucking factors. Carrier411 tracks and evaluates all your carriers' safety ratings, CSA 2010 BASIC scores, insurance, operating authority, FreightGuard reports, and more.

For a flat and affordable monthly fee, register all the trucking companies you want to monitor through its website (www.Carrier411.com) and you are notified when changes happen. Change alerts are available instantly by email, fax and online regarding Unsafe Driving, Fatigued Driving (Hours-of-Service), Driver Fitness, Controlled Substances/Alcohol, and Vehicle Maintenance.

Transcredit

Transcredit (www.transcredit.com) provides three products to trucking factors:

1. Its PremierReport provides financial information, business profiles, and credit scores

2. CreditTrac, which for a flat monthly rate provides updated credit scores and credit alerts, and

3. GoCollect, which can send you email alerts of past due invoices, make pre-collection phone calls on your behalf, and/or take professional collection action for invoices seriously past due.

Observation

We have seen in the chapters in the Risk Management section that spreading the concentrations of your funds among many clients and customers is the most prudent way to run your factoring business. The same principle applies to your underwriting.

The words from Credit.net's report quoted earlier ("in no event should the information contained on this report be used as the sole source in making a credit decision") is actually very good advice no matter what service/s you use. Don't use just one report to decide if you'll accept a prospective client or customer – find as much information as you can. Obtain as much data from as many sources as your budget, time, and sense of comfort allow.

Clearly there is far more information available to the small factor than one can possibly use or need. The information is presented in this chapter so you know what's out there and can get an idea of what is useful without being overwhelmed by what you can get.

Refer to the chapter "Due Diligence" on just how much underwriting is really needed for the level of business you do and the comfort level you need. You can't look at every single report available, but neither should you look at only a single report and stop.

Credit reports from different providers can both complement and (sometimes) contradict each other. A UCC filing, judgment, tax lien or other item may show up in one report but not another. One agency may give the business a fairly high score while another's score for the same company might be rather low. Thus the more information you gather the more complete the picture you see.

As you can tell from previous chapters, underwriting may be more art than science; however, you need to start somewhere. Once you have studied the various providers out there and the reports they offer, make a preliminary checklist of underwriting steps you will perform for prospective clients and another one for new customers. They'll probably be somewhat similar but not identical.

New factors often ask me for a Due Diligence checklist, which gives exact step-by-step underwriting actions they should follow. While I encourage each factor to develop his/her own checklists and procedures, the next chapter gives some suggestions as to where to start and what your preliminary checklists might include. Feel free to adapt these to your own company's processes as you gain experience and confidence in this important part of your business.

16
Checklists

We now have a foundation for performing your due diligence – that is, what to look for and where to find information regarding companies with whom you are considering doing business. The next step is to organize your underwriting into step-by-step procedures that make retrieving, compiling, and analyzing the data (and thus your decision) a lot easier. The best way to get organized is with checklists.

FactorFox provides a feature that gives the ability to make and edit customized checklists for prospective clients, prospective customers, and schedules. While using this feature is optional, those who do find it quite convenient, and it can be adapted to the checklists below quite easily.

Checklists for Preliminary Due Diligence

Prospective Client Checklists. Below is a generic checklist you might use when underwriting your prospective clients. Keep in mind that using at least two of the "Services available" resources in the checklists below is advisable.

Checklist – Due Diligence for Prospective Clients

____ 1. Application Form received; all answers provided
    ____ Due diligence fee if required

____ 2. Free internet searches:
    ____ Client's web site
    ____ Google business
    ____ Google owner's name
    ____ Google/Bing maps of residence, business
    ____ Review entries in LinkedIn, Facebook, Google +
    ____ IFA watch list (if a member of IFA)

____ 3. Preliminary documents/information:
    ____ Business license/Corporation Articles/Driver's License
    ____ Aging report
    ____ Financial statements

___ Existing bank loans/lines
___ Previously filed tax forms to show taxes are current, if required
___ 4. Company background checks:
    ___ UCCs:
      Methods available:
      ___ Secretary of State website
      ___ UCC service
    ___ Liens, judgments, UCCs
      Services available:
      ___ Accurint
      ___ KnowX
      ___ Experian
      ___ D&B
      ___ Smyyth
      ___ Cortera
      ___ Ansonia
      ___ Credit.net
      ___ Other
    ___ Tax Guard Due Diligence Report
___ 5. Owner/s background checks:
    ___ Liens, judgments, criminal background, UCCs
    Services available:
      ___ Accurint
      ___ KnowX
      ___ Experian
      ___ Other

Prospective Customers Checklists. Once you feel a prospective client looks acceptable you need to consider her customers. Some factors review the customers first but that's up to you. Either way you're looking for quick deal-killers, so if you can find those with little or no expense, so much the better. The more you look, the more time and money you tend to spend.

Checklist – Due Diligence for Prospective Customers

___ 1. Review client's aging and customer payment histories if available
___ 2. Free internet searches:
    ___ Customer's web site
    ___ Google businFess
    ___ Google/Bing maps of business
___ 3. Check business credit
    Services available:
    ___ Experian
    ___ D&B
    ___ Smyyth
    ___ Cortera
    ___ Ansonia
    ___ Credit.net
    ___ Other

Making the Decision to Accept or Decline

After you have done as much underwriting as you feel you can or is necessary, you must make the decision to accept or decline a client or customer. Finding good information (which may be limited to finding no *bad* information) is what you hope you'll uncover, and usually leads to your acceptance of the account. However, often you find little or no information at all on a client or customer. What do you do then?

Very small prospective companies often have little or no information, especially if the business is new or young. They just haven't been in business long enough for companies to report anything. However, finding poor credit scores on client companies and their owners is not at all unusual and is often the reason they need to factor: banks and other lenders won't accept them. While you may not find much on a client's company, you certainly want to find all you can on its owner. Accurint and Experian reports are usually quite helpful in providing this information if it is to be found at all.

On the other hand, suppose you find little or no credit history on a prospective customer. What do you do in this case? If a client looks good but you can find little or no information on a customer (which is common with very small companies whose other vendors do not report their payment history and/or who pay cash), ask for a payment history on that customer from the client. If they have done business with this customer for a year or more they should be able to provide some kind of data showing invoice amounts and dates, and payment amounts dates.

If the customer is new to the client and you can't find any credit information, a wise course is usually to tell the client you can't fund invoices to this customer with the information available. If the client wants to do business with the customer, they might do so on a 6-month trial basis. While you won't factor invoices to them yet, giving the customer a little rope (at no risk to you) can help you see how they pay. Advise the client to start off with COD terms, then maybe extend that gradually to 10 or 15 day terms. If they pay dependably, extend the terms to 30 days. Once they've been paying dependably at that level for several months, you may feel safe factoring these invoices.

Alternately, if your client *really* needs to factor this customer and you're feeling especially adventurous (a rare attribute among seasoned factors) you could agree to factor such a customer on a very limited trial basis. During the time it takes to establish a good payment history (again six months usually gives you enough time to feel comfortable) you might give a low advance, such as 50% or just enough to meet the client's costs, charge a higher discount, and allow a shorter than usual recourse period, perhaps 60 days if you usually give 90.

While you have some funds at risk this way (as opposed to just not funding until the client has established a proven record without your money involved), your exposure should be pretty low and you can always cut him off any time you think is prudent. However, the client should have other, solid customers' invoices in the equation so you have funds available in escrow, rebates, or advances to use to cover these if they go bad. Once you're comfortable with the payment history, you can provide a better advance, discount, and recourse period.

However, be careful of your exposure with unknown customers you "try out" like these. Closely watch your concentrations with unrated companies and keep an eagle eye on their aging reports to track their payments. If you don't they can fall behind and getting paid can become a very difficult. Monitor the invoices closely and look for any signs the customer is delaying or avoiding payment, doesn't want to talk to you, or other red flags. Always remember the Cardinal Rule of Money with new, unknown customers.

Once you have made the decision to accept a client and customer, the following checklists can help you set up their accounts.

Checklist – Establishing a New Client's Account

Establishing a Client Account
___ Contract signed and on file
___ File UCC
___ File IRS 8821
___ Establish Tax Guard Monthly Monitoring Report

Checklist – Establishing a New Customer's Account

___ Notices of Assignment to new customers
___ Verify Accounts Payable has received the NOA
___ Verify Accounts Payable has changed the remittance address to yours
___ Verify first factored invoices

Checklists for Ongoing Due Diligence

A sound practice is to check UCC-1 filings annually to see if a tax lien or other UCC-1s have been filed against your clients, or with customers with whom you have a lot of funds outstanding. Tax liens have priority over UCCs even if the tax liens are filed later. Checking this using Tax Guard's Monthly Monitoring Report, and/or alert services from credit reporting services, will keep you informed. You want to know if your collateral is at risk because your client hasn't told you about a tax problem that has arisen (which can happen easily), or a customer's credit rating has dropped for any number of reasons.

Making these annual checks or paying for ongoing alerts can be a bit costly but if they turn up a problem, can more than pay for potential losses. They may show your lien position or client's or customers' finances weren't what they were when you started factoring.

Checklist – Ongoing Due Diligence for Clients

___ Notices of Assignment to new customers
___ Verify invoices as necessary
___ Follow up on slow pays
___ Check UCC filing status yearly
___ Re-submit 8821 filings yearly
___ Review Tax Guard Monthly Monitoring Report
___ Look for alerts of changes in credit score from credit services

Checklist – Ongoing Due Diligence for Customers

___ Contact customer when payment sent to client
___ Verify invoices as necessary
___ Follow up on slow pays
___ Look for alerts of changes in credit score from credit services

Checklist for Closing an Account

When the time comes for a client to stop factoring, you need to follow a few simple steps to formally close the account.

Closing an Account
___ File UCC-3
___ Notify customers of termination of Notices of Assignment
___ Return Escrow Account funds if necessary

In this chapter we've provided specific steps to pull together and utilize the numerous underwriting resources available to make the best possible decision as to whether you will accept or decline an account. We've also provided steps you can take to monitor your accounts, but haven't gone into much detail about such monitoring. That's what the next chapter, "Preventive Maintenance" is all about.

17

Preventive
Maintenance

This is one of the most important chapters in this book, and readers often are surprised by that. The topic is pretty mundane, easy to put off, and something most folks aren't thrilled about doing. But if you skip this chapter or ignore what it says, you'll live to regret your inattentiveness. Believe me.

Most small factors love to have clients like one of mine I called "Alan the Pit Bull" (see the story called "The Secret to Getting Paid" in the chapter "Additional Resources"). Alan was absolutely the best client I ever had for collecting his slow-paying receivables. I wish all my clients were so tenacious about customer payments.

But reality is, most clients are not like Alan; in fact, most are as different from Alan as a Chihuahua is from a Saint Bernard. Alan made his own calls on slow payers and was extremely effective at getting paid. But these calls are something *you* must do routinely for most of your clients, and doing so is often as thrilling as changing the oil in your car.

Some time ago I had a small pickup truck I drove for years. It had been my dad's, had sentimental attachment for me, and was just a good old dependable workhorse. It wasn't beautiful but it was as dependable as the setting of the sun and it got the job done.

It certainly wasn't the hottest set of wheels on the road but it was mine and I drove it everywhere...much to the chagrin of my kids, who always referred to it (with the slightest hint of a smile and the barest touch of sarcasm) as the "Piece of

Wonder." But whenever they needed something hauled, guess who wanted to use it.

Anyway, at one point, the old pickup was overdue for an oil change. When I finally got around to taking care of it, the oil that came out was dark, dirty and pretty ugly. It contrasted starkly to the clear, clean oil that went into the engine to replace it. Not only was the old oil dirty, there wasn't much of it. My truck took four-plus quarts but this time there were probably no more than two quarts drained out of the engine.

Simply put, I wasn't taking proper care of my old friend and if I had let this go much longer the engine could have been in very bad shape. Anybody who owns an auto knows the value of such simple preventive maintenance as regular oil changes…especially if you've had to pay for repairs that regular maintenance would have made unnecessary.

Your factoring business needs some regular preventive maintenance too. It's pretty easy and inexpensive to do, just like an oil change: you must follow up on the slow paying customers of your clients. You can spend all the time and money you want getting accounts set up with proper due diligence, careful checking of credit reports, and so on…but if you don't do what's necessary to keep your receivables running smoothly, all that earlier work may be wasted.

Think of it as going out and buying that nice, new expensive car you've had your eye on for a long time. What is it – a Mercedes, Lexus, BMW, Cadillac, Jaguar, a sports car, a classic antique? Whatever it is, do you have a picture of it in your mind?

Ok, now imagine yourself spending time and energy researching the consumer guides and learning everything you can about the car's features and benefits. See yourself shopping around at various dealers, negotiating the best deal possible, and then finally driving your dream car home with a happy smile on your face and sense of satisfaction in your heart. And now imagine driving this work of art everywhere you go, and all your friends and everyone you drive by staring and admiring your beautiful new machine. What a great feeling!

And now imagine driving this fantastic car everywhere for the next four years...and *never once changing the oil.* Aaaugh! Who in their right mind would do that?

Well that is exactly what factors do who spend large sums on nice office equipment, software, carefully planned marketing campaigns, fancy websites, thorough due diligence, and all the bells and whistles...but then never make calls to customers who are late paying their overdue bills. It makes as much sense as never changing your dream car's oil.

It is very easy to just let your clients watch your aging reports and make calls to their slow paying customers. After all, you reason, these clients are on recourse and if the bills don't pay in 60 or 90 days you can take a charge back. Right? Yes, but wrong thinking.

One of the most important services you provide your clients is tracking their accounts receivable and knowing their customers' payment habits. That is, over time you will learn which customers pay like clockwork in two weeks, which take 30, 60, or 80 days as a normal course of business, and which ones are completely unpredictable. Often clients can tell you what length of time is normal for many of their customers, so be sure to ask.

When you learn these payment habits and find a blip on the radar – like a two-week payer is suddenly at 35 days, or a 30-day payer has slipped to 45 – this is the flag to alert you they need a call. Being on top of slow payments this way is crucial to your value as a factor, and if your clients' cash flow dries up because of slow payments due to *your* being lax on needed calls, their business may soon be in peril. And guess what – that in turn puts your investment in their invoices in jeopardy.

Perhaps you think you're too busy with other more important things to do anything as mundane as calling slow payers to see what's happened to the money they owe you. Well you know what? Changing your oil is pretty mundane too. Do you skip that?

The more consistently you follow up on overdue payments the more likely you are to catch problems and get paid.

Collection calls – I prefer to use the term "follow-up" calls – are very important to both you and your clients and need to be handled professionally. If your manner comes off as threatening or heavy-handed you can alienate the customer – which is a very reasonable concern most clients have when they first consider factoring.

The great majority of overdue bills are late not because the customer is unwilling or unable to pay; with good due diligence you will usually avoid such customers. Most bills are not paid on time (my guess would be around 80%) because the accounts payable person responsible for paying a bill doesn't have the invoice.

This can be due to being mailed to an incorrect address, or incorrect routing to them, or they simply lost it, or just about any reason you can think of. Believe me, you'll hear them all. Therefore when you make a follow-up call, it's best to use this approach.

If the customer is a large company, call and ask to speak to the accounts payable department; once you're there ask to speak to the person who handles the payables for this particular client. Accounts are often distributed among payables clerks alphabetically: Mary handles companies whose names start with A to D, Tony handles E through H, and so on. If the customer is a smaller company, ask to speak to the person who handles their bookkeeping. Get right to the person who cuts the check so you don't waste a lot of time explaining who you are and what you want to people who can't help you.

Once you have the right person, say, "Hello, I'm _____ and I handle the receivables for ABC Widget Company. I'm showing an invoice that's getting a bit old and I want to make sure you received it. Can you help me with this?"

This engages the person by enlisting their help to solve your problem, rather than making them defensive with the blunt, accusatory approach of "Why haven't you paid this bill yet?"

After taking a moment to check, most of the time she will say she "never received it" or "has no record of it" and if you can just fax or email her a copy of the invoice she'll take care of it right away. (Be sure you keep invoice copies!) Check to see you have the correct fax or email address as that may be why she never received it. Then again, there's a good chance she just lost it.

Be sure to write down the name of the person you talk to and keep a log of these calls – date, time, and who said what. FactorFox has a built-in Invoice Notes system where you can track every call about every invoice; if you're using spreadsheets you can track these conversations using the Telephone Log below.

<u>Telephone Log</u>

Date	Time	Company	Person's Name	Tel./ Ext. #	Re: Client	Message

You should end the conversation with a rough estimate of when to expect to receive the payment. If she's evasive or won't give you one, that's a red flag that you may not get paid so watch that customer carefully! Inform your client when a customer concerns you this way, as he may want to put the company on COD or cease dealing with it altogether. You probably don't want to buy any more invoices to such customers.

If the bill still hasn't been paid a week or two after you expected you now know whom to call. You phone that person to "follow up on the payment status" of the invoice you spoke to her about earlier. Armed with your Invoice Notes or Telephone Log information you'll have exact dates and what she said. This will make you come off as professional and on top of things, which makes an impression on people who pay bills.

If there's another reason an invoice hasn't been paid besides "I never received it," the payables clerk or bookkeeper can usually tell you: it's not been approved for payment, someone has been on vacation, they're short handed and behind, something was wrong with the product or service, and so on. Sometimes the invoice and/or check must cross several desks and it just takes a while to get signed and mailed (common with larger customers). Other times the check will have already been scheduled for next week's print run and is all set to go, but just won't get signed and mailed until then. Again, log this information and follow up if you don't receive payment in a reasonable time based on the information given.

A friendly relationship with the payables people at customers' companies can not only make your job easier and your (and their) day brighter; it can also ensure you get paid in a timely fashion. That can go a long way to keeping your client's (and thus your own) business solvent, plus you will be a hero in your client's eyes. You'll make him look good, save him money, keep his and your cash flow stable, and maintain both of your businesses on firm footing.

Get in the habit of regularly watching your flagged invoices and aging reports, and regularly make needed follow-up calls to people with overdue bills. Account managers at large factoring companies understand this as a key part of their job and they spend a lot of time doing it. This kind of monitoring and follow up had a lot to do with what made their company big. Translate: follow-up calls make you money.

If payables staff and bookkeepers come to know you as friendly and also diligent, they will be sure to pay your clients' invoices in a timely manner when those invoices arrive...and frequently before other invoices that are also awaiting payment.

So keep your and your clients' businesses running smoothly with the routine preventive maintenance of regularly watching for overdue customer payments and making timely follow-up calls. It's a painless way to avoid what can become costly repairs that never should have been needed in the first place. Do this long enough and consistently enough and maybe in time your factoring business will provide the funds for that dream car you've always wanted. Remember the nice feeling as you pictured yourself driving it home?

Just remember to change the oil.

18

24 Common Mistakes

There are numerous mistakes new factors can make not just early in their business, but any time. Unfortunately, you may not realize the potential hazard of what you're doing. While there are no doubt more mistakes you can make than those described below, what follow are mistakes I've observed others make or have made myself.

#1. Failure to Plan

The chapter "Charting Your Course" provides guiding questions to point you in the direction you wish to take your factoring business. While this manual doesn't provide similar specific questions for a marketing plan, it's not a bad idea to commit this part of your business to writing as well. These are the two key parts of piloting a successful ship.

While you probably don't need to plot every detail years in advance, failure to plan, at least in general terms, is planning to fail: trite but true. Compose the map you will follow, make adjustments for detours as they appear along the way and you'll arrive at your destination a lot more smoothly and quickly than if you just wing it.

#2. Getting Sidetracked

In the course of looking for (and finding) clients, you will inevitably run into requests for loans or venture capital, acquaintances who offer other "opportunities," and numerous other temptations which can lure you away from factoring. It is very, very easy to get sidetracked by these, and your business will not fare as well if you wander off the path. Be able to say, "No thanks," stick with factoring, and do it better than anyone else.

The proverbial "Jack-of-All-Trades, Master-of-None" result is all too common among people who get sidetracked. Lack of focus will retard the growth of your factoring business while you chase after venture capital or other money for a prospect. Requests for loans and venture capital are easy to come across, but extremely hard to place with a funding source. One local venture capitalist told me he funds about 1% of the requests that come across his desk, all of which are presented in carefully constructed business plans.

Unless you already have experience and multiple contacts in a related cash flow business, stick to factoring and stay clear of brokering loans or venture capital. There's plenty of business out there for the small factor who does nothing else.

#3. Being Under Capitalized

This can creep up on you whether you have $50,000 in factoring money or ten times that much. You constantly need to have a good handle on how much money your clients are going to need for advances and how long their accounts take to pay. If you're off on either of these, you can end up in a very embarrassing situation.

Take the small factor with $20,000 to use as advances. He takes on a client who has only one customer who wants to factor $2,000 every week, and who swears up and down his customer always pays in 30 days. After a month, $8,000 is out. The first invoice is paid, but the next two drift into 45 days each. Another invoice with the same client/customer is factored, but then the client takes on a new customer he wants to factor. Now more advances are needed and the factor has a cash flow problem himself. He must scramble to come up with the funds to meet his client's need.

The above scenario can play if you have one client or a dozen. Factoring, by its very nature, enables companies to increase business. That means their invoices will grow in size, number, and frequency. If you're not in a position to meet that need for more and more funds as demand increases, your reputation as a "money person" can go down the tubes. Don't take on more than you can handle – both in the number of clients and the volume they factor. If you expect your client base to grow, be positioned to fund that growth and you'll be a savior in their eyes. Alternately, don't hesitate to refer clients who have grown to a factor who has greater capacity or handles larger clients.

Nothing is more embarrassing or stressful than to have clients submit invoices and expect advances in 24 hours...and you can't come up with the money. If the phone or fax rings and you hope it's not a client wanting an advance, you're under funded. Believe me, that's under fun.

#4. Complicated or Misleading Rates

Some new factors start with discount rates that are way too complicated. For example, one may charge .1% per day for the first 30 days, an additional .15% per day for the next 15 days, then 2% more for the block of the next 15 days, and finish with an additional 3% for the remaining days until 90. Then after recourse at 90 days it's an additional 1% for every five days thereafter forever.

You got all that? If so, please repeat it aloud without looking. And if you can repeat it, calculate in your head how much the client is paying at day 47.

A convoluted rate might be concocted by someone who is trying to "incentivize clients for rapid receivables turnaround in order to maximize returns and minimize risk." People with rates like this often talk like this.

The problem is while both the rates and the words may make perfect sense to this factor, prospective clients are going to look at these numbers and say, "Uhhh...what?"

If your prospect doesn't understand what you're saying and can't easily calculate what you're charging, he *might* think you're some kind of financial wizard. Unfortunately he's not going to want to work with you because he won't understand how much he's being charged and will always have a hollow numbness in his mind when he wonders how much he's paying to factor his invoices. This in turn can make him wonder if he's being overcharged when he realizes he'll never be able to figure out how his rates are calculated, and eventually this can lead to distrust of you, his factor. That's not good.

In a similar way, I've seen other factors (usually more experienced ones) offer rates or advances that sound really, really good – until you get the contract and read the fine print. This is often done among factors where competition is fierce, such as transportation, and they're jockeying hard for an inside position in the race for new business.

On the internet you'll probably find factors who advertise 100% advances and teaser discounts far below the competition. "How can they do this?" one legitimately wonders. Well the truth is, mathematically you can't give a true 100% advance rate and make income from factoring. A factor giving a full 100% advance is paying the full value of the invoice – which therefore can't be purchased "at a discount." There is simply no room for a discount when you advance 100%!

So what do factors who advertise these advances really do? Usually their angle is to give the 100% advance minus the discount; that is they deduct the discount from the advance at the time of funding. So if they have a flat 5% discount, 5% is deducted from the "100% advance" and they effectively advance 95%.

This is nothing more than a 5% discount taken from the front end rather than the back end. They're not advancing 100%, they're advancing 95%. It may make for appealing ad copy on their website and an attractive sales pitch, but it's certainly not a 100% advance. It's misleading to my thinking.

Likewise, exceptionally low discount rates that are simply too low to provide an adequate profit to the factor are likewise deceptive. Factors who advertise these rates to get prospects' attention always – and have to – tack on additional fees and charges with fancy names they don't advertise. When all the discounts and all these fees and charges are added up, their rates are comparable to everyone else's.

None of these practices are good for prospective clients, nor for the factors who practice them, nor for the factoring industry as a whole. Such methods lead people to suspect that if factors are this slippery in their advertising then they probably can't be trusted in their operating procedures and who knows what else.

Therefore, keep your advance and discount rates simple to understand and free from smoke and mirrors as to how they're calculated. Be honest and straightforward with what you advance, what you charge, and how you do business. It pays far better dividends in the long run than a bunch of hocus pocus baloney.

#5. Inadequate Due Diligence

Once you have prospects knocking on your door, you need to decide if you'll fund them, how much to advance, and how much to charge. Your due diligence will guide you here but if you're just starting out, have no experience with credit reports, and have no one to advise you, what due diligence procedures should you follow? What are the credit reports telling you? How do you know whether the due diligence you're performing is "adequate"?

Even with directions to follow, most of us get a queasy feeling the very first time we do something new. Because of our inexperience, we don't know exactly what we're doing or supposed to do; moreover, we don't know how much we don't know. This is especially true with due diligence which requires reading credit reports and related material, and trying to determine if someone will be a good client or customer. The best approach is to have an experienced colleague review your due diligence before you agree to take on a client or customer, or before you advance funds. See the chapters entitled "Due Diligence" and "Credit Reports" for help in this area.

A mistake I've observed is the tendency of an inexperienced factor to overlook a customer's true credit worthiness. The new factor may be fairly thorough in checking out a client, but often learns little or nothing about the client's customers. As these are the ones paying the invoices you're buying, it is critical to know as much as you can about them too. In credit reports, look for payment trends; number of days beyond terms (DBT), that is days past due; occurrence of bills sent to collection; comments by other vendors; general risk guidelines; bankruptcies; positive, neutral and negative account profiles, and so on. In particular, look for judgments against this company or individual and be wary of factoring a prospect with past judgments.

As you read the report ask yourself, "What is the general picture painted in this credit report? How stable is this business? Is this someone who will pay his bills? (They're going to be my bills, after all!) How long will he probably take to pay? Do I want to wait that long?" Check out the customers as well as the clients!

#6. Accepting a Client as a Favor

At some point in your factoring business, you will very likely be presented with a prospect who, based on your due diligence or simple gut feeling, you would ordinarily decline as a client. However, extenuating circumstances may sway you to accept this prospect as a favor to someone.

Here are three scenarios.

1. The prospect comes from a broker who has brought many good clients in the past and you want to keep this person happy, so you'll do him a favor and approve this client.

2. The questionable prospect is your favorite aunt's next door neighbor, and she's told you how much this person would benefit from your help. She's also told him what a great person *you* are and how your service will benefit him. Since this aunt is a dear woman you've loved since you were in diapers, you decide to do her and the neighbor a favor and accept his account.

3. A charming prospect just tugs your heart strings in such a way that you'll overlook some glaring shortcomings to her account and take her on because you just inexplicably feel like you should.

Be very careful of letting your heart rule your head in such circumstances. When you are inclined to turn someone away you usually have very good reasons for doing so. The extenuating circumstances – your relationship with the consultant, your affection for your aunt, or your desire to help a winsome prospect – may lead you to overlook very good reasons for rejecting the account. But when you step back from these emotional elements of the decision, you may realize that accepting this client is just not a good idea. In fact, it's probably a downright *bad* idea.

Most factors who have accepted new clients as a favor to someone usually end up regretting the decision. Consider very carefully whether this is one of those times that your head needs to rule your heart. Remember: *no* client is better than a *bad* client.

#7. Making Loans to Clients

You will be looked upon by your clients as a person of means because you're providing cash they don't have. As a result, a few clients may ask you for loans instead of, or in addition to, factoring. This is especially possible if your client is in financial trouble, gets hit with an unexpected tax bill, or experiences some kind of financial crisis – medical expenses, lawsuit, divorce, car/truck/mortgage/building balloon payment due...you name it.

First, he may come to you and ask for a relatively small loan, perhaps $1,000 or $2,000, just to get him out of this temporary situation. Because he's a good client, honest and hard-working and you like him, you want to help. So you loan him the money, probably at an interest rate far lower than your factoring discounts.

That crisis passes, then a few months later another problem arises. He's behind in his truck payments. If he doesn't have $3,000 in the truck dealer's hands by noon tomorrow, he'll lose his truck which is vital to his delivery business. If he loses his truck, he'll go out of business and you'll lose both the client and the $2,000 you're still owed from the first loan. Against your better judgment, you loan him another $3,000. Two months later...five months later...ten months later...one crisis after another is met with more nervous requests. The tension in his voice is clear. By this time you're more than several thousand dollars into this client but if you pull the plug, the house of cards will come crashing down, he'll be out of business and you'll never see your money again.

Avoid getting into a situation like this by declining such requests right off the bat. You are a factor, not a lender. You buy invoices, you don't give loans. If your client would like to factor some receivables to get out of a bind, you'll be glad to help; but you don't do loans. Period.

If you start loaning money, you won't make as much in interest as you would from factoring discounts (even if they pay back the loan). And you'll have less factoring money available. You stand to lose a lot in the long run if the above scenario develops; unfortunately it's not just possible, it's very likely. Again, stick to one thing and do it well: factoring.

#8. Being Rushed

It is very common in this business to run into potential clients, or brokers with potential clients, who absolutely MUST get funding by tomorrow or sooner, or dire consequences will befall them. This can be a two-edged sword, but by and large be careful with people who want money too quickly.

While you want to find clients who have sincere cash flow problems which put them in a pinch (which is why we're in business), never allow yourself to be rushed. You must act expeditiously with new clients, as unnecessary delays can cost them money and create further problems. However, rushing to help someone out of a crisis (usually of their making) may not be in your best interest. Someone who needs instant money may be either

1) a bona fide good prospect
2) a prospect with poor management skills and therefore questionable as a good client (see the section, "Making Loans to Clients")
3) a prospect who knows hurrying up the process can cut corners to his benefit, or
4) a con artist ready to take you for a ride.

If the prospect wants you to hurry up your procedures, beware. Don't be rushed. Take the time necessary to do the due diligence you feel is needed. If the prospect isn't willing or able to wait for this, she probably won't be the kind of client with whom you want to work. If she's legitimate, she can almost always wait a couple days for you to do your homework. While you should move quickly, don't short-circuit your underwriting: you may end up getting burned.

#9. Purchase Order Funding

Quite often, new prospects think the only receivables they have to factor are purchase orders. These are orders from a customer for work to be done, but which has not begun. Thus, there is no invoice generated yet, and no completed service or product for you to verify with a customer.

Sometimes factors will advance against purchase orders, but usually decrease the advance to the amount of the client's cost from his supplier. Thus a first advance is sent to the supplier, not the client for the client's cost of goods. When work is eventually completed and the invoice is cut, the factor then pays the remaining amount of the advance to the client. For example if a normal factoring advance is 80% and the P.O. advance is 50%, the remaining advance for the invoice becomes 30%. It becomes a normal factoring transaction from there.

Often with government transactions, all you'll have is the equivalent of a purchase order. While the government is obligated to pay (in their own sweet time) as long as the client delivers, the same is not necessarily true with business purchase orders. This makes funding purchase orders, especially with a new client, terribly risky, and you are wise to avoid doing so.

Early in my business, I funded a new client's three purchase orders from some nurseries that had ordered wholesale trees from him. There was no supplier for my client since he dug the trees up in the mountains himself so the advance went to him. He delivered the trees to the nurseries which they acknowledged receiving; unfortunately, the nurseries later claimed the trees died and they refused to pay. Because my client guaranteed his products, the nurseries didn't have to pay for them. Worse, he had a bad year, no personal financial reserves, and therefore couldn't make good the money he now owed me. Eventually he filed for bankruptcy and I lost everything I advanced him. It was an expensive lesson in purchase order funding, as well as buying receivables for perishable goods.

#10. Chaining Clients

The business of one of my clients was to locate and arrange new accounts for janitorial service companies. His customers, the janitorial services, paid him the first two months' worth of billing for accounts provided, after which all income was the customer's (janitor's) to keep. The client wanted to factor one of his janitorial service customers who in turn wanted to factor some of the accounts the original client had secured. It sounded like a good deal: in a sense, two clients for the price of one.

However, the companies being cleaned didn't pay for the janitorial service, and the janitorial company therefore didn't pay me for the invoices factored for the original client. The domino effect took place and all three of us ended up with a mess. If it had worked well, wonderful; but chaining clients like this is doubly risky. If the customers who paid the janitorial services were tried and true, it should have worked. Lesson: don't do transactions like this unless you have a solid history showing that the customers at the end of the chain have always paid and will continue to pay their bills in a timely and dependable manner.

What's more, having a new client who is also another client's customer is not a good idea anyway, as his credit rating is probably not good yet. Remember, you want solid, creditworthy customers paying your client's invoices. Most very small new factoring clients don't fit that description.

#11. Advancing Too Much to Start

Your greatest risk with most clients will be the first funding you provide. You have no first-hand experience with receiving payments, the client's and customer's honesty and integrity, or that the payment will come to you instead of the client. All of these put you in a vulnerable position. So prudence dictates that the first advances to a new client should usually be the smallest advances they receive.

However (especially when you're first starting out), the tendency is to move ahead more quickly than cautiously and to get the client under way. Fight the temptation to give more than is wise. Make it clear that you will only advance so much, and no more, until you start to receive customer payments. Once a track record is established and you feel comfortable with your client's customers' payment patterns, you can gradually ease your earlier restrictions. Remember the Cardinal Rule of Money: don't risk more than you can afford to lose – especially with a new, untested client.

#12. Giving Advances for Work Not Completed

This can happen very easily with even your best clients, and with clients who are either new or have been factoring for some time. It will creep up on you if you let it.

Similar to making loans described above, a client will come to you saying there's an unexpected bill or he wants to make a special purchase to help his business, maybe some new equipment he can get at a great price if he grabs it right away.

Knowing you don't do loans, he asks if it would be okay to give your advance for an upcoming invoice now rather than when the work is done and the invoice is ready to send. The invoice may be for next week's work or perhaps next month's work. Obviously you won't be able to verify the invoice because the work's not finished or perhaps not even started.

But he pleads that helping him in this way will really get him out of a jam, or enable him to make both of you more money with that new equipment. Especially if he's been a good client for some time, you honestly expect him to complete the work as usual; after all, the invoice will be to a regular customer who is routinely factored and a good payer (maybe). Why not help him out, after all? He's honest and a good client. and you like to help people.

If you agree to do this with a good, trusted client, most of the time everything works out smoothly. But it only takes once for a snag to develop. What can happen? Just about anything, though none are likely. Maybe the weather suddenly turns bad, a severe storm washes out roads, and he can't get to the job site for months. Or perhaps the client gets injured or falls ill and isn't able to do the work as expected. A family emergency can arise (death of a parent, a child is severely hurt or very ill...you name it) which takes the client out of town or away from work for a few weeks – precisely the time he *would* have done the work for which you just advanced him. Worse, the client could have a heart attack, be in a serious car accident, or anything else catastrophic and just drop dead. Not likely, but not impossible.

Heaven forbid, if your client turns out to be a crook and is smooth enough to gain your trust after working with you for some time, he's also learned your operation's vulnerability. He's figured out this is a perfect way to fleece you, pulls it off, and is long gone or declares bankruptcy by the time you realize what's happened.

Again these are unlikely scenarios but stranger things have happened. The longer you factor the more likely you are to get a request like this. Sooner or later, someone will ask for it so be ready with your answer.

On the other hand, suppose none of these dire scenarios happen at all and you fund the invoice with the work incomplete. The roof doesn't cave in and life carries on quite normally. However, in this case, what will this early advance do to his cash flow next month?

Because this advance will not be forthcoming then, will he be able to pay regular bills, meet payroll, or pay for some unexpected expense that crops up then? If he can't you'll likely find him on your doorstep asking to do the very same thing again, and when this becomes a pattern you have a problem.

Abusing factoring like this is a big reason clients go out of business due to cash flow problems, even when they're factoring. Experienced factors simply don't advance on invoices before the work is complete; neither should you. Make it your policy not to advance on *any* invoice until the work is finished and is signed off by the customer or can be verified. Period. (Just like you don't do loans. Period). Make this clear from the very beginning so he never even thinks to ask in the first place...though he very likely will ask anyway just to test you. Kind of like your kids.

Standing by this policy protects you both from intentional fraud and from situations which truly are not expected but which put your money at risk anyway. You'll feel a little like a parent turning your teenager away who's asking for money to go somewhere fun, but you need to be firm.

What's more, when you say yes just one time the precedent is set. It'll be harder to say no the next time and chances are high your client will ask you to do it again if you've said yes just once. Count on it.

#13. Buying "Pay When Paid" Invoices

Quite frequently you'll find clients, usually who provide a service and do work for larger companies in their industry as a subcontractor, who are on a "pay when paid" basis with their customers. What does this mean?

Let's say a small janitorial company lands a new account with a large national janitorial firm to clean all the restaurants of a national chain in his region. This sounds like a good account since the restaurant is a household word and has good credit. The large janitorial company has been in business for years and your underwriting shows they are quite stable.

He does the work, submits his invoice to factor at the end of the month, and receives his advance. A month goes by and while you're still waiting for payment from this invoice, he submits his next invoice because he needs to meet payroll. Fair enough, that's not unusual; now you're out the advances for two months of invoices. When the end of the second month arrives and you're still waiting to get paid for the first, he submits his third month's invoice and expects his advance promptly. After all, he has payroll tomorrow.

Wondering what's happened to the first invoice you ask him why it hasn't paid yet. "I don't know," he says, "they're just slow. That's why I needed to factor them." Quite true.

Going back into your files, you dig out the customer contract he provided when he first wanted to factor this debtor, and you read it much more carefully this time. There, you find this company will pay your client 60 days *after* the original customer pays them – not 60 days from your client's invoice date! That means if the restaurant chain pays 60 days after the client's customer bills them (which is probably a few weeks after your client sent them his bill), these invoices are going to take at least 120 or more days to pay from the time you advance. Yikes!

Further, suppose the restaurant claims your client's crew didn't show up to clean several times in a month and won't pay for those days. They short pay the client's customer's invoice, who in turn takes this deduction and adds a penalty (also stipulated in the contract) for the crew's absence. Thus you've not only waited over four months to get paid, you're severely short paid and had no idea this would happen.

Pay when paid arrangements add extra layers of risk because you're far removed from the company for whom the work is done and pretty powerless to do anything when slow and/or short payments happen. Clearly this is not the best scenario to factor.

So before you take on a client who is subcontracting for a larger customer, be sure you are clear about the full agreement, and know if it is a pay when paid arrangement. Have a realistic grasp on how long you'll wait to get paid, and know whether you will have access to the original paying company if problems occur.

#14. Blindly Batching Invoices

When you work with very small companies, several have especially small invoices whose amounts make big factors run for the hills. Ten, twenty, and fifty dollar invoices are the bane of any factor no matter how small, and most experienced factors avoid them. Why? They funded them once or twice earlier in their factoring careers and decided there were bigger and better fish to fry.

Tracking very small invoices individually is just as much work as tracking invoices ten or a hundred times the size, and if your discount is the same percent as it is for the larger invoices, you're making practically nothing on each very small invoice. For example, if you charge 5% for 30 days on a $10 invoice and it pays in 30 days, you make 50 cents. Whoopie. And even if you have fifty $10 invoices, you make $2.50. For all the time you take to enter and track these dinky invoices individually, this is not the kind of business you want.

Therefore, a factor who takes on a client with a lot of really small invoices needs to get creative. Usually weekly or monthly he will batch a large number of very small invoices into a single transaction. He gives the transaction an "invoice number" for tracking, and advances on this transaction that contains hundreds of itty bitty invoices, often totaling one or two thousand dollars. That makes it an amount worth factoring.

A month later the customer pays. His check stub or other payment breakdown may or may not itemize the client's original job numbers for each $10 job, and it won't include the "invoice number" the factor assigned because the customer has no record of that. But whether or not the job numbers and payment amounts for each are provided really doesn't matter because the factor hasn't tracked these – it's too much work. He's tracking the larger "invoice number" he assigned to the batches he bought.

When payment arrives, the factor doesn't know if the amount paid covers all the invoices on a particular batch, if some were skipped or short paid, or perhaps if this payment spans two, three, or more batches. He just doesn't have that information.

So typically you, the factor, just assign each payment to your open invoices on a first in, first paid basis. That is, you apply the payment to the oldest unpaid invoices you have and really don't know if these are the invoices the customer is actually paying. The payment amount probably doesn't equal the oldest batched invoice amount, so you apply the payment to all of the oldest "invoice" outstanding, and perhaps part of the next one. You're simply applying every payment to the oldest unpaid transactions you have.

As long as you don't advance too much, the customer consistently pays on time, and the invoices you show as unpaid don't get older and older, this can work. But if you notice over several months that some of your blindly batched invoices appear to be taking longer and longer to pay, what is probably happening is this: the customer isn't paying every single $10 invoice. They may be short paying some and/or not paying others at all for what could be legitimate reasons. But because you're not tracking each $10 invoice individually and have applied all payments to the oldest batches, you have no way of knowing what batches contain short paid and unpaid jobs, and how much these add up to.

Therefore it's crucial to be in very close touch with the customer and have immediate knowledge of any jobs not being paid in full or at all. You can make adjustments or take chargebacks as needed as long as you know this right away; but if you don't know, and short paid and unpaid invoices begin to pile up over time, you can end up with a problem. Let me tell you a true story to illustrate.

A small factor we'll call Jeanette had been factoring a relatively short time and had a client who was a one-person courier service. The courier had many, many micro invoices. Every day he made several runs for a larger courier for which he was paid $10 or $20 apiece. She factored the client over a year or so, blindly batched these mini invoices, and funded and tracked only the batched amounts. When payments arrived, she applied them to the oldest batches as described earlier.

After some time Jeanette developed health problems and had to close her factoring business. She sold her portfolio to a couple other small factors, and this courier's account was bought by one we'll call Tom. Jeanette was honestly not aware of any problems with the account and told Tom the customer paid quite regularly, which was true and verified in the payment records she provided. She hadn't paid much attention to the fact that the customer's payments very gradually were slowing slightly over the course of the year. Since they paid consistently, she figured the account was fine and never felt the need to speak with the customer about any payments.

Tom was fairly new to the business and this looked like a good account since the client factored weekly and the customer paid regularly each month. He bought the batches of unpaid invoices from Jeanette, continued funding the client, and everybody was happy...for a while.

Over the next several months, Tom noticed the batches of invoices were taking longer and longer to pay. He asked the client why this was so, who didn't really know. In the client's mind, keeping track of the receivables was the factor's job. He just did his job (driving every day), submitted the invoices each Friday, and received his advances. That's all he knew and cared about.

However Tom was becoming concerned and finally called the customer. After a considerable time spent digging through numerous payment reports from the customer and long lists of $10 and $20 driving runs from the client (which Jeanette and Tom both had batched), he found that many of the runs were never paid for various legitimate reasons, and never would be.

As a result, he was out several thousand dollars in advances and discounts. The client didn't feel he was responsible for that money; after all, managing the paperwork and payments was Tom's job, not his. If Tom had messed up something, that was his problem. Even though they were on a recourse basis, the client barely lived week to week on his advances, didn't have any extra money to cover the chargebacks, and deducting them from advances would put him out of business. Any way you sliced it, Tom couldn't recoup his money from the client. Recourse with this client under these circumstances meant nothing.

Tom contacted Jeanette and explained what had transpired, and indicated he felt she should be responsible for the invoices from the original buyout that would not be paid. Even though she sincerely thought the account was sound and it was bought and sold in good faith, she understood Tom's position. They agreed she would pay him back what he had paid for the unpaid invoices from the buyout, which she did. Fortunately for Tom this was only a few thousand dollars, If Jeanette's bills for her declining health had been significantly higher, or the amount owed from the buyout had been several tens of thousands of dollars, things would likely have gotten quite messy and the story probably would not have ended as well.

Think long and hard before buying micro invoices as they can raise all kinds of complications. Before you decide to buy them determine if blindly batching is a good solution. Prior to investing a dime, find out from the customer if, when you receive funds, you will be notified of any jobs not being paid in full. If you need to blind batch everything and you won't be notified, you don't want to buy them.

If you can be notified, realize this is likely going to be a high maintenance account and you'll need to stay on it like white on snow. Budget your time accordingly and charge enough of a discount to make it profitable. In other words, make sure the account is worth accepting in the first place. If it's not, pass. Don't make the next common mistake, which is....

#15. Not Saying "No"

Many of the common mistakes mentioned so far happen as a result of the factor not saying "no" – no to getting sidetracked, accepting a client as a favor, making loans, being rushed, purchase order funding, chaining clients, advancing on uncompleted work, buying "pay when paid" invoices, and blindly batching invoices. If the factor had simply said "no" to any of these scenarios, the bad result that followed wouldn't have happened.

A few more mistakes described below also result from the same error of not saying "no": allowing payments to be sent to the client, developing over-concentrations or not enforcing limits, and letting down your guard. Clearly not saying "no" is one of the most common of common mistakes.

Many people, especially those who want to help others, find it hard to say "no." It's even harder when you've struggled for months to get your business under way, find that first client or two to factor, and can almost taste your first discount income. At this point, all you have are your instincts to guide you because you don't have much experience.

If a potential client and/or his customers have terrible credit reports (or none), and you have an uneasy feeling in the pit of your stomach in some intangible way, *listen to your instincts.*

Too often people who turn out to be flaky at best, or crooked at worst, have burned new factors right out of the starting gate. You may be tempted to accept someone questionable because you don't want to say no, and don't want to start all over finding another new client.

Again, always remember this maxim: **no client is better than a bad client**. The longer you factor the more you'll realize how true this is. Just like the Cardinal Rule of Money, repeat it out loud several times and memorize it. *No client is better than a bad client.*

What's more, you'll quickly find there are other fish in the sea. If you get a bite from a prospect who ends up making you nervous, let him go and put your line back in the water. For some reason, interested prospects tend to come in waves, and you may well get another bite quickly from someone who could be a far better catch. Saying "no" doesn't bring the world to an end.

#16. Payments Not Sent to You

You want all customer payments sent directly to you for one very good reason: you have a far better chance of getting your money back. Allowing payments to go to clients routinely should never be done. You can lose a lot of money if only one client receives and keeps payment due you. Never rely on her promise she's going to "pay you back" – she may become very hard to find.

This happened with one client I had (with her first and only invoice I bought) who was a published author in the medical field. A mutual friend who was a member of her church referred her. My daughter even babysat for her. Sounds like a good risk, right? Someone you'd think will keep her word and pay you? She skipped town owing me and a number of other people a collective pile of money.

When a client intentionally pockets a payment for a factored invoice, that client is committing criminal fraud because she is literally stealing what is yours. She was already paid for the invoice with the advance you provided; the payment from the customer was legally assigned to you and therefore is your property. *You* own it and the second she accepted the advance and assigned the payment, her rights to that payment ceased. Make sure every client fully understands this, and also make it clear from the start that such activity is a criminal offense you and your attorney take very seriously.

The other reason not to allow payments to go to the client is the simple fact that an honest mix-up or human error can easily occur. The client, client's spouse, secretary, bookkeeper, or whoever gets the mail may not realize that an invoice was factored and innocently deposit its payment into their bank. Several weeks later when you haven't received payment, the discount for that invoice has probably increased with the elapsed time.

Assuming you're made whole (an assumption, not a guarantee), your loss is your factoring money hasn't turned as quickly as possible to make more money for you; your client's loss is paying an unnecessarily higher discount. The headache and loss of income is bad for both of you. This reason alone is good for explaining why payment must come to you.

Be clear from the beginning that payments will always come to you or you won't be able to be their factor. Sweet and simple. Make certain your address appears prominently on the invoice as the "Remit to" address. This is discussed further in the chapter, "Record Keeping."

Despite your best efforts, a client will occasionally receive checks for factored invoices. When that happens, do *not* allow him to deposit the check and write you a check from his bank account. Many clients' accounts are run "on the edge" and chances are good the check they give you will bounce. In my years of factoring, about 99% of the NSF checks I've received have come from clients. Almost no customers' checks come back because I'm careful to fund invoices to solid customers. If a client receives a check, tell him to simply get it to you as quickly as possible – to keep his discount as low as possible. You know the other reason, though you don't need to say it.

To keep the client on his toes when he receives checks paying factored invoices, clearly state in your contract a 15% penalty is charged (on the invoice amount or check amount, whichever is larger) if a client deposits or cashes a factored payment. This is called a "check conversion penalty" or "misappropriated funds penalty." Experienced factors do this for a good reason: it works. Be sure to tell him right from the start of the consequences of his depositing a check – even if unfactored invoices are also paid with the same check. Then follow through. If he converts a check, pays the penalty, and wants to continue factoring, chances are very good it won't happen again.

#17. Poor Follow-up on Late- and Non-Payers

Because this is one of the most important aspects of your ongoing factoring business, the chapter "Preventive Maintenance" is devoted to it. Overlooking follow-up on late and non-paying customers is a not only a very common but a very costly mistake.

As anyone who's ever collected money knows, the longer the wait to receive payment the less likely you are to be paid. Collection agencies have statistical graphs that illustrate this and the results are indisputable. That's why they charge more and more to collect the older invoices become.

Therefore, the wise factor will carefully monitor how long customers take to pay bills and will take regular, definite steps to assure payment is made. When you don't make a point of regularly checking on the payment status for overdue debt, all too often the debt will be ignored and can become impossible to collect.

For example, I had a client with two long-overdue invoices. Eventually the client was confronted on a very consistent and direct basis. After checking into what had become of these payments, the client stated that one of the customers claimed to have paid the invoice. The client and customer traced the check and found it was made out to the client's company and cashed. What had happened?

Several months earlier, with the client's permission, an employee of the client had gone to the customer and offered a 25% discount if the customer paid the invoice immediately. The check was made out to the client's company and given to the employee...who promptly cashed it, pocketed the money, and never returned to work. The client agreed she still owed my company the money, but this problem could have been avoided if I had been in close touch with both client and customer as soon as the payment was overdue.

Good factoring software will provide a means of tracking past due invoices, but you want more than just aging reports. Aging reports show how old invoices are but not customers' payment patterns.

FactorFox allows you to "flag" invoices at the time of approving the schedule and any time after that. If a particular customer consistently pays in 30 days, you might set their default flag days at about 40. Thus if you notice an invoice is flagged, you know the customer is later than usual and action is needed. If a customer routinely pays in 60 days, you set their invoices to be flagged at 65 or 70.

Used this way, watching flagged invoices is a built-in warning system for telling you a customer's payment is later than expected and needs follow up. This is much more helpful than an aging report because it's not just based on number of days out; it's based on each customer's payment history and trends.

As mentioned, a good way to handle slow pays is discussed in the chapter "Preventive Maintenance." Once your business is under way and you have money on the street, refer to this chapter, understand and consistently practice what it suggests, and your company will be far more likely to succeed. The old saying fits perfectly here: the squeaky wheel gets the grease.

#18. Over Concentrations and Lack of Limits

In the chapter, "Reducing Your Risk," we look at client and customer concentrations. Look at the charts in that chapter of client concentrations. Note the risk involved in putting too many eggs in one basket: if the basket spills, most of your eggs are history. The very best risk management technique costs absolutely nothing and is very easy to implement: **avoid over-concentrations.**

A new factor had $100,000 in factoring money and took on his first client who was soon factoring $80,000. All of this was concentrated in one customer. The things that could go wrong with that arrangement are enough to make one shudder.

As a matter of standard practice, put limits on how much you'll have in outstanding advances with a given client and customer, as well as the largest invoice size you'll buy. Make sure the client understands your limits; it's up to you to enforce them. Not doing so can lead you to the over-concentration problem just mentioned, as well as becoming under-capitalized.

#19. No Structure to Pay Yourself

Unless you need absolutely no income from your factoring business, arrange your company's budget from the start to pay you something, even a nominal amount, every month. If all the income your company makes is routinely put back into the business and you never personally enjoy the fruits of your labors – at least a little – there can be a psychological side effect which is not healthy, especially if this is your full-time work. You need to feel that your efforts are benefiting your clients and providing you income. Nothing can sap your enthusiasm for work and the enjoyment of running your own business like working your fingers to the bone and not making a dime of take-home pay. The worker deserves his wages: that includes you.

The temptation as your business grows and you accumulate clients is to channel all net income back into advances. That can be a necessity at times (and a definite sign of under capitalization), but it's a bad idea to do this regularly. Make your salary a part of your operating budget, pay yourself every month or every other week, and make your business revolve around you...not the other way around.

If you've loaned your company money, pay yourself interest like any other lender. If you devote an entire room in your home to your business, have your company pay you a fair rent amount. Either of these will put money in your pocket which, though taxable, is not subject to payroll taxes and can cost your company (and you personally) less. Talk to your accountant about the best way to structure this. As far as IRS is concerned, you may need to pay yourself some kind of salary; again, your accountant can advise you how much that may be.

If your income is not enough to pay you what you need or have established as goals, you must either obtain more funding and/or clients, cut expenses, charge higher rates, or reconsider whether factoring will meet your income needs.

#20. Poor Record Keeping

Accurate, organized record keeping is vital to your factoring service, and a separate chapter is dedicated to it. It may appear to your clients that you don't do much – just verify invoices, advance money, wait to get paid and give rebates. But in order to keep this financial information accurate and accessible (as well as client, customer, participant, and broker data), you have to be well organized when it comes to keeping records.

Unless you intend to have only one or two clients and work with a very small number of brokers, you'll need a computer with a good data base for the above organization. You'll certainly need good and flexible factoring software and adequate financial software to track your business.

You'll also need to have your filing system organized and have a solid method of backing up what you have stored on your computer. If you don't and your computer crashes, or you need a copy of an invoice, payment, or proof of some aspect of a transaction, you'll be stuck. That's not to say you need paper copies of every little thing – you don't. Thanks to PDF files and a cloud-based back up system I'm nearly 100% paperless and very glad of it. Just be organized in a way that you'll be able to quickly pull what you need.

Poor record keeping makes you look unprofessional to clients, customers, and colleagues. It can cost you dearly if there are ever tax questions, or a dispute as to whether an invoice was sent, factored, its payment received, rebates paid, and so on.

#21. Inadequate Software

If you have no more than two or three clients, you can probably track your factoring information on spreadsheets and be satisfied. However, as your client base grows, you will outgrow spreadsheets and wish you had started with software written expressly for factoring.

I started my business with spreadsheets for tracking factoring transactions, but it became unwieldy by the time I had about six clients. When I reached a dozen, it was a terrible burden on my time and energy. Once I started using database software written specifically for factoring, hours of entry and reporting work were lifted which enabled me to dedicate more time to other aspects of the business. I only wished I had started using this approach in the first place.

Don't pay for software you don't need if your business is simple, but when you reach a certain level you really need to spring for good software. Once you do, you'll be amazed at how much easier running your business is. Having good software you need is like quitting smoking – you just feel better, food tastes good again, and you wonder why you waited so long to do this.

#22. Letting Down Your Guard

After you have been factoring for a long time you will enjoy having some clients who have been with you for years. Working this long together means you know these clients and their customers quite well and have made very decent money with them. They have stayed with you because factoring has been good for them, they trust you, and getting regular advances has become a routine and successful long-term way of running their businesses. In short, factoring has worked very well for both of you. You wish all your clients would turn out like this.

Because you have worked with and known these clients for so long, their accounts are practically running on auto-pilot and you likely consider them friends. You've probably lightened up on your verifications (if you do any at all), and don't pay much attention to aging reports since their customers have always paid. You might even allow them to do things you would never let new clients do, like getting checks from customers and sending them to you. After all, you've worked together for quite some time with nary a problem.

In other words you let down your guard.

In practically all cases, good long-term clients like this are trustworthy and nothing bad ever happens. However, that doesn't mean every single client you ever have will never pull a fast one. When unforeseen circumstances develop and a client feels financially cornered, he can end up lying and defrauding you. Or he can just get greedy and do something stupid. Even long-time clients you know well and trust are capable of either. A couple clients I factored for several years provide perfect examples[5].

The first one factored regularly for three or four years and was one of my best clients – steady, good volume, nice to work with. However he never told me he had gradually fallen into arrears with IRS and in fact was tens of thousands of dollars in the hole with the tax man. To pay IRS just enough to keep them at bay, he needed to come up with money from somewhere.

When I asked why payments from a once good customer were getting slower, he played dumb. "I sure don't know. I think they have someone new in payables maybe?" It didn't take long to find out the real reason.

I contacted the customer's payables department (sure enough, there was someone new there), and asked when payment would be made for various late invoices. The new person knew the answer without even looking up the invoices: "Oh, those checks were done a month or more ago. He's been coming in as soon as they're cut and picking them up."

I asked her to provide copies of the checks, which clearly showed he had endorsed and deposited them. A day or two later, because I had filed IRS form 8821 when we started factoring, I received notification from IRS he was seriously in arrears and owed a lot of money. I called to speak with him about all this, but he wouldn't answer my calls and didn't return them. The puzzle pieces now fit together perfectly and the picture was clear.

What always amazes me about clients who divert checks like this is they inexplicably assume I won't find out. While I may

---

[5] For several more real life stories that illustrate many important factoring lessons, read *Factoring Case Studies* by the author.

not realize what they've done immediately, sooner or later the truth comes out. Do they really think I won't notice a payment is long overdue? Tracking receivables I've bought is what I do for a living! What do they think I do all day, watch soap operas and eat cookies? A craving for cash followed by dishonest and deceptive acts cloud their reason, extinguish their common sense, and make them do very foolish things.

They're like the boy the day after Halloween, who made a huge haul of candy the night before and put his stash on the kitchen counter. Despite his mother's warning to eat only a couple pieces and no more, within hours the pile was half gone, his face green, and his stomach obviously upset. When his mom asked how much candy he'd eaten, he vehemently denied eating any (while holding his stomach) and plaintively suggested the dog or his sister must have done it. He didn't fool anybody for a second, especially his mother! Nor do clients who pull this check conversion/"I don't know nuthin'" stunt.

Another good, years-long client did the same thing but for a different reason. When I was a less-experienced factor, I had allowed him from the start to receive checks from his customers, and for all that time he dutifully overnighted them to me immediately. I allowed this because he said early on he didn't want me to contact them (always a red flag). He was afraid they wouldn't do business with him if they found he was factoring – a common new client fear but in fact a *very* rare customer response.

After a few years without any problems, an occasional check would not arrive on my doorstep when expected. I would let him know and he would make calls to the customer to see what had happened, then give me a date when payment would arrive. Sure enough, checks would appear – but the stubs indicated they were paying other invoice numbers, some he had factored, some he hadn't. I was to apply the payment on the check for invoice 2571 to invoice 2489 that had not been paid, and payment for invoice 2577 was to cover invoice 2502. Because I was being made whole I went along with it, but keeping track of paid and unpaid invoices started to get complicated.

After a while the number of invoice payments being applied to other invoices became numerous. The confusing jumble of this invoice number paying that invoice number made it very hard to know what had and hadn't been paid. It was clear the formerly good-paying customer was behind on several thousand dollars' worth of factored invoices; I just couldn't tell which ones. Since the client lived across the country I couldn't go to his office and sit down with check stubs and invoices and sort it out.

When I finally admitted to myself he was being less than straightforward and I'd had enough of the record keeping mess, I contacted his customer. I quickly learned he had been depositing checks ever since the numbering switcheroo had started. He had been playing the slight-of-hand "which shell is the pea under?" game as he switched around the invoice numbers quickly and constantly to deceive me. I played the game because he had been a good client for so long. Too late I realized that out of greed he had become nothing more than a flimflam man.

When I told him what I had learned he denied any wrongdoing and became quite angry (since he'd been caught red-handed) and threatened to sue me if he lost the account. I told him he'd already lost it. The minute the customer learned what he had done they were finished with him – not because he was factoring, but because of his fraud. He lost his factor the same day for the same reason. Nobody wants to work with a crook.

Once you have proof a client has endorsed checks after claiming he never received them, the jig is up. You have a lying, fraud-committing weasel who has taken advantage of your trust, goodwill, and long-time relationship. That is not only profoundly disappointing and hurtful, once the hurt wears off you get extremely mad at the former friend turned thief.

In short, never let your guard down, even with clients you've factored for a very long time and consider friends. While the vast majority of long-term clients never, ever do this, remember: **anyone can cheat you.** *Anyone.* If you factor long enough, when (not if) you have this experience you'll be just as stunned as every other factor who has funded a trusted client for years, only to learn the "friend" had the gall to pull this off.

#23. Not Following Your Own Rules

The times I've run into trouble factoring are when 1) because of my inexperience, I took on clients or customers I didn't recognize as bad risks, and 2) I didn't follow my own rules. While you're in this business to help others and make a decent living, you'll do neither if you can't separate your heart from your head when tough decisions must be made.

Count on it: you'll have people with hard luck stories that can tear your heart, prospects with good customers but one nasty glitch, and all sorts of circumstances which force you to decide: do I accept this situation or not? This chapter describes rules I've made to avoid making costly errors; you will develop your own rules. But if you have rules and choose to ignore them, the risk of losing your money or even your business is greatly increased.

Establish and test your parameters, limits, types of businesses you'll fund, and whom you'll turn away and why. Once you have a good set of guidelines, **follow them**. Being firm does not mean you're cold, calculating, and heartless; it means you'll be around for the next prospect you can truly help.

#24. Giving Up

When your factoring business is fairly young, discouragement can set in if you don't find what you consider to be enough clients. Often people new to the business make little headway finding clients the first several months. Some people take over a year or more before they actually close deals and begin to make money.

If this happens, realize it's not unusual and you're not a complete incompetent, though you may feel like one at times. Discouragement can be your greatest enemy when you begin any new endeavor, especially factoring. So don't give up. Keep at it.

Once you have a book of business, sooner or later you'll have some bad experiences as described in this chapter. You'll see factoring is, in a sense, like any other part of life: you have good days and bad days. You'll thoroughly enjoy working with some wonderful people, and you'll come to regret working with others you'd like to see burn in hell. You'll make very good money, but you'll also make mistakes and lose money sometimes. During these bad days it's natural to feel like throwing in the towel.

If your losses have completely put you out of business (which won't happen if you follow everything in this book), or the bad experiences with dishonest people have jaded your outlook on humanity to the point you feel you need to do something else, perhaps you should hang it up. Otherwise, hang tough. Don't quit. Keep plugging away. Factoring is a good business despite the wild ride at times.

Endurance has its own rewards; people who have remained in factoring for a very long time understand this and that's why they're still around.

Part 5

Operations

19

Factoring Software

Make no mistake: factoring software can be one of the largest expenses you face in your fledgling operation. If everything else suggests "all systems go" don't let the cost of software be the only reason to keep you from entering the factoring arena.

Very small factors who decide not to purchase a database when they start, often begin with spreadsheets. Spreadsheets were used by factoring companies for quite some time before dedicated database programs became sophisticated enough to replace them. Now the databases are many, many times more powerful than spreadsheets.

Good factoring programs are readily available and you will make life easier on yourself down the road if you can start your business using one. If you have adequate funds when you begin, starting with dedicated database software will make your record keeping far easier, and new software will be one less thing to learn later. If you feel you must start with spreadsheets, making the move to higher end software can be a logical growth step and an indication that you are running your business successfully.

When I started my factoring business in 1994. only one factoring data base existed which cost much more than I was willing to pay. So I started my business with the bare bones – Quicken to keep my business finances and Excel to manage factoring records.

As my business slowly grew I graduated to QuickBooks and a FileMaker data base I designed just for myself. As more time went by, I outgrew the FileMaker database and began developing the program that is now FactorFox, which itself has evolved light years past what it was in its early days. In short, as your business matures and technology advances, so will the way you track your data and your profitability.

You can spend unnecessary hours and exorbitant costs in developing custom-made software for your factoring business. Thankfully, that is not necessary unless you're extremely picky about what you want your software to do. However, writing a program to track factoring transactions can become unbelievably complicated as you try to allow for every possibility of what can happen with an invoice. Developing your own software is an enormous undertaking even if you plan to use it only in-house. I have spoken with several people who tried to do just that, and after spending months and even years – and many thousands of dollars – every one simply gave up in frustration.

As you look for factoring software, you want to find a package that will meet your needs both now and in the future. I suggest any factor considering purchasing software carefully study each company and their offerings mentioned in this chapter. Software is one of the most significant investments in your factoring business you will make in terms of dollars paid, the amount of time you spend with it, and the image of your company it projects.

Does one specific software program exist that has every single feature, every bell and whistle, you want for your factoring business? In all honesty, probably no. Since writing your own software from scratch is likely to provide far more frustration than satisfaction, your best choice is to find the software that most closely fits your needs and budget, then adapt your operation to the software.

Too often I see factors try to force factoring software to perform exactly the way their business is run. That's backwards; such thinking can be the proverbial attempt to fit a round peg in a square hole, especially with a very unique factoring niche. A much wiser approach is to make your business – how you calculate discounts, charge other fees, make advances, give rebates, track reserves, and so on – conform to the software. That's far easier and less costly than paying for expensive customizations you may not really need…once you learn to think outside the box of how you've always done business.

Because products and prices of the software companies below constantly evolve with technology and industry trends, I have simply listed the products, companies, and websites of those who provide software to the factoring community. You are encouraged, as you were in the "Factoring Franchise" chapter, to thoroughly research which solution is the best fit for your operation both as you begin and as you grow. A list of questions to consider is provided to facilitate your research, followed by a chart to record your answers for each company below.

Factoring Software Companies

Here are software programs and their respective companies whose products are sold to smaller and medium-sized factors:

FactorFox
FactorFox Software, Inc.
www.FactorFox.com

WinFactor
ePolk, Inc.
www.WinFactor.com

Factor/SQL
Distinctive Solutions, part of 3i Infotech
www.dissol.com

CADENCE | FactorSoft
Bayside Business Solutions, Inc.
www.baysidebiz.com

Factoring Plus
Capital Software
www.cap-soft.com

FactorIn
Aditya Birla Minacs
www.minacs.adityabirla.com

Factoring Software Questions

When researching software companies, answers to the following questions can help you determine the factoring software that best suits your needs.

1. **Company History**
   - When and why did your company start developing software for the factoring industry?

2. **Ownership**
   - Describe the present ownership of your company and their factoring experience.

3. **Product/s**
   - How many different products do you offer?
   - How are they different from each other?
   - What market does each address?

4. **Differentiation**
   - How is your product or products different from other factoring software?

5. **Installation**
   - What steps are needed to install your software on my system?
   - Do you provide this service or do I need to do the installation myself?
   - What is the cost of installation if your company does it?
   - How long does installation take?

6. **User Base**
   - How many active users presently utilize your system (not including those who bought it but no longer use it)?
   - Describe some typical characteristics of companies who use your products, including:
     - number of staff
     - number of clients
     - portfolio size
     - location

- Do you have companies in my factoring niche using your product?
- Can you give me the names and contact information of at least five companies using your software that I may contact?

7. User Licenses

- How many factoring staff may use your product with the entry level license you provide?
- What do you charge for a license providing additional staff to use it?
- Is there a limit as to how many staff can view data, make entries, or run reports at the same time or from any particular location?

8. Data Restrictions

- Are there restrictions to the number of schedules, invoices, clients, customers, brokers, etc. that can be entered?

9. Non-Staff Usage

- Can my clients use your software to enter schedules and/or view reports?
- Can my accountant, brokers, investors, and others use your software to view reports?
- If yes to either or both of the above, can I prohibit access if I don't want them to view the data directly?

10. Web-Based or Disk-Based

- Is your product web-based (in the cloud) or disk-based (on my computer)?
- Is there extra cost for web access if that's available?

11. Additional Hardware

- Do I need to purchase any additional hardware (server, scanner, etc.) to use your software?

12. Integration

- Does your software integrate with QuickBooks or other accounting programs? If so, how?
- Are bookkeeping entries of data from your software made via exporting, other electronic means, or can these accounting entries only be made manually?

- Does your software integrate with any credit reporting websites?
- Are integrations with other services available or planned?

13. Free trial
- Do you provide free trial of your product before purchase? If so:
  o How long is the free trial?
  o Is the free trial version a full-featured product or are some features unavailable?

14. Training
- Do you provide training to new users?
- If so, where and how is it done?
- What is the cost?

15. Documentation
- Do you have online or written Help files to assist with learning the program?
- If so, where are they and how do I access them?

16. Support
- Describe your software support methods and cost.

17. Price
- How much do your products cost?
- How frequently am I billed?
- How do I make payments?
- Do you provide a guarantee?
- Can I cancel my subscription and receive a refund for unused time?

18. Customization
- Can the software be customized to my particular needs?
- If so, what can be customized?
- What is the price of customizations?

19. Other Products or Services
- Does your company provide any additional products or services for factors besides software?

20. Choice
- Why should I choose your company and product over your competition?

FactorFox   www.FactorFox.com

#	Item	#	
1	Company History	1	
2	Ownership	2	
3	Product/s	3	
4	Differentiation	4	
5	Installation	5	
6	User Base	6	
7	User Licenses	7	
8	Data Restrictions	8	
9	Non-Staff Usage	9	
10	Web-Based or Disk-Based	10	
11	Additional Hardware	11	
12	Integration	12	
13	Free Trial	13	
14	Training	14	
15	Documentation	15	
16	Support	16	
17	Price	17	
18	Customization	18	
19	Other Products or Services	19	
20	Choice	20	

WinFactor   www.WinFactor.com

#	Item	#	
1	Company History	1	
2	Ownership	2	
3	Product/s	3	
4	Differentiation	4	
5	Installation	5	
6	User Base	6	
7	User Licenses	7	
8	Data Restrictions	8	
9	Non-Staff Usage	9	
10	Web-Based or Disk-Based	10	
11	Additional Hardware	11	
12	Integration	12	
13	Free Trial	13	
14	Training	14	
15	Documentation	15	
16	Support	16	
17	Price	17	
18	Customization	18	
19	Other Products or Services	19	
20	Choice	20	

Factor/SQL www.dissol.com

#	Item	
1	Company History	1
2	Ownership	2
3	Product/s	3
4	Differentiation	4
5	Installation	5
6	User Base	6
7	User Licenses	7
8	Data Restrictions	8
9	Non-Staff Usage	9
10	Web-Based or Disk-Based	10
11	Additional Hardware	11
12	Integration	12
13	Free Trial	13
14	Training	14
15	Documentation	15
16	Support	16
17	Price	17
18	Customization	18
19	Other Products or Services	19
20	Choice	20

CADENCE | FactorSoft www.baysidebiz.com

#	Item	
1	Company History	1
2	Ownership	2
3	Product/s	3
4	Differentiation	4
5	Installation	5
6	User Base	6
7	User Licenses	7
8	Data Restrictions	8
9	Non-Staff Usage	9
10	Web-Based or Disk-Based	10
11	Additional Hardware	11
12	Integration	12
13	Free Trial	13
14	Training	14
15	Documentation	15
16	Support	16
17	Price	17
18	Customization	18
19	Other Products or Services	19
20	Choice	20

Factoring Plus   www.cap-soft.com

1	Company History	1
2	Ownership	2
3	Product/s	3
4	Differentiation	4
5	Installation	5
6	User Base	6
7	User Licenses	7
8	Data Restrictions	8
9	Non-Staff Usage	9
10	Web-Based or Disk-Based	10
11	Additional Hardware	11
12	Integration	12
13	Free Trial	13
14	Training	14
15	Documentation	15
16	Support	16
17	Price	17
18	Customization	18
19	Other Products or Services	19
20	Choice	20

FactorIn   www.minacs.adityabirla.com

1	Company History	1
2	Ownership	2
3	Product/s	3
4	Differentiation	4
5	Installation	5
6	User Base	6
7	User Licenses	7
8	Data Restrictions	8
9	Non-Staff Usage	9
10	Web-Based or Disk-Based	10
11	Additional Hardware	11
12	Integration	12
13	Free Trial	13
14	Training	14
15	Documentation	15
16	Support	16
17	Price	17
18	Customization	18
19	Other Products or Services	19
20	Choice	20

Comment

As you know, I am the owner and developer of one of the software products and companies mentioned above, FactorFox. While I obviously have a bias toward this software, I am the first to acknowledge it is not the only solution for every factoring company in existence. It was originally developed for smaller factors, but it has been used by both smaller and medium-sized factors for quite a while now.

A great deal of time has gone into creating and updating FactorFox's design and features so it incorporates the factoring procedures in this book, as well as many more. If you closely follow the directions and practices described in these pages, FactorFox will look familiar to you and be suitable for a great many factoring operations.

20

Factoring from a Virtual Office

Factoring from a virtual office starts by going paperless, or at least moving in that direction as completely as you can. If you want to work remotely, especially if you plan to have people working with you without a central location, you can't be dependent on paper documents all the time.

With a business that relies so heavily on written contracts, movement of funds, tracking transactions, reports, and everything else involved in factoring, the question is fair: "Can a factoring company really be paperless?" The answer is an unequivocal "yes." My company and the companies of several small factor colleagues are living proof. So where do you start?

Going Paperless

PDF Files

Adobe Acrobat is a program which creates and reads files in a format called PDF (Portable Document Format), which is a universally recognized file format. It is one format just about everyone can use no matter what kind of computer you have.

Printing files to PDF instead of paper is the key to a paperless office. Once you're in the habit of printing PDF files you'll realize how much paper you once used, and how time consuming and what a hassle filing papers was. By making your operation paperless you'll save a lot of money on paper, toner, and filing cabinets. Paperless is the way to go, no question.

You can get Acrobat <u>Reader</u> for free but it only *reads* PDF files. To *create* PDF files (which you must do to create your own

PDF files and thus become paperless), you need Adobe's full-featured program, Acrobat, which unfortunately costs several hundred dollars. Its regular updates also are pricey.

However, several non-Adobe PDF creator programs are available that range in price from free to around $100. While these don't have the depth of features of Acrobat, the price difference is considerable and for most people one of the substitutes work just fine.

To find these, Google "PDF program," "PDF creator," "PDF convertor" or something similar. You'll find several programs that create, read, and do lots of cool PDF things. Most of those that cost money have free trials. Veronica and Anne, who work with me, both use Cute PDF (www.cutepdf.com) and are quite happy with it, though there are many others from which to choose.

Another paperless tool is FactorFox, which enables a paperless office because all reports can be saved to numerous file formats including PDF. What's more, because your clients have access to reports themselves, you never need to create a report and send it to them as a PDF, on paper, or anything else. Because all reports generated in FactorFox are always available within the online program, keeping a separate copy of them – paper or electronic – isn't necessary most of the time. FactorFox also comes with a document sharing feature called DocuFox which enables clients to electronically send you their invoices and any other documents you need to share; you can send clients files as well. This feature can also provide file storage if you choose.

Backup

When you go paperless, backing up your computer files is critical. I'm a big fan of online backup services rather than backing up to onsite hardware. If my home were to be hit by a natural disaster, have a major fire, be robbed, or any number of unpleasant things I don't want to think about, my backup would be gone right along my other equipment, and my business records would vanish to the ether.

Thus the value of an offsite, online backup system. There are many out there and I use Carbonite (www.Carbonite.com),

258

which is priced quite reasonably and works just fine. Once you setup your instructions, you don't have to lift a finger because backups are done automatically whenever your computer is on and idle – not just at the end of the day.

Carbonite has a handy feature in which it puts a little green or yellow dot on each file's icon. Backed up files have a green dot, those awaiting backup are yellow. You can right-click on any icon/s with a yellow dot, select Carbonite from the popup window, and tell it to back up the file immediately. Normally within a minute or less the dot changes from yellow to green, and the file is backed up. Cool.

If disaster strikes and your hardware is gone, get new equipment, restore your online backup files from Carbonite's site, and you're back in business. Like everything else, Carbonite has plenty of competition which you can find by Googling "online backup," "offsite backup," etc.

eFaxes

Fax machines are going the way of the buggy whip, but sending and receiving faxes is still a very common and convenient way of sending documents. Paper faxes have been replaced with eFaxes and if you aren't using an eFax service you should be.

eFaxes are available through online services that enable you to receive faxes to the fax number your service provides. When someone sends a fax to your eFax number (and multiple faxes from different people can be received simultaneously), you are instantly sent an email with an attachment (usually a PDF) of the faxed document. Open the attachment, read it, then delete or save it on your computer. Handy, quick, and another tree spared. You can also send files in common formats (PDF, Word, etc.) directly from your computer as an outgoing eFax for just pennies a page.

There are a multitude of eFax services and prices can vary considerably, so shop around. I've been using eFax services from OneSuite (www.OneSuite.com) and am happy with its price and dependability. Search the net for "internet fax,"

259

"paperless fax," "online fax," and "electronic fax," and you will find a large selection of services from which to choose.

Electronic Signatures

Because the contract with your client is the basis of your working relationship and protects you in court, the signatures on your contract must be legally binding. The old way of printing contracts and having both parties sign them with a pen is giving way to electronic signatures which are much faster and more convenient, and have held up in court as valid.

Like everything else, many companies provide this service and you should spend some time doing your research. Search keywords "electronic signature," "e-signature," or "digital signature" and you'll find them. Prices and features vary but the basic idea is the same; use the free trial of a few to compare them. I use RightSignature.com and it works well for me. What follows are RightSignature's two methods of creating and e-signing a contract.

The first method is to create a template that can be used for all clients, brokers, or any particular type of contract you have. To create a client contract template, first use Word to produce the contract, with blanks for the company name, address, etc. which the client will fill in. You also leave blank spaces where the signatures, initials, dates, etc. will go. Upload the file and indicate where the signatures, initials, and dates go throughout the document. Mark any field you want as "Required" (which should be all of them) – the contract can't be completed if any required box is left empty by the signer. Finally save it as a template; you now have a generic document for e-signature you can use for any type of business for which the template is used.

The second method is to provide, on each contract, the client's company name, address, and so on, making it customized to each client. Again, in Word leave spaces where the signatures go in the document before uploading. Enter the name and email address of the client (or broker or anyone else you want to sign) on the site. Upload the file, then insert the appropriate type of fields into the empty spaces on the document. Once everything is ready, click "Done"; the document is saved to the site and the client receives a notification by email from

RightSignature, letting her know the document is awaiting her signature.

The client then opens the document by clicking a link in the email. Instructions are included on the site. The individual has the choice of typing her name using a signature-type font, or using her mouse to create an original signature. She inserts her signature, initials, date, etc. in all the right places by clicking a button, and the document is signed very quickly. No fields are accidentally skipped because the program will not allow any required fields to be left blank. Finally she clicks a button that accepts everything as final.

The contract is then emailed as a PDF file to both the client and you, with a page added at the end that includes official information which makes the document legally binding. The pages of this PDF file cannot be edited or deleted. Store the record in your paperless filing system (it remains on the service's website as well), and you have a signed contract, no paper involved. If you ever need to provide a paper copy of the contract, just print the PDF, including the last page, and there you have it.

Now that we're familiar with the basic tools needed to go paperless, we can turn to running your factoring company from a virtual office. Let me describe how I run mine.

My Virtual Office

By reading this book you have learned I have been a factor for many years. Unlike numerous factors in business this long, I have chosen to remain a very small operation. Why? Because rather than making the most money possible and living with the responsibilities that involves, remaining small is a life style choice for me.

I like working from home with very few staff. I like wearing comfortable and very casual clothes every day (my wife might call them frumpy, but we've been married far too long for her to do that). I like spending zero time commuting daily. I like having my dog by my side all day. For me, small is good and bigger is not necessarily better. For many years I was a one-person operation.

However, between running three businesses simultaneously (Dash Point Financial, Dash Point Publishing, and FactorFox), I reached the point some time ago when I needed help. I have been most fortunate to find highly capable people to work with me in each business. And because of FactorFox and other technology commonly available, I can select people to work with me who live anywhere: they don't need to live in or move to my area.

Several years ago I brought on board my co-worker, Veronica, to run much of the day-to-day factoring operations. She had all the skills I was looking for – she had worked for other factoring companies, understood the business well, and also wanted to work from home. As the business progressed and we needed help with follow-up calls, we added Anne, a veteran factoring broker and colleague I had known for several years. Anne also worked from home and wanted to keep it that way.

Neither of them lives anywhere close to me: I'm near Seattle on the West Coast, Veronica is over 2000 miles away near Toronto, Ontario, Canada, and Anne is in Rhode Island, 1000 miles east of Veronica. Despite our distant locations and different time zones, all of us are able to do our jobs and find all the company information we need right at our fingertips, any time, every day. How?

Because our entire business is paperless and web-based, we each can work from our homes, and none of us need to come to a central office to access the information we need to do our work. We all can use any computer, tablet or smart phone wherever we happen to be, as long as we can access the Internet.

With online banking and a lockbox, I almost never need to go to the bank. If I receive a check, I simply mail it to the lockbox and save the time and gas used in a bank run. We view online banking information at any time and can see what electronic payments have arrived first thing in the morning. Once the day's checks have arrived in the lockbox, its daily report is available online about noon my time. Thus we both know by then the total funds that have arrived for the day. Veronica enters the day's receipts quite quickly into FactorFox, where Anne can see what payments have arrived.

We each log in to FactorFox with our unique user names and passwords, and get right to work. We can all simultaneously view summary and complete aging reports, instantly check flagged invoices to see which customers have overdue payments, and determine which need attention. For follow up calls, any of us can add invoice notes about any invoice, and all of us (as well as the client) can read these notes any time. We can also read invoice notes our clients enter as well. We have taught them to submit schedules, send invoices, enter notes, and access their reports all through FactorFox, saving us all much time and providing great convenience for everyone.

Veronica, Anne and I communicate daily via Skype (video cameras available but not required), instant messaging, email and phone. If we want to have a three-way conversation, Skype easily accommodates that. Though we are thousands of miles apart every day, we all know the status of every account – and can talk about it – at any time. Free.

Through our online fax number we receive incoming faxes which are simultaneously emailed to all three of us as PDF files. For pennies we can send files on our computers as faxes through the same service, which costs only a few dollars a month for unlimited incoming faxes. We don't print faxes or anything else on paper, including checks – we only send ACHs and wires.

So the three of us work very closely together in our virtual office every day...yet we are physically many miles apart. With a web connection, smart phone, FactorFox, Skype, online faxes, and a lockbox, I can run my business from anywhere, not just my home office. Whether I'm out of town at a conference, visiting family out of state, or enjoying a working vacation just about anywhere, with these simple tools I can run my business from literally almost any place I want to be.

Who needs a big fancy office with dozens of employees in a single location to be happy? Not me. I'll work in my frumpy clothes at my virtual office with a snoring dog at my feet any time.

21

Record Keeping

As you can tell from the many forms in this manual, factoring involves a lot of record keeping. You have to enjoy this end of it (or work with someone who does), because it will consume much of your office time and energy.

What is offered here is what works for me and continues to evolve with time. Decide what you will use based on your own judgment, and consult your attorney as to what might be best for you, especially in regards to any laws in your area which might affect your factoring practices. Ask your attorney about usury laws and licensing requirements in your state (for example, in California you need to obtain a state lender's license) and be sure your practices are in compliance. If your attorney doesn't know the answers to these important matters, get a referral to one who does.

Preliminary Steps to Set Up a Client

On your website, include a page that explains factoring, a summary of your company and what you do (distinguishing yourself from other factors as specifically as possible, your contact information, your application form, and eventually a page with testimonials from satisfied clients.

Once you have a prospect, the first step is to have her browse your website to become familiar with your company and operations. She might then call you with questions; after speaking and assuming you both want to move forward, the next step is for her to complete your application. You should set up your online application form so that when the prospects completes it and clicks "Submit," an email is sent to you with the completed information and arrives as text. Stay as paperless as possible.

Alternately, the prospect may simply complete the application and you'll receive it without previous contact. If that's the case, call the client to get acquainted, learn about her company, customers, products or services, business experience, and get a feel for her need and suitability for factoring. After this discussion you should have a feel as to whether you want to work with this person, pending your due diligence.

If your conversation makes clear that she doesn't meet your parameters (which usually emerges quickly) but know of another factor who might be interested, make the referral and earn a broker commission. If she does meet your parameters, let her know you're interested in her account and will begin underwriting right away. Give her an accurate indication of how long that will take and that you will contact her as soon as it's complete. If you then decide to decline this prospect, let her know right away so she doesn't wait days wondering.

If you accept the prospect, let her know immediately by phone or email with a congratulatory first paragraph saying her account has been approved. Everyone likes to be accepted and this gets the account off to a positive start. Tell her the next step is for you to create the contract and setup documents (below) which you will provide as soon as they're ready. Do that quickly.

You will save a lot of paper and (once you've set up with a provider) time by having your contract signed electronically. There are several companies that provide this service, such as RightSignature (www.RightSignature.com), EchoSign (www.EchoSign.com), RPost (www.RPost.com), DocuSign (www.DocuSign.com) and others. Search "electronic signature" or "e-signature" to find them. Compare them for price, features, ease of use, clarity of instructions (keep your more technically challenged clients in mind), and if free trials are offered, take advantage of them.

Electronically signing your contract documents saves the trouble of providing a checklist for turning in all needed documents because you can make required fields of all the signatures, initials, and dates throughout the document. The e-signature provider confirms that no required field has been overlooked so you don't need to review it to make sure something wasn't skipped. The service sends an official PDF file of the completed document to you and the client – entirely legal and acceptable in court, no paper involved. The trees thank you.

Once you have the signed contract and accompanying documents in hand, complete whatever remaining due diligence you have like sending NOAs to the customers, filing your UCC and 8821, and anything else needed. Prepare her account in your software and receive the first batch of invoices she wants to factor. You're now ready for first funding.

Documents You Need

The following documents are those I utilize to establish a client's account. Samples are shown in the same order as described on the next several pages, followed by a more detailed description in some cases.

- **Application Form** – with a signed approval for credit checks (on your website).

- **Term Sheet** – a one-page summary of your factoring arrangements including discounts, other charges, advances, recourse period, and anything else important to the factoring relationship.

- **Factoring and Security Agreement** – this is the core of your business agreement, often referred to as the "contract."

- **Discount Schedule** – specifies the discount agreed and how it is calculated.

- **UCC-1 Form** – must be filed in the state as described in the chapter "UCCs."

- **Certificate of Corporate Resolution** – if the company is incorporated, or Partnership Agreement if a partnership. This document can be skipped for Sole Proprietors, and is not needed for small corporations in which one person fills all the officer roles.

- **Request** for Business & Personal Financials; an Aging Report is most helpful. Some factors also request or require the client's most recent tax returns, just to make sure they've been filed and the client isn't behind in this regard.

- **Personal (or "Continuing") Guaranty** – Occasionally a potential client will balk at this; it's your call as to whether you'll require it. I do in every case.

- **Validity Guaranty** – This document says the invoices the client will submit are all genuine, valid and have no offsets or counterclaims that will be deducted from payments by the customers.

- **Notice of Assignment** – A letter to customers indicating assignment of Accounts Receivable and that payments are to be sent to your address.

- **Schedule of Accounts** – Clients must sign and turn in one of these with each batch of invoices factored. Provide a sample as well as some blank ones to get them started. This document is built into FactorFox, and can be entered online by the client or you.

- **IRS Form 8821** – Available from IRS's website, have the client sign this form, then be sure you send it in. It instructs IRS to notify you of any notification from IRS to your client regarding a delinquency in their taxes and if IRS is planning to lien their assets. If they do, your UCC will fall into second position behind IRS. But you'll have 45 days to work out a program out to keep IRS happy and you in first position.

- **Delivery of Funds** – This gives you instructions as to how to transfer funds to the client, and whom the client authorizes to sign the Schedule of Account form.

- **ACH Direct Deposit Request** – This provides needed bank account information if you offer ACH direct deposits, and the client desires this service. Make sure it is approved by your ACH provider.

- **Instructions for Factored Payments Received by Client** – This gives specific instructions to the client regarding

what he is required do if he receives payment for a factored invoice.

Some will say this documentation isn't enough, while others will say only some of the above are needed. The forms you use are up to you: I've seen an Application that had nothing more than the owner's name, company name, address, phone number, and Social Security number on it, period. You're the boss and need to balance the security you gain from thorough due diligence, with the client's needs and inclination to not factor small receivables because of a mountain of paper work. But remember: the more a client needs cash, the more willing he will be to sign the documents you put in front of him.

Below are samples of many of the documents described above. You will no doubt want to adapt several of these to your own purposes; they are provided here to get you started.

ABC Financial Services

(253) 555-5555   PO Box 9999
(253) 555-5555 Fax   ABC Town, WA 99999

Application Form

Date:_____	Title:_____
Name:_____	Phone:_____
Company Name:_____	Fax:_____
Address:_____	Cell:_____
City, State, Zip:_____	Email:_____
Referred by:_____	

Describe Your Company_____
& the business you do:_____

☐ Sole Proprietor ☐ Partnership ☐ LLC ☐ Corporation FEIN# _____

How long in business industry   _____   Factored Before? ☐ Yes   ☐ No
Gross Revenue last 12 months   _____
Avg volume to factor - Monthly   _____   Other Factors Name: _____
                    Annually   _____   Approx # of customers: _____
% Yearly growth   _____   Approx # to factor: _____
Avg Invoice Size   _____   Range of Invoice sizes:_____

Please explain in detail: _____
                                 _____
                                 _____

Taxes due or past due: ☐ None   ☐ Local $____ ☐ State $____ ☐ Federal $__

Litigation / Judgements: ☐ Yes   ☐ No   (If yes, please describe on separate sheet)

UCC Filings: _____   Bank Loans   _____
             _____   Collateral   _____

Principals of Company:

Officer Name	Title	Home Address	City, State ,Zip	SS#	% Owned

(continue on back)

270

Application, page 2

Customers you wish to factor:

Company Name Company Address City,State, Zip	Approx. size of Co. ($ Sales/Yr)	Type of Business	Avg. Invoice Amount	Credit Terms You give	Avg Payment Time
1)					
2)					
3)					
4)					

3 Business References:

Name	Phone	Business / Company	Association with you
1)			
2)			
3)			

Other Information:

_____

_____

_____

Banking Information
   Name of Bank _____   Branch _____
   Checking Acct # _____   Contact Person _____
   Bank Routing # _____   Phone # _____

Professional References
   Name of Attorney _____   Phone _____
   Name of Accountant _____   Phone _____

Agreed and Consented to
   Signature _____   Print Name _____
   Title _____   Date _____

The **Application** is used to obtain preliminary information about your prospective client, his customers, his experience in the business, and potential deal killers. This form should be included on your website. Look at online applications of several other factors to get ideas of what you want to include on yours.

After your due diligence and your approval of a client, the information on the Application is used to create the contract, and also in FactorFox to track a client's transactions. While the information on this application may have some data you may not use, be sure to get at least the following:

- Demographic information (name, phones, address, etc.)
- Business type (S- or C-Corporation, LLC, etc.)
- Federal ID number
- Existence of liens from loans, tax delinquencies, judgments, etc.
- Owner/officer information
- Customers to factor including company name, address, city, and state (so you can find credit information).

Unless you have an SSL-secured website, do not request a person's full social security number, and do not have them email it to you. The number can be "hacked" with these insecure transmissions and subject the person to identity theft. Asking for the first five digits of a Social Security number and the owner's date of birth ensure you're looking at the right person when performing your due diligence with Accurint.

Term Sheet

from
ABC Financial Services
to
Client

ABC Financial Services proposes the following preliminary terms for factoring receivables:

- Initial credit line of $_____.
- $___ charge for ACH electronic direct transactions. Bank wires $___ client cost (additional charges from your bank will be incurred to receive bank wires).
- Recourse period of _____ days. Client with option to request chargeback sooner if desired.

Advance Rate and Reserves
____% Advance on all approved invoices, less ____% deposit to Escrow Reserve until cap is reached.
Escrow Reserve cap equals of ____% of credit line.

Discount Rates

	Days out	Percent of gross invoice amount
0 - ____ days		____%
Each ____ days thereafter		____% additional

Minimum discount of $_____ per invoice

These terms are offered provided account is established by ___/___/___.

Agreed and accepted:

	ABC Financial Services
_____	
Company Name	
_____	John Q. Factor
by (name)	by
_____	President
Title	Title
_____	_____
Signature	Signature

The **Term Sheet** is a summary of all the important aspects of the factoring relationship you are establishing: the initial credit line, cost of funds transfers, factoring advances and discount rates, fees you charge, reserves held, recourse period, and so on. Though they aren't stated on the sample Term Sheet, if you have due diligence fees, credit check charges, and/or term contracts, this information should be included as well.

The **Contract** – usually called **Factoring and Security Agreement** or **Accounts Receivable Purchase Agreement** (not shown) is the heart of your factoring relationship, and also the longest of your documents. If you have a client who wants to make significant changes to this document (which happens occasionally), consult your lawyer before doing so. In my experience, such clients may become quite difficult if they sense you will let them make substantial changes to your factoring agreements and processes. You need to be in control of the factoring relationship and what you will and won't allow.

Attorney David Jencks has prepared complete legal document templates especially for small factors, which I recommend. They are called Basic Legal Documents, Additional Legal Documents, and Complete Legal Package, and are available for purchase and download from www.DashPointPublishing.com.

Most new small factors will find what they need in the Basic documents. More specific legal needs, plus two hours of Mr. Jencks' time, are provided in the Additional documents. If you decide you want everything in both the Basic and Additional Legal Documents, they are available together in the Complete Legal Package.

The names of specific documents included in the Basic Legal Documents are:

- Factoring and Security Agreement
- Term and Rate Sheet
- Schedule of Charges
- Certificate of Resolution
- Notification of Assignment
- Account Debtor Release, Complete

- Account Debtor Release, Conditional
- Account Debtor Release, Pay New Factor
- UCC-1 Collateral Description
- Waiver of Defenses by Account Debtor
- Continuing Guaranty
- Validity Guaranty
- Power of Attorney

The Additional Legal Documents include:
- Intercreditor Agreement
- Buyout Document – Outgoing
- Buyout Document – Incoming
- IRS Quasi Subordination Letter
- Marshaling Letter

And the following services from Mr. Jencks:
- Assistance with proper UCC-1 Filings
- One Intercreditor Agreement Completed if and when necessary
- Full personalization of the above documents, which includes:
  o The name of the factor in all documents.
  o Any industry specific language for the type of industry being factored.
  o Future factoring documentation questions. (Does not include any type of litigation or assistance in putting a deal together.)
- Two hours of legal counsel (in ¼ hour billing increments) for discussing the documentation, answering questions, beginning to put a deal together or whatever issues may arise. After 2 hours of tracked time, additional hourly charges for consultation, assistance, drafting, etc.

The Complete Legal Package includes all the above from the two sets combined.

ABC Financial Services
Discount Schedule

The discount earned by Factor for purchasing the Accounts Receivable shall be the following percentage of the face amount of the Account Receivable purchased.

1.   ____% if payment of an Account Receivable is collected up to ____ days;

2.   ____% if payment of an Account Receivable is collected between ____ and

      ____ days.

3.   An additional ____% for every ____ days after if payment of an Account Receivable is collected after ____ days.

Number of days out calculation clock starts of the date the advance is paid by factor and stops on the day factor receives payment.

Seller (Company):   _____

Signed by: _____

(Please print your name): _____

Title: _____

Date: _____

The **Discount Schedule** is a simple yet detailed explanation of how your discounts are calculated on a day-by-day basis. If the client had any questions about how your discount is calculated, this should answer them.

Be sure to point out the sentence, "Number of days out calculation clock starts on the date the advance is paid by factor and stops on the date factor receives payment." This clearly states that the clock does not start on the invoice date, but the date you gave the advance – and that it stops when *you* receive payment, not when the *client* receives payment, if that happens.

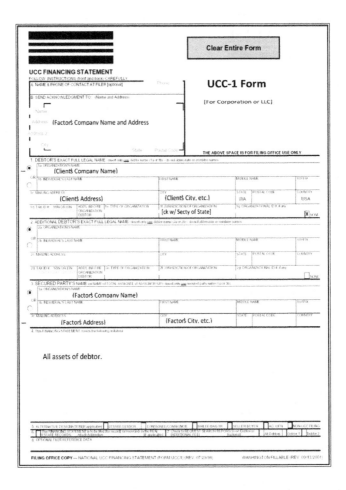

Note: wording in #4 above should be identical to wording in contract's section on Security Interest. The Basic Legal Documents package provides additional wording that should be used when "All assets of debtor" is written, as above.

Some states require an entry in the box "Jurisdiction of Organization" in #1. Contact the Secretary of State's office to learn what this is for your client (usually a city). Many states also require you to either include the client's Organizational ID or check "None" in #1. Again, ask the Secretary of State what to enter here.

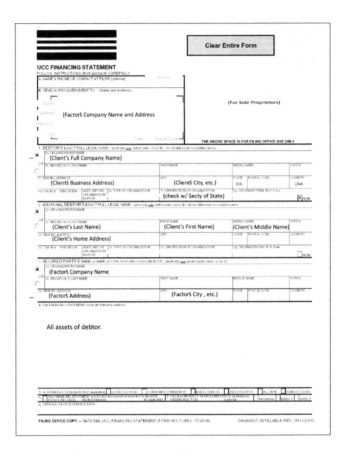

Note on Sole Proprietors. Some clients who come to you for factoring will be Sole Proprietors. Many factoring attorneys discourage you from factoring Sole Proprietors as doing so can expose you to tax or legal liabilities that are not present with Corporations or LLCs. Discuss this with your attorney before funding a Sole Proprietor, or simply require a prospect become incorporated or an LLC before accepting him. Such a legal registration is usually better for the client anyway, and many may already be considering this move.

The **UCC-1** form is important for securing your investment and protecting you, in the event your client goes bankrupt or his debtors garnish his assets. A few states will have unique requirements, so be sure you follow the instructions so you don't omit any required box's information. If you do omit something, your filing will likely be returned and you'll probably have to re-file, and perhaps be required to pay the filing fee again.

The client does not need to sign this document.

Form 8821
(Rev. August 2008)
Department of the Treasury
Internal Revenue Service

Tax Information Authorization

♦ Do not sign this form unless all applicable lines have been completed.
♦ Do not use this form to request a copy or transcript of your tax return. Instead, use Form 4506 or Form 4506-T.

OMB No. 1545-1165
For IRS Use Only
Received by:
Name
Telephone ( )
Function
Date

1   Taxpayer information. Taxpayer(s) must sign and date this form on line 7.

Taxpayer name(s) and address (type or print)	Social security number(s)
Client Company Name	000 : 00 : 0000
Client Address	Employer identification number
Client City, State, Zip	00 0000000
Daytime telephone number	Plan number (if applicable)
(000) 000-0000	

2   Appointee. If you wish to name more than one appointee, attach a list to this form.

Name and address
ABC Financial Services
PO Box 9999
Anytown, USA 99999-9999

CAF No. 000000 (assigned to you by IRS)
Telephone No. 253 000-0000
Fax No. 253 000-0001
Check if new: Address ☐   Telephone No. ☐   Fax No. ☐

3   Tax matters. The appointee is authorized to inspect and/or receive confidential tax information in any office of the IRS for the tax matters listed on this line. Do not use Form 8821 to request copies of tax returns.

(a) Type of Tax (Income, Employment, Excise, etc.) or Civil Penalty	(b) Tax Form Number (1040, 941, 720, etc.)	(c) Year(s) or Period(s) (see the instructions for line 3)	(d) Specific Tax Matters (see instr.)
Income	1040	2005 - 2015	Collections
Employment	940	2005 - 2015	Collections
Employment	941	2005 - 2015	Collections

4   Specific use not recorded on Centralized Authorization File (CAF). If the tax information authorization is for a specific use not recorded on CAF, check this box. See the instructions on page 4. If you check this box, skip lines 5 and 6 . ♦ ☐

5   Disclosure of tax information (you must check a box on line 5a or 5b unless the box on line 4 is checked):

a If you want copies of tax information, notices, and other written communications sent to the appointee on an ongoing basis, check this box _____ ♦ ☑

b If you do not want any copies of notices or communications sent to your appointee, check this box ___ ♦ ☐

6   Retention/revocation of tax information authorizations. This tax information authorization automatically revokes all prior authorizations for the same tax matters you listed on line 3 above unless you checked the box on line 4. If you do not want to revoke a prior tax information authorization, you must attach a copy of any authorizations you want to remain in effect and check this box _____ ♦ ☐
To revoke this tax information authorization, see the instructions on page 4.

7   Signature of taxpayer(s). If a tax matter applies to a joint return, either husband or wife must sign. If signed by a corporate officer, partner, guardian, executor, receiver, administrator, trustee, or party other than the taxpayer, I certify that I have the authority to execute this form with respect to the tax matters/periods on line 3 above.

♦ IF NOT SIGNED AND DATED, THIS TAX INFORMATION AUTHORIZATION WILL BE RETURNED.

♦ DO NOT SIGN THIS FORM IF IT IS BLANK OR INCOMPLETE.

Signature _____ Date _____   Signature _____ Date _____

Print Name _____ Title (if applicable) _____   Print Name _____ Title (if applicable) _____

☐☐☐☐☐ PIN number for electronic signature   ☐☐☐☐☐ PIN number for electronic signature

For Privacy Act and Paperwork Reduction Act Notice, see page 4.   Cat. No. 11596P   Form **8821** (Rev. 8-2008)

IRS 8821 Form gives instructions to IRS to inform you of any activity or communication from IRS to your client. To download it in PDF format go to the IRS website at www.irs.gov and in the site's search field type "8821." Be sure to use the most current form (the revision year is in the upper left corner of the form). If the client is behind in her taxes, this is an early warning system so the receivables you've purchased aren't garnished by the IRS.

A few notes about completing this form.

1. If your client **is a Sole Proprietor** (and you accept Sole Proprietors):
   a. Section 1
      - On the left enter their personal name followed by "DBA 'Business Name.' "
      - On the right enter their FEIN number (if different from their social security number, otherwise enter their social security number), and phone number.
   b. Section 2
      - On the left enter your company name and address.
      - On the right enter your CAF number (assigned to you by IRS after your first 8821 filing), telephone, and fax numbers.
   c. Section 3
      - Column a, Type of Tax: put "Income" in the first line and "Employment" in the second and third lines.
      - Column b, Tax Form Number: put "1040" in the first line, "940" in the second line, and "941" in the third.
      - Column c, Year(s) or Period(s): In each line make the box a 10-year spread, going back seven years and ahead three years. For example, if the present year is 2012, enter "2005 – 2015."
      - Column d, Specific Tax Matters: put "Collections" in all three lines.
   d. Sections 4 and 6 leave blank
   e. Sections 5: *be sure* to check box 5a. It's the reason you're filling out this form.
   f. Section 7: the client must sign and enter the date here. You can pre-enter their name and title below the signature and date lines.

2. If your client **is a C-Corporation or LLC**:
   a. Section 1
      - On the left enter their business name and business address.

       • On the right enter their FEIN number and phone number.
- b. Section 2
  - On the left enter your company name and address.
  - On the right enter your CAF number (assigned to you by IRS after your first 8821 filing), telephone, and fax numbers.
- c. Section 3
  - Column a, Type of Tax: put "Income" in the first line and "Employment" in the second and third lines.
  - Column b, Tax Form Number: put "1120" in the first line, "940" in the second line, and "941" in the third.
  - Column c, Year(s) or Period(s): In each line make the box a 10-year spread, going back seven years and ahead three years. For example, if the present year is 2012, enter "2005 – 2015."
  - Column d, Specific Tax Matters: put "Collections" in all three lines.
- d. Sections 4 and 6 leave blank
- e. Sections 5: *be sure* to check box 5a. It's the reason you're filling out this form.
- f. Section 7: the client must sign and enter the date here. You can pre-enter their name and title below the signature and date lines.

3. If your client **is an S-Corporation**:
  - a. Section 1
    - On the left enter their business name and business address.
    - On the right enter their FEIN number and phone number.
  - b. Section 2
    - On the left enter your company name and address.
    - On the right enter your CAF number (assigned to you by IRS after your first 8821 filing), telephone, and fax numbers.

c. Section 3
- Column a, Type of Tax: put "Income" in the first line and "Employment" in the second and third lines.
- Column b, Tax Form Number: put "1120-S" in the first line, "940" in the second line, and "941" in the third.
- Column c, Year(s) or Period(s): In each line make the box a 10-year spread, going back seven years and ahead three years. For example, if the present year is 2012, enter "2005 – 2015."
- Column d, Specific Tax Matters: put "Collections" in all three lines.

d. Sections 4 and 6 leave blank
e. Sections 5: *be sure* to check box 5a. It's the reason you're filling out this form.
f. Section 7: the client must sign and enter the date here. You can pre-enter their name and title below the signature and date lines.

Note: IRS keeps only one 8821 filing on a business or person. So if another party files an 8821 after you, your filing is "bumped" and you won't be notified. Therefore it's a good idea to re-file these every year or so.

The **Certificate of Corporate Resolution** (not shown) is needed only if the client's business is incorporated and has multiple members on the board of directors. Its purpose is to show that the corporation's board has given the person signing your factoring documents the authority to do so.

For many small companies that are incorporated, the board often consists of the president and no one else, making this document superfluous. If the business is a partnership, the Certificate of Corporate Resolution is unnecessary but all partners need to sign all the other documents. If the business is an LLC, the members of the LLC should sign everything as well.

The **Personal** (or **"Continuing"**) **Guaranty** (not shown) is one of the Basic Legal Documents from David Jencks. It is a document which commits the person signing to pay you back from his personal assets if the business is unable to do so. As such this document carries some punch in your favor in case an account goes sideways. If you must turn over an account to collections, this is often the first document the collections people will ask if you have.

Occasionally you'll find a client who is unwilling to sign a personal guaranty. You will need to decide if this will kill the deal or you can live without it. However, if the person signing the guaranty has little or no personal assets, this document won't be worth much. Be careful if a business owner will not sign this document but obtains the signature of another person for the personal guaranty; that individual may have no net worth. Doing this protects the business owner's personal assets at your, and perhaps this other person's, expense.

If the person signing has personal assets but does not want to take the personal risk of signing this document, you might want to satisfy yourself as to his perception of his risk. If he doesn't have enough confidence in his company to guarantee his personal assets, this might give you pause as to working with him in the first place. However, many attorneys discourage their clients from signing personal guarantees of any kind, and the person may be acting on his attorney's advice.

If your client is married and lives in a community property state, the client's spouse should sign this personal guaranty as well.

Be sure the client does *not* write his title and/or the company name by the signature line, as doing so makes this a *corporate* guaranty and defeats the purpose of a *personal* guaranty.

The **Validity Guaranty** (not shown) is a guaranty stating the client will give you valid invoices and that there are no offsets or other reasons the customer will not pay his invoices' full amounts. It also includes statements that the client is solvent, the sold goods are the property of the client and not someone else, and are free of other liens and security interests other than yours.

This guarantee is essentially a promise the client will be honest with you. He won't factor phony invoices, he isn't about to declare bankruptcy, the invoice amounts are correct and what the customers will pay, and the client will send you payment for factored invoices should he receive them.

It is highly unlikely a client will refuse to sign this document. After all, why would someone promise *not* to cheat, lie to, or defraud you?! But if he refuses to sign, run for the hills. Automatic deal killer.

The **Notification of Assignment** letter (not shown) is another of the Basic Legal Documents from David Jencks. This letter is the notification to your client's customers of the factoring relationship and assignment of receivables. This letter also gives you protection from a client receiving payment for factored invoices.

Here, the customer is given notice that the client's receivables have been assigned to you and the customer must now pay you in lieu of the client. The letter makes clear that payments to the client do not relieve the customer of the obligation to you. That means a customer will have to pay you, even if he has already (yet erroneously) paid the client for a factored invoice.

Legally, this letter can be from you on your letterhead and does not require either your client's or the customer's signature to be binding; you only need to show proof the customer has received it. Proof is usually obtained via registered mail from the post office or registered email using a service like RPost (www.rpost.com). Therefore some factors omit the customer's signature lines from this document and simply send the letter to the customer. This is done so the customer doesn't think he can pay anyone he wants if he refuses to sign the letter.

Other factors want the customer's signature on file so they know the customer has received the letter, made the remittance address change, and is aware of his responsibility to pay the factor directly. The customer's signature is also clear proof you can use should they "pay over notice," that is pay the client instead of you. Personally, I have both my signature and my client's signature at the bottom of the letter so there is no question in the customer's mind that the client is agreeing to this.

I also require a customer to sign and return this letter before I fund the client's first factored invoice to any new customer. While legally this is procedural overkill, I find it is just a better way to get the customer on board and send payments where they should, right off the bat.

Also, the Notification of Assignment makes clear the client is not allowed to redirect funds or inform the customer of the release of the assignment. Only an officer from your company can release the Notification of Assignment, and only in writing. This is to keep the client from telling the customer he's not factoring anymore and to send the payments to him. That's clearly fraud, but it happens more than you want to know.

The **Notification Release** letter need not be lengthy and three variations are provided in the Basic Legal Documents package. It should be on your letterhead and addressed to the customer. All it needs to say is your company no longer has a financial interest in the client's receivables, and provides instructions as to where future payments should be sent.

Despite all these steps, as mentioned in the chapter "Banking and Funds Transfers" I never cease to be amazed how frequently payment over notice occurs. With apologies to any readers who work or have worked in payables departments (and admittedly some people there are quite competent), dealing with AP departments for many years has led me to develop a kind of conspiracy theory against factors.

I suspect that large corporations intentionally put their least intelligent workers in their payables departments. I also suspect that within the payables departments, the least capable people are given the responsibility of addressing and cutting checks for companies who factor their invoices. How else do you explain how frequently clients *still* get paid directly, despite everything factors do to properly notify customers as to where to send payments? Murphy's Law (if something can go wrong it will) and the Peter Principle (people rise to their level of incompetence) are both alive and well in payables departments nationwide. I swear, it's a conspiracy.

End of theory.

```
┌─────────────────────────────────────────────────────────────────────────┐
│                      Schedule of Accounts                      11/1/2012  │
│                      ABC Financial Services                               │
│                      Gina's Sheening Cleaning                             │
│                                                                           │
│   Schedule Number      GINA-0001                                          │
│  ┌──┬─────────────────────────────┬──────────┬─────┬──────────┬──────────┐│
│  │  │ Customer                    │ Invoice #│ PO #│Invoice Date│Invoice Amount││
│  ├──┼─────────────────────────────┼──────────┼─────┼──────────┼──────────┤│
│  │1 │ Golden Valley Real Estate   │ 1050     │     │ 11/01/12 │ 2,000.00 ││
│  │2 │ Good Grub Restaurant        │ 1051     │     │ 11/01/12 │ 4,000.00 ││
│  │3 │ Creaky Joints Chiropractic Clinic│ 1052│     │ 11/01/12 │ 2,000.00 ││
│  │4 │ Stressless Dresses Boutique │ 1053     │     │ 11/01/12 │ 1,000.00 ││
│  └──┴─────────────────────────────┴──────────┴─────┴──────────┴──────────┘│
└───────────────────────────────────────────────────────────────────────────┘
```

	Customer	Invoice #	PO #	Invoice Date	Invoice Amount
1	Golden Valley Real Estate	1050		11/01/12	2,000.00
2	Good Grub Restaurant	1051		11/01/12	4,000.00
3	Creaky Joints Chiropractic Clinic	1052		11/01/12	2,000.00
4	Stressless Dresses Boutique	1053		11/01/12	1,000.00

This is to certify that the parties named above are indebted to the undersigned in the sums set opposite their respective names, for merchandise sold and delivered or for work and labor done and accepted.

The undersigned hereby sells, assigns and transfers all of its right, title and interest in the above listed accounts receivable ('Invoices') to ABC Financial Services pursuant to that certain Accounts Receivable Purchase Agreement between the undersigned and ABC Financial Services.

Total	9,000.00
Advances	7,200.00
Escrow	550.00
Discount	0.00
Adjustments	0.00
Net Advance	6,750.00

Payment Type	ACH
Payment Date	11/01/12

Submission Date: 11/1/2012

Company: Gina's Sheening Cleaning

Signature: *Gina Steening*

Name/Title: Gina Steening, President

FactorFox

ABC Financial Services
PO Box 9999
Seattle, WA, 98100
206 999 0000

Schedule of Accounts
Page 1 of 1

The **Schedule of Accounts** is included in FactorFox (the above page is a screenshot from the software) and must be completed and signed or authorized by your client each time she has invoices to factor. This document is referred to in the contract and is an extension of the contract. A completed Schedule of Accounts record is generated in FactorFox, and a copy of one is included in the chapter "A Sample Factoring Transaction."

By completing this form, the client provides a record of which invoices are factored, and by signing or authorizing the Schedule, legally assigns the receivables to you. If this document isn't completed properly, the invoices aren't assigned and they are not your property. Therefore don't advance funds until this form is complete.

__Delivery of Funds__

Select one the following as your default delivery of funds method.

____ 1. ACH direct deposit. Funds appear in your account 1-2 business days following the transfer. No charge.

____ 2. Bank wire. Funds usually appear in your bank account the same day as transfer though this is not guaranteed. $____ is deducted from the amount wired plus an additional deduction is made by the receiving bank.

____ 3. Check

     ____ a. Client pick up. No charge

     ____ b. Regular first class mail. No charge

     ____ c. FedEx next afternoon delivery. $____ charge.

For ACHs and Bank Wires:

Name of Bank: _____

Bank Routing #: _____

Account #: _____

Name of Account: _____

Bank Address: _____

Bank Phone #: _____

- -

Please complete the following in addition to the above.
At least one person must be authorized to sign the Schedule of Accounts form.

Company Name _____

Authorized Person 1: _____

Authorized Person 2: _____

Approved by: _____

Date: _____

The **Delivery of Funds** form gives you instructions as to how your client wishes to receive advances and rebates. Put only choices you offer here; if you don't issue checks, don't include them. Likewise, if you are charging for any of these delivery methods, make the charges fair and cover your costs.

Include the option for ACH deposits only after you have been approved for this by your bank or ACH provider.

Instructions for Factored Payments
Received by Client

If you receive a customer payment for any factored invoice, <u>do not deposit the funds into your bank account nor cash the check</u>. Doing so is committing **fraud**. Handle the payment the following way:

1. Immediately email a copy or fax the check and its stub to ABC Financial Services (fax 253-000-0001). Include a note indicating how you are delivering the payment to us (1st class mail, Priority Mail, hand deliver, overnight).

2. Deliver the check as indicated on your note. Your account will be credited for the payment as being received the business day we receive it, not when you fax it. The remittance addresses are:

<u>USPS Delivery</u>   <u>FedEx/UPS Overnight</u>
ABC Financial Services   ABC Financial Services
P.O. Box 9999   123 Main Street
Anytown, USA 00000-0000   Anytown, USA 00000-0000

3. To avoid improperly routed payments in the future, contact your customer's Accounts Payable department or bookkeeper to thank them for payment and remind them to send future checks to your Accounts Receivable remittance address:

P.O. Box 9999
Anytown, USA 00000-0000

I understand these instructions and will immediately forward all payments for factored invoices to ABC Financial Services as directed above. I understand that by depositing or cashing such payments I am subject to a Misdirected Payment Fee per incident, a breach of contract that may result in termination of the factoring agreement, and am committing criminal fraud that can carry severe penalties.

Company Name: _____

Signature: _____

Print Name: _____

Title: _____

Date: _____

The **Instructions for Factored Payments Received by Client** form is not part of the Basic Legal Documents package, but is something I created in a fit of disgust after one too many clients converted a check. It makes me feel better to include it in my contract package, so I do.

This document gives very specific instructions to the client regarding what he is required do if he receives payment for a factored invoice. While the client agrees to send such payments to you in the Validity Guaranty, this document gives specific instructions as to where to send them.

This document also clearly spells out the consequences if clients get sticky fingers: a Misdirected Payment Fee, breach of contract possibly resulting in termination of the relationship, and the significance of criminal fraud. Clients can't claim ignorance as to what to do with these checks if they read and sign this document (but some will anyway).

Sooner or later (usually sooner), a client will receive a factored customer payment and if the check is made out to him – despite this document – he may be inclined to deposit the check and "pay you back" from his own bank account. This is not something you want to occur. In my experience, even honest clients sometimes see nothing wrong with doing this. However, that is a practice you *never* want to allow as it can lead to multiple problems.

Once Under Way

Keeping careful and accurate records is absolutely critical. Organization helps you stay on top of things, protects you if the client disagrees with some invoice, discount, or other item, and is your audit trail if you need it. The more complete, accurate and systematically filed your records are, the better for everybody.

Customer Payments

The idea behind a limited power of attorney is to allow you to deposit checks made out to your client. Unfortunately, most banks do not allow a third-party (you) to deposit checks made out to someone else (your client). Talk to your bank to learn what they will and won't allow here.

You may require that checks be made to your company only, or have checks made out like this:

"Pay to the Order of ABC Factoring Company, FBO Client Company" [FBO stands for "For Benefit Of"].

Why have the check be made this way, or only to you? If your client obtains a check, he can't deposit it if it's made out to your company. I now use a lockbox for all customer check payments, and my bank is not concerned about to whom the checks are made, as long as they're sent to the lockbox. This is a very good reason to use a lockbox if you have enough factoring volume to make the expense worthwhile.

Invoices

Invoices are about as diverse as the businesses who create them, but generally include a date, number, company name and address, bill to name and address, terms, quantity of product or hours of service rendered, description of product or service, subtotal, tax, and freight and/or miscellaneous charges. What you want to pay most attention to with invoices is that YOUR company's address is on them, conspicuously evident under words that say something like "Remit to" or "Pay to." You can have your name and address put on with a sticker or inked stamp as many factors do (though some clients think this looks tacky...I tend to agree).

If your client is generating invoices on a computer, it's usually not hard to add your "remit to" address. If you're creating the invoices for your client (and some may want you to) you can make the invoice look like and say anything you want. Ideally, yours would be the only address on the invoice, with the client's phone number listed. (See the sample invoice in the next chapter.) I prefer having only one address on the invoice since customers often pay to the client's address if there are two addresses on the invoice. It's best to have only your address, and print "please remit to this address."

I've seen various ways of getting invoices out the door. Some factors say if the client generates paper invoices, you should have the client mail both the originals and copies to you. Then you put your sticker on the originals, keep copies for your records, verify them, and mail them as you pay the advance. That works well but is time consuming and you're paying the postage. I've seen one factor supply an inked stamp that says "payable to" the factor's name and address, and give a stamp to each client. The client then faxes to the factor a copy of each invoice with the Schedule of Accounts, from which the factor makes the verification calls (including verification about the proper remittance address), and the client mails the invoices (using the client's time and expense). Once the factor verifies the invoices, the advance is given.

A variation is to have the client print your remittance address on their invoices which are created by their computer so it looks professional, and then wait for their fax. This works well, though receiving faxes or copies does leave you open to fraud, as you don't know for certain the client sent the invoice, changed the amount on it after faxing it to you, and/or sent it with your address on it. For this reason many factors require the client to supply the factor with the original invoice plus a copy. The factor then mails the original. However, if you feel safe letting the client mail the originals, it will save time stuffing envelopes and the cost of postage. Alternately, the client could email the invoice to the customer and copy you on the email. That way you can see both the customer and you are receiving the same invoice.

Invoice Verifications

Ordinarily, the more you verify invoices the safer you'll be. Some factors say that being "consistent in your inconsistency" is a good practice for verifications. That is, if you have an unpredictable pattern to your verification practices, a dishonest client will have a harder time getting away with fraudulent invoices and/or phony customer approvals.

Some types of business lend themselves well to verifications signed by the customer, indicating payment is approved. A good example is time cards signed by the customer for employees hired through a temporary agency. Temp agencies often make great factoring clients, and verifications can be a snap if time cards are agreed by all as a promise to pay. Simply have the signed time cards faxed or mailed to you with the invoices. A document signed by the customer will protect you better in any dispute than a note you make from a verification made by phone.

However, never underestimate the nerve of dishonest clients. I had one temp agency client forge every time card she submitted for months and I didn't verify them; I just assumed the time card signatures were legitimate. It was only when the invoices weren't paid that I called the customers. Incredibly, they had never heard of her or her company. If I had verified only a handful of these at the beginning, I would have avoided a lot of problems.

The following two verification forms are included in FactorFox, providing a convenient and easy means of recording every verification. The first is created as a report that can be emailed to the customer, who signs and sends it back.

ABC Financial Services
PO Box 9999
Anytown, USA 00000-000
253 000-0000 * Fax 253 000-0001
joefactor@abcfinancialservices.com

INVOICE ACKNOWLEDGMENT FORM

Good Grub Restaurant
321 Hollow Wood Road
Willows Bend, WA 00000-0000
Mabeetle@goodgrub.com

**FOR SERVICES RENDERED AND/OR PRODUCTS PROVIDED
FROM YOUR VENDOR (our client): Gina's Sheening Cleaning**

Invoice #	Invoice Date	PO/ Reference	Amount	Notes

Please verify and note any invoices that have been paid as of today's date.

The authorized signature below acknowledges and represents to ABC Financial Services that all goods and services relating to the invoices listed above have been completed and accepted. There are no defenses, set offs or other claims which would prevent payment in full of the invoices listed above.

Please email or fax signed copy to ABC Financial Services.

Customer Signature _____

Print Name _____

Title _____

Date _____

The second form is used when making phone verifications; it can also note the presence of written verifications.

▶ Customer

Customer: Invoice Status:

Phone: Verification Complete:

Contact Person:

Other Contact:

▶ Invoice

Client: Invoice Date:

Invoice #:   PO #:

Amount:

▶ Phone

Date of Call [   ]   Time of Call [   ]

Talked To [   ]

▶ Written

☐ Letter   ☐ Bill of Lading

☐ Invoice   ☐ PO

☐ Invoice Acknowledgment Form   ☐ Rate Confirmation

☐ Other [   ]

▶ Product

Did you order the goods?   Have you received the goods?
○ Yes ○ No   ○ Yes ○ No

Have you inspected the goods?   Are the goods satisfactory?
○ Yes ○ No   ○ Yes ○ No

▶ Service

Was the service performed?   Are you satisfied with the service?
○ Yes ○ No   ○ Yes ○ No

Notes

[   ]

Unfactored Invoices

If a client factors some, but not all, invoices with a given customer, tell him to have **all** payments sent to you to save confusion on the part of the customer. When you receive a payment for an invoice which you can't find in FactorFox, you'll know you didn't factor that invoice. You then rebate 100% of the unfactored invoice upon receipt of payment, less a processing fee if you charge one. The client must trust you with this, since it's the best way for you to handle a client's customer with some invoices factored, and some not factored.

Factoring Record

The name and format for this document are my creation, but every software package and factor uses his or her own variation. You don't need to copy mine exactly, as I've seen factors get by with less information than this. However, I like this form for its completeness and so do my clients.

If you're using spreadsheets, when you receive a Schedule of Accounts you'll transfer the information from it onto the Factoring Record. Check to make sure all invoice information is written accurately on the Schedule – invoice number, date, amount, and customer name. As customers make payments, you enter them into the Factoring record and the rebates and factoring discounts due will be calculated. If you're using FactorFox· either the client or you can enter the invoice information; you just need to be sure they're entered accurately if the client makes the entries. The Factoring Record is one of many reports FactorFox automatically generates.

Rebates

These can be done numerous ways, and the client needs to be clear about which you're going to do when she signs the application papers. Rebate methods are designed to provide the factor with security, but can easily lead to misunderstanding (and with it, distrust) in you from your client.

An old method is to pay back rebates due from a given Schedule when all the invoices on the Schedule have been paid.

This may sound a bit unfair, but when you have advanced money and are waiting to be paid, you're vulnerable and this protects you by creating a temporary reserve. Again, explain this clearly when you review how to do the Schedule, and your client will understand why you're doing it (your security, not to rip her off). It will keep her paying attention to particular invoices that are slow, and encourage her to contact the slow paying customer. Believe me, clients want their rebates! On the other hand, a client may be resentful if all but one invoice on a Schedule with twenty invoices isn't paid. Always find creative ways to keep yourself safe and the client happy with your service.

A second method of rebates gives you better security but is more complicated, and is the method some larger factors use. It's more complicated because you utilize a specific factoring discount (the most you can charge per your Agreement) and then rebate part of that discount based on when the invoice is paid, in addition to rebating the security deposit when it reaches a certain percentage of total invoices. If that sounds confusing, the following example should clarify.

Suppose you want to charge 5% for the first 30 days, and 2% for each 15 days thereafter, up to 90 days. It looks like this:

5%	30 days
7%	45 days
9%	60 days
11%	75 days
13%	90 days

The highest discount you'll collect is 13% at 90 days. The contract is so worded that your discount is 13%, and you give rebates on the fee when the invoice is paid before 90 days: if paid in 30 days, the discount rebate is 8%, thereby making the discount 5% (13% - 8% = 5%); if paid in 45 days, the rebate is 6%, making the discount 7% (13% - 6% = 7%), and so on. In addition, you are also holding a security deposit reserve. If you advance 70% and your total discount is 13%, your security deposit is 17% (30% - 13% = 17%).

With this method of calculating rebates, you don't pay rebates according to any Schedule of Accounts, but on a calculated percentage of the total outstanding balance of invoices due, which accrues from this 17% security deposit plus discount rebates. This calculated percentage is usually 50%.

Getting lost? Okay, say you factor a $5,000 invoice; with a 70% advance, $850 (17%) is kept as security deposit. Then you factor another invoice with the same client, again for $5,000; another $850 is kept. $1,700 is now in reserve ($850 + $850 = $1,700). Even if the first invoice is on a Schedule by itself and is paid, you do not pay the rebate because only $1,700 is in reserve (not yet 50%, or $2,500). The reserve continues to build up on unpaid invoices until you go over 50% of the unpaid balance of total invoices factored, at which point you begin paying rebates and only pay enough to keep the reserve at 50%. Confusing?

Yes, and somewhat different from how I (and most clients) first understood how rebates are paid: "You're paid the advance immediately, and when your customer pays the factor, you get what was withheld, less the factor's discount." With this method, getting paid a rebate is not that simple and if a factor were to do this to me as a client without explaining this extremely carefully before I signed my life away, I'd think he was trying to pull a fast one when I expect a rebate and it doesn't come. The first and third (see below) methods make the contract language much simpler, are easier for the client to understand, and are easier to track by both the factor and the client. The disadvantage is that you, the factor, are not as well covered by the reserve. Fortunately, you can be protected another way which we'll describe shortly.

A third method is to simply pay rebates on a regular basis and whenever a client factors a new schedule. If you pay rebates weekly, pick a day you total all rebates due and provide the rebates that day. You probably want to set a minimum rebate due amount if paying weekly (mine is $250) to avoid constantly paying very small rebates.

While you are least protected with this method, clients are happier as there is almost no wait for rebates. Further, you don't end up paying large sums that have accumulated from payments on a single schedule, which may be difficult to cover if your available cash is low. If your client has some invoices nearing recourse, draw her attention to that fact, and indicate you intend to withhold all or part of the upcoming rebate to cover the charge back. This way, you won't need to take charge backs out of her next advance or require her to pay you directly...both of which can wreak havoc with the client's cash flow. If you've clearly explained that you're a recourse factor and she understands her responsibility for unpaid invoices, she will grasp what you're doing.

Regardless of how you pay rebates, make sure you describe the one you use and explain carefully to the client how the rebate is calculated. If you don't, you may have an understandably grumpy (or worse) client who expects a rebate that may not be as quickly forthcoming as she expected.

Separate Reserve Account

Creating a separate reserve account is discussed in the chapter "Reducing Your Risk," and bears repeating here. I have found this tool to be exceptionally helpful and an excellent means of protecting both myself and the client when customers short pay invoices or don't pay at all. Here's how I do it.

First, I explain that for all clients I create a "rainy day" fund that will help if and when a customer doesn't pay in full or at all. This reserve money will be a small, temporary deduction from their first few advances, and the client will still receive the lion's share of his advance, plus his full rebate payments when customer checks arrive.

The reserve fund will gradually build up to equal 10% of the client's credit limit. Since I start my new clients with a $10,000 credit line, their reserve has a $1,000 cap to start. How is money put into this reserve? Each time an invoice is factored, 5% of that invoice is placed into the reserve from each advance.

Here's an example. Let's say a client receives an 80% advance. When a $1,000 invoice is factored, $800 or 80% is paid for the advance, $50 or 5% of which is set aside into the escrow reserve; so the client actually receives $750 in cash. Once the $1,000 cap is reached, no more is put into the escrow reserve and the client receives the full 80% advance.

Structured this way, the client continues to receive rebates in addition to advances, while concurrently setting aside reserve money for potential problems. Over time, the client will build up to $1,000 in her reserve account. Then, if a customer pays, for example, only $600 for a $1,000 invoice, the money owed from that short payment can be taken from the reserve fund, and not from the client's next advance or rebate. This can be a great help to a client's cash flow. To replenish the amount used, future payments then refill this reserve fund (as was done before the draw on the reserve) until its cap is again reached.

When a client's business grows, her factoring volume increases, and her credit limit is increased; the reserve fund grows with it simply by remaining at 10% of the credit limit. So if you increase the credit limit from $10,000 to $15,000, the reserve fund cap increases from $1,000 to $1,500 (thereby remaining at 10% of the credit limit).

Because this reserve fund accumulates from money that would have been paid the client as advances, this is the client's money. Therefore the funds remaining in the reserve when the client stops factoring are paid in full to the client.

When explained carefully to new clients and the rationale made clear, most prospects see the prudence of setting aside funds in this reserve and willingly agree. The client's cash flow remains steady even with short payments or non-payments, your funds are at less risk, and everyone feels better.

My Electronic Filing System

Everyone has his own filing system and yours will evolve. For what it's worth, what follows is how my electronic filing system is presently organized. Like everything else, this continues to progress and change with time.

First of all, because I need to share many documents with Veronica and Anne, we use a service called Dropbox (www.Dropbox.com) which enables us to access the same files without having to constantly email them to each other. Set up a Dropbox account, create a Dropbox folder on your computer, and put the folders with files you want to share into the Dropbox folder. Then grant access to whatever files you want to whomever you want to share the files. They accept the sharing invitation, and presto! No more sending files back and forth.

You must be absolutely sure to backup your Dropbox files to a service like Carbonite. Why? If someone makes changes to a file in your Dropbox folder, that changed file is saved to your folder, her folder, and Dropbox's online folder – but the previous version of the file is overwritten. However, if you didn't want this change, the old version of the file is gone unless it was backed up. Take this a step farther – if a disgruntled employee decides to delete all your files and the files are not backed up, you are up the proverbial creek.

If you work alone you really don't need Dropbox so the filing system described below can simply go wherever you want. But if you do use Dropbox, you need to rethink how to organize your files. Put everything you need to share with others into the Dropbox folder; personal and non-business items should be left out of it. Here's how the files I share with Veronica and Anne are structured.

First I have a DPF folder (which stands for Dash Point Financial, my factoring company). Inside are several folders viewed by Details and therefore listed alphabetically. They are:

- Banking
- Brokers
- Clients
- Collections
- Customer Credit Reports
- Daily Invoices
- Daily Receipts
- Docs Needed
- Letters
- Loans
- Marketing
- Miscellaneous
- Participations
- Staff
- Taxes

- UCCs & 8821s

Most folders have subfolders. Here are a few examples:

- Banking
  - 2010 Bank Statements
  - 2011 Bank Statements
  - 2012 Bank Statements
- Brokers
  - Broker Packet
  - Signed Agreements
- Prospects
  - Active
  - Duds
- Staff
  - Anne
  - Veronica

For example, my Prospects folder has two subfolders, Active and Duds. When I receive an application from a prospect, I create a subfolder for the prospect and put the application document in the prospect's subfolder. As I do my underwriting, save copies of credit reports, and gather PDF copies of their business license and everything else, these files go into the prospect's folder.

When a prospect becomes a client, I move their folder from the Prospects folder to the Clients folder. If I turn them down or they just go away, their folder is put into the Duds folder.

Some folders inside my main DPF folder have many more subfolders than the Prospects folder. For example, the Clients folder has a subfolder for each active client, and a subfolder for Inactives. I use the first four letters of the client's company name as an abbreviation which is easier to read than using their full names. (FactorFox also uses this convention in naming schedules.) Thus the Clients folder's subfolders look like this:

- Clients
  - 1STC
  - ACLE
  - AFFI
  - AGUI

- o BRAN
- o BUGS
- o CART
- o EAST
- o …etc.
- o zzInactives

I've forced Inactives to the bottom of the list by putting "zz" before its name. That way I can find that folder quickly – it's always last. When a client becomes inactive, at the beginning of the year after deactivation they are moved to the Inactive folder. Thus the Inactives folder has multiple subfolders of all the inactive clients:

- zzInactives
  - o ABOV
  - o ACTI
  - o BRYC
  - o BUDG
  - o CALI
  - o CLEA
  - o …etc.

Inside each client's folder I keep everything important regarding that client: application form, underwriting credit reports on the client, UCC filing, PDF copies of their signed contract, signed NOAs from their customers, and anything else significant. Having everything in one central place for each client makes finding their important documents very easy.

Two other folders Veronica, Anne and I are into constantly are the Daily Invoices and Daily Receipts folders. Each has subfolders of each year's transactions:

- Daily Invoices
  - o 2010
  - o 2011
  - o 2012

Each year's subfolder includes all the PDF files of each client's schedules and invoices they factored that year, organized by client. Thus, 2012's subfolder looks like this:

- 2012
  - 1STC Invoices 2012
  - ACLE Invoices 2012
  - AFFI Invoices 2012
  - AGUI Invoices 2012
  - BRAN Invoices 2012
  - CART Invoices 2012
  - ...etc.

Within each client's subfolder, the schedule and invoice PDF files are entered for clients who don't factor too often. So for the not too active client CART, all his PDF files just go into his yearly file:

- CART Invoices 2012
  - CART Invoices 2012.02.17 Sched 001.pdf
  - CART Invoices 2012.04.03 Sched 002.pdf
  - CART Invoices 2012.07.22 Sched 003.pdf
  - CART Invoices 2012.08.30 Sched 004.pdf
  - CART Invoices 2012.11.10 Sched 005.pdf

For more active clients, the schedules and invoice PDF files are placed in subfolders by quarter. The quarterly subfolders for the more active client ACLE looks like this:

- ACLE Invoices 2012
  - 1Q ACLE Invoices 2012
  - 2Q ACLE Invoices 2012
  - 3Q ACLE Invoices 2012
  - 4Q ACLE Invoices 2012

Inside ACLE's 2Q subfolder are the PDF files of schedules with invoices factored that quarter:

- 2Q ACLE Invoices 2012
  - ACLE Invoices 2012.04.17 Sched 017.pdf
  - ACLE Invoices 2012.04.29 Sched 018.pdf
  - ACLE Invoices 2012.05.12 Sched 019.pdf
  - ACLE Invoices 2012.06.15 Sched 020.pdf

A very active client has monthly subfolders inside his quarterly folders, and the PDF schedules and invoices files are placed in each month:

- 3Q SWEE Invoices 2012
  - o 2012.07 SWEE Invoices
  - o 2012.08 SWEE Invoices
  - o 2012.09 SWEE Invoices

→ - 12.07 SWEE Invoices
  - o SWEE Invoices 2012.07.08 Sched 122.pdf
  - o SWEE Invoices 2012.07.12 Sched 123.pdf
  - o SWEE Invoices 2012.07.18 Sched 124.pdf
  - o SWEE Invoices 2012.07.24 Sched 125.pdf
  - o SWEE Invoices 2012.07.29 Sched 126.pdf

Thus, the folder tree for the schedules and invoices of a not very active client like CART looks like this:

DPF
- Daily Invoices
  - o 2012
    - o CART Invoices 2012
      - o CART Invoices 2012.02.17 Sched 001.pdf

The more active client ACLE's folder tree looks like this:

- Daily Invoices
  - o 2012
    - o ACLE Invoices 2012
      - o 2Q ACLE Invoices 2012
        - o ACLE Invoices 2012.04.17 Sched 017.pdf

The very active client SWEE's folder tree looks like this:

- Daily Invoices
  - o 2012
    - o SWEE Invoices 2012
      - o 3Q SWEE Invoices 2012
        - o 2012.07 SWEE Invoices
          - o SWEE Invoices 2012.07.08 Sched 122.pdf

Like the Daily Invoices folder, the Daily Receipts folder also has many subfolders. Copies of every lockbox daily report and the day's check copies are organized much like the Daily

Invoices folders, but the years include a division between Bank Receipts and Client Receipts:

DPF
- Daily Receipts
  - 2011 Bank Receipts
  - 2011 Client Receipts
  - 2012 Bank Receipts
  - 2012 Client Receipts

The Bank Receipts folders contain a PDF copy of the daily lockbox report plus all the check and stub copies from the lockbox for the day.

The Client Receipts folders contain a PDF copy of the daily lockbox report only, without the check and stub copies. Since some of the PDF check and stub copies' files can be rather large, I omit the check and stub copies from the Client Receipts folder to save disk space. If I see a client received a payment on a particular day and want to see the check and stub, I can find it in that day's Bank Receipts folder.

Inside a year's Bank Receipts folder, the first subfolders are for each month of the year:

- 2012 Bank Receipts
  - Bank Receipts 2012.01
  - Bank Receipts 2012.02
  - Bank Receipts 2012.03
  - Bank Receipts 2012.04
  - Bank Receipts 2012.05
  - Bank Receipts 2012.06
  - ...etc.

Within a month's folder are the daily PDF files of each day's deposit:

- Bank Receipts 2012.06
  - Bank Receipts 2012.06.01.pdf
  - Bank Receipts 2012.06.02.pdf
  - Bank Receipts 2012.06.03.pdf
  - Bank Receipts 2012.06.04.pdf
  - ...etc.

Inside a year's Client Receipts folder, the subfolders are for each client:

- 2012 Client Receipts
  - o 1STC Receipts 2012
  - o ACLE Receipts 2012
  - o AFFI Receipts 2012
  - o AGUI Receipts 2012
  - o BRAN Receipts 2012
  - o CART Receipts 2012

Each client's Receipts folder is broken down as is done with Daily Invoices folder – for clients who aren't very active, all their daily receipts go in their year's receipts folder. If a client is more active, quarterly folders are next, into which the daily PDF files are put. For very active clients, monthly folders are provided into which their daily receipts PDF files are placed.

22

A Sample Factoring Transaction

Gina's Sheening Cleaning

Let's walk through a sample factoring transaction, from start to finish, using all the due diligence, setup documents, and other tools now at our disposal. We'll use a sample client – Gina's Sheening Cleaning, a fictional company that cleans commercial office buildings. The company is owned by Gina Steening.

Gina hears about you from an associate, Lacey Washington, who recommended you because you are factoring her receivables and she is happy with the service you provide. (You spent a lot to find Lacey, and that is finally beginning to pay off! She'll also enjoy the finder's fee you pay.)

You talk with Gina on the phone and learn she cleans for a local restaurant, a retail store, a couple of medical offices, and a real estate office. Her business has grown steadily and she is having trouble meeting weekly payroll because her customers take 30 - 45 days to pay. She has been in business for only a year, the banks won't help her, and you hear a note of concern in her voice that her success may swamp her young company.

She has learned more about your factoring service from your website and completed the online application. Her customers have good credit, you have found no red flags on public records searches, and you have approved her as a client.

She has signed your contract documents, you have created her account in FactorFox, and you're training her to enter her first schedule there. You follow these steps as outlined on the Transaction Flowchart below:

1. Receive the Schedule of Accounts (see below) and invoice/s (or create the invoice/s within FactorFox), and the Notice of Assignment letter/s from customers as needed (see below).

2. Make sure the customer/s, invoice number/s, and invoice amount/s are accurately entered on the Schedule.

3. If errors or omissions are found, notify the client.

4. Verify the invoices with the customers using a signed invoice or making a phone call. Record the information gathered on the Verification form.

5-6. If there is a problem with the goods/services, notify the client.

7. Be sure your company name and address are on the invoices before they are sent to the customer.

8. Advance funds for the Schedule. Reference the Schedule number. (E.g., GINA-0001 refers to Schedule of Accounts #1 for her. Advance funds via ACH, wire, or check. This starts the clock for calculating your discount.

9. Now you simply wait to receive payment on the invoices, keeping an eye on the aging and a slow payment flag for this transaction.

10.-11. If a problem surfaces or recourse is looming, notify the client. If the customer is slower paying than usual, make a follow-up call saying you manage the receivables for this client and "want to be sure they received the invoice" or that you are "checking on payment status." Log the date, time, person's name, and what she said.

12-13. When payment arrives (see sample customer check below), verify its accuracy and notify the client if the amount received is significantly different from the invoice amount. If acceptable, the clock stops for your discount calculation.

14. Deposit the check and enter the receipt information in FactorFox. The Discount and Rebate Due for each invoice are calculated automatically in FactorFox.

If you're using a spreadsheet, the formula for calculating your discount is:

Discount Amt = Invoice Amt x Discount % Rate.

The formula for calculating the rebate is:

Rebate = Amt Recd – (Adv Amt + Discount Amt + Adjustments [Fees]).

Enter the deposit record into your filing system. If using spreadsheets, transfer the receipt with its splits (advance, rebate, discount, and broker commission) into your bookkeeping program. (This is done automatically in FactorFox.)

15.-17. If a rebate is due, pay the client. Clients are always glad to get this! Give the client an updated copy of the Factoring Record with it (unnecessary with FactorFox). If this client was introduced to you by a broker, client, or other person, calculate commission due and pay according to your agreement.

18. Thank your client for the business and ask if she knows when and about how much the next Schedule will be. Keep her thinking ahead...with you in mind. Every so often, remind her you give finder's fees when she refers you to someone who becomes your client.

Remember, the first couple of Schedules will be the slowest with each client, so be somewhat flexible yet clear as to what you need to make everything go smoothly. After a client has done a few Schedules, you'll both get into a groove and factoring will become an easy, and hopefully pleasant, relationship for everyone involved.

Transaction Flowchart

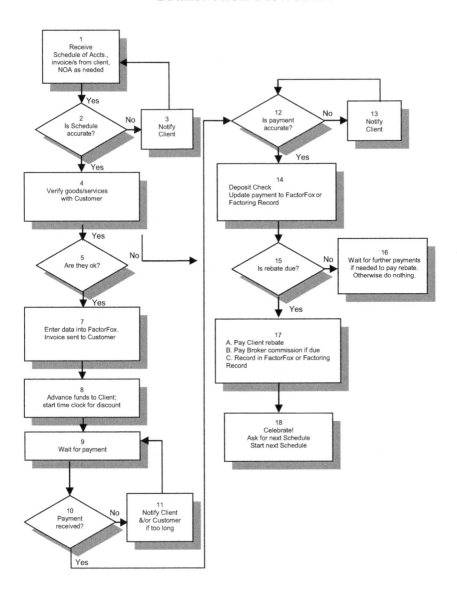

Completed Schedule of Accounts

<table>
<tr><td colspan="6">Schedule of Accounts</td><td>11/01/12</td></tr>
<tr><td colspan="7">ABC Financial Services</td></tr>
<tr><td colspan="7">Gina's Sheening Cleaning</td></tr>
</table>

Schedule Number GINA-0001

	Customer	Invoice #	PO #	Invoice Date	Invoice Amount
1	Golden Valley Real Estate	1050		11/01/12	2,000.00
2	Good Grub Restaurant	1051		11/01/12	4,000.00
3	Creaky Joints Chiropractic Clinic	1052		11/01/12	2,000.00
4	Stressless Dresses Boutique	1053		11/01/12	1,000.00

This is to certify that the parties that the parties named above are indebted to the undersigned in the sums set opposite their respective names, for merchandise sold and delivered or for work and labor done and accepted.

The undersigned hereby sells, assigns and transfers all of its right, title and interest in the above listed accounts receivable ("Invoices") to ABC Financial Services pursuant to that certain Accounts Receivable Purchase Agreement between the undersigned and ABC Financial Services.

Total	**9,000.00**
Advances	7,200.00
Escrow	450.00
Discount	0.00
Adjustments	0.00
Net Advance	**6,750.00**

Payment Type	ACH
Payment Date	11/01/12

Submission Date: 11/01/12

Company: **Gina's Sheening Cleaning**

Signature: *Gina Steening*

Name/Title: **Gina Steening, President**

ABC Financial Services
PO Box 9999
Seattle, WA 98100
206 999 0000

FactorFox
Schedule of Accounts
Page 1 of 1

Notice the Schedule is signed by the client, making the assignment valid.

Completed Notice of Assignment

ABC Financial Services
PO Box 9999
Seattle, WA 98100
206 999 0000
206 999 0001 Fax

October 31, 2012

Attention: Accounts Payable
Good Grub Restaurant
1010 Pubhub Road
Seattle, WA 908100

Notice of Assignment and Change of Payee

We are pleased to inform you we have established a working relationship that provides Gina's Sheening Cleaning with a working capital line of credit. These funds will enable further growth and expansion from which Gina's Sheening Cleaning and their customers will benefit, both now and in the future. Accordingly, Gina's Sheening Cleaning has assigned all present and future Accounts Receivable with your company to ABC Financial Services.

To the extent that you are now indebted, or may in the future become indebted to Gina's Sheening Cleaning on an account, payment thereof must be made payable to ABC Financial Services and not to Gina's Sheening Cleaning or any other entity.

This letter hereby instructs you to remit your payment of all invoices from Gina's Sheening Cleaning directly to ABC Financial Services, and to continue to do so until notified otherwise by ABC Financial Services. Payments made to any party except ABC Financial Services will not relieve your obligation for Accounts Payables due Gina's Sheening Cleaning and will expose you to multiple liability. This notice may not be revoked except in writing by an officer of ABC Financial Services.

Please make your checks payable to, and send them to:

ABC Financial Services FBO Gina's Sheening Cleaning
P.O. Box 9999
Seattle, WA 98100

Your cooperation is appreciated. Please make the needed changes in your Accounts Payable system and keep a copy of this letter for your records.

Should you have any questions concerning this letter, please call ABC Financial services at 206 999-0000 or Gina Steening, President, Gina's Sheening Cleaning at 206 333-4444.

Sincerely,

Joe Factor

Joe Factor
President
ABC Financial Services

Gina Steening

Gina Steening
President
Gina's Sheening Cleaning

Received and acknowledged by <u>Good Grub Restaurant</u>, customer of Gina's Sheening Cleaning:

Signature: _____*Betty Beetle*_____

Print Name: _____Betty Beetle_____

Title: _____Manager_____

Date: _____November, 1, 2012_____

The Notice of Assignment has been signed and returned by the customer. When you verified the invoice with Betty, you also made sure she has changed Gina's remittance address in her system and will send all checks directly to you.

Invoice Included on Schedule

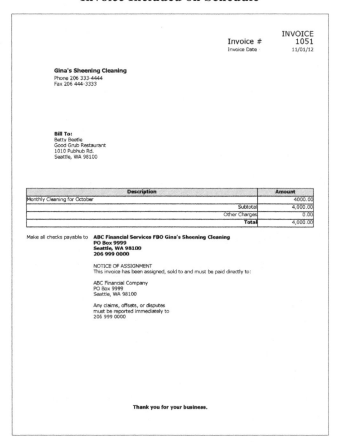

Above is an invoice on schedule GINA-0001, whose NOA was received and shown on the previous page. Note the proper assignment wording; also the client's address is not on the invoice – only yours.

Invoice Verification

▶ Customer

Customer: **Good Grub Restaurant**	Invoice Status: Approved
Phone: 206 111-2222	Verification Complete: Yes
Contact Person: **Betty Beetle**	
Other Contact:	

▶ Invoice

Client: Gina's Sheening Cleaning	Invoice Date: 11/01/12
Invoice #: 1051	PO #:
Amount: $4,000.00	

▶ Phone

Date of Call 11/01/12	Time of Call 09:30 AM
Talked To Betty Beetle	

▶ Written

- [ ] Letter
- [ ] Invoice
- [ ] Invoice Acknowledgment Form
- [ ] Other [　　　　　　　　　　]
- [ ] Bill of Lading
- [ ] PO
- [ ] Rate Confirmation

▶ Product

Did you order the goods? ○ Yes ○ No	Have you received the goods? ○ Yes ○ No
Have you inspected the goods? ○ Yes ○ No	Are the goods satisfactory? ○ Yes ○ No

▶ Service

Was the service performed? ● Yes ○ No	Are you satisfied with the service? ● Yes ○ No

Notes

[　　　　　　　　　　　　　　　　　　　　　]

The factor has verified the invoice with the customer and recorded the verification information on this form. The staff person making the verification, date and time of the verification, and record of the customer's comment and approval, are shown.

Assuming the same preparations have been done with the other invoices on this schedule, everything is now in place to pay Gina her advance.

Factor's Advance to Client

ABC Financial Services		5035
PO Box 99999		
Seattle, WA 98100		November 1, 2012
Pay to the		
Order of	Gina's Sheening Cleaning	$ 6,750.00
	Six thousand seven hundred fifty and 00/100	Dollars
For	GINA-0001 advance	*Joe Factor*
		NON-negotiable

If the factor pays the advance with a check it would look like this. If paid via ACH or wire, the factor would have a record of the transfer from the bank.

Now that the schedule has been approved and the advance sent, the Factoring Record showing Gina's first schedule looks like this:

Factoring Record after the Advance Is Paid

Factoring Record
Gina's Sheening Cleaning

			All Invoices
			11/1/2012
Invoices:	9,000.00	Credit Line:	10,000.00
Advances:	7,200.00	Credit Used:	9,000.00
Adv. Adjustments:	0.00	Credit Available:	1,000.00
Discounts:	450.00	Invoice Count:	4
Rebate Paid:	0.00	Escrow Reserve:	450.00

GINA-0001

Customer	Inv #	Inv Date	Inv Amt	Adv Amt	Adv Adj.	Net Adv	Date Adv Pd	Days From Inv	Adv	Discnt %	Discnt	Escr	Date Pmt Rcd	Amt
Golden Valley	1050	11/01/12	2,000.00	1,600.00	0.00	1,500.00	11/01/12	0	0	5.00	100.00	100.00		
Good Grub	1051	11/01/12	4,000.00	3,200.00	0.00	3,000.00	11/01/12	0	0	5.00	200.00	200.00		
Creaky Joint	1052	11/01/12	2,000.00	1,600.00	0.00	1,500.00	11/01/12	0	0	5.00	100.00	100.00		
Stressless	1053	11/01/12	1,000.00	800.00	0.00	750.00	11/01/12	0	0	5.00	50.00	50.00		
			9,000.00	7,200.00	0.00	6,750.00					450.00	450.00		

ABC Financial Services
PO Box 9999
Seattle, WA 98100
206 999 0000

FactorFox

Many weeks later the customer pays the invoice with the following check.

Customer's Payment Check to Factor

Good Grub Restaurant	384525
1010 Pubhub Drive	
Seattle, WA 98200	December 18, 2012

Pay to the   ABC Financial Services
Order of   FBO Gina's Sheening Cleaning | $ 4,000.00

Four thousand and 00/100 ... ... **Dollars**

For   Invoice 1051   *Betty Beetle*

NON-negotiable

The factor receives the customer's check, then pays Gina her rebate. If paid with a check it would look like this.

Factor's Rebate Payment

ABC Financial Services	5062
PO Box 99999	
Seattle, WA 98100	December 27, 2012

Pay to the
Order of   Gina's Sheening Cleaning | $ 400.00

Four hundred and 00/100 ... ... **Dollars**

For   Inv 1051 rebate   *Joe Factor*

NON-negotiable

If paid via ACH or wire, the factor would have a record of the transfer from the bank.

The next Factoring Record shows this rebate as being paid 12/27. Shortly after that Gina submitted her third schedule. Both the second and third schedules, as well as other receipts and rebates, now show on the Factoring Record:

Updated Factoring Record

Factoring Record
Gina's Sheening Cleaning

Invoices:	28,000.00	
Advances:	22,400.00	
Adv. Adjustments:	0.00	
Discounts:	950.00	
Rebate Paid:	2,250.00	

		All Invoices
Credit Line:	15,000.00	1/4/2013
Credit Used:	14,000.00	
Credit Available:	1,000.00	
Invoice Count:	12	
Escrow Reserve:	1,500.00	

Customer	Inv #	Inv Date	Inv Amt	Adv Amt	Adv Adj.	Net Adv	Date Adv Pd	Days from Date of Inv	Adv	Discnt %	Discnt	Escr	Date Pmt Rcd	Amt Rcd	Rebate	Rebate Pd	Date Rebt Pd
GINA-0001																	
Golden Valley	1050	11/01/12	2,000.00	1,600.00	0.00	1,500.00	11/01/12	17	17	5.00	0.00	100.00	11/18/12	1,500.00	100.00	100.00	
Good Grub	1051	11/01/12	4,000.00	3,200.00	0.00	3,000.00	11/01/12	49	49	10.00	0.00	200.00	12/20/12	4,000.00	800.00	800.00	12/27/12
Creaky Joint	1052	11/01/12	2,000.00	1,600.00	0.00	1,500.00	11/01/12	39	39	7.50	0.00	100.00	12/10/12	2,000.00	400.00	400.00	12/12/12
Stressless	1053	11/01/12	1,000.00	800.00	0.00	750.00	11/01/12	32	32	7.50	0.00	50.00	12/03/12	1,000.00	200.00	200.00	12/12/12
			9,000.00	7,200.00	0.00	6,750.00					0.00	450.00		8,600.00	1,500.00	1,500.00	
GINA-0002																	
Good Grub	1054	12/03/12	4,000.00	3,200.00	0.00	3,000.00	12/04/12	26	25	5.00	200.00	200.00	12/29/12	4,000.00	600.00	600.00	01/04/13
Creaky Joint	1055	12/03/12	2,000.00	1,600.00	0.00	1,500.00	12/04/12	31	30	5.00	100.00	100.00	12/31/12	1,000.00	150.00	150.00	01/04/13
Stressless	1056	12/03/12	1,000.00	800.00	0.00	750.00	12/04/12	28	27	5.00	50.00	50.00	12/31/12				
			7,000.00	5,600.00	0.00	5,250.00					350.00	350.00		5,000.00	750.00	750.00	
GINA-0003																	
Good Grub	1057	01/03/13	4,000.00	3,200.00	0.00	3,000.00	01/04/13	1	0	5.00	200.00	200.00					
Creaky Joint	1058	01/03/13	2,000.00	1,600.00	0.00	1,500.00	01/04/13	1	0	5.00	100.00	100.00					
Stressless	1059	01/03/13	1,000.00	800.00	0.00	750.00	01/04/13	1	0	5.00	50.00	50.00					
Flean Jim's Gym	1060	01/03/13	2,000.00	1,600.00	0.00	1,500.00	01/04/13	1	0	5.00	100.00	100.00					
Hyper Day Care	1061	01/03/13	3,000.00	2,400.00	0.00	2,250.00	01/04/13	1	0	5.00	150.00	150.00					
			12,000.00	9,600.00	0.00	9,000.00					600.00	600.00		0.00	0.00	0.00	

FactorFox

320

Part 6

Reinforcements

23
Additional Resources

This final chapter provides more resources to help your small factoring business. We'll start with three true stories mentioned elsewhere in this book that teach poignant and illustrative lessons for smaller factors. These are followed with more detailed information about the International Factoring Association, a website for my web-based training program, periodicals and websites of interest to smaller factors, and other books and ebooks available.

Three True Stories for Small Factors

✛ ✛ ✛

A Small Factor's Thoughts about Big Factors' Concerns

Some time ago I attended Bob Zadek's Lenders' Podium conference on "The Law & Business of Factoring" in San Francisco. This was my first experience in person with Mr. Zadek, who, true to form, is entertaining, witty, and extremely knowledgeable about factoring law. He is also full of very helpful and practical suggestions about how to run a factoring operation.

For the most part those in attendance were from banks and larger factoring companies. This is Mr. Zadek's audience, and understanding that helped me appreciate even more the value of being a small factor. Compared to factors who fund larger companies with bigger volumes (and with them, much higher stakes), I factor especially small companies with very low volume.

Being an attorney, much of Mr. Zadek's presentation focused on the legal documents and procedures larger factoring operations need to utilize to minimize their risk. He told many stories of factors having problems collecting, and how the documents he provides stand up in court and protect his clients, the factors. When factors have hundreds of thousands of dollars at stake in a single client, litigation is usually the only means of recouping lost money. However, such factors can easily end up paying $50,000 in legal fees to recover a $500,000 debt they are owed. That kind of expense is not only within their means, but worth spending to recover such a large potential loss.

As I sat there considering transactions with so many zeros, I realized how my operation is in a whole different league than those of the folks sitting around me. If this were baseball, I'd be playing in a B League, while they're in AAA or the Majors. Like most medium-sized and larger factors, these people have no interest in clients factoring $10k per month. They commonly factor $100,000 - $2,000,000 each month per client. And at that level, they'd certainly *better* have good legal documents and counsel.

Many of my clients factor around $15-20k per month; several others are under $10k. Considering my comparatively humble portfolio, I felt a sense of relief throughout the conference. I was relieved that once my clients need to factor more than $50k-$60k per month, I usually pass them on to a larger factor.

By limiting my exposure in this way, I will never go to court to try to recover $500,000 from any client. I will never need to spend $50,000 to *try* to recover an amount of money that would devastate my company if it were uncollectible. In fact, as long as most of my clients remain near or under $50k per month, I'll probably never go to court in the first place.

If I'm owed $5,000 or $10,000 and need to spend that much in attorney fees to collect, there's no sense in going to court at all. It's far wiser to simply hand an account over to collections and if necessary take the bad debt write off, and move on. I won't like it, but my business will easily survive and I won't waste an inordinate amount of time, energy, stress, and money trying to collect.

The most unpleasant aspect of factoring, to my thinking, is trying to collect from clients or customers who have become unresponsive and elusive. If you run your operation properly and efficiently, the time you spend doing that will be minimal. Therefore, like larger factors, we small factors cannot be sloppy with our setup documents or lackadaisical in our due diligence and follow up. Either is a surefire blueprint for losing money.

Our clients must understand there can be ramifications and unpleasant results if they intentionally try to defraud us. However, if we small factors are minding the store and don't take on more clients than we can efficiently manage, or dollar volumes than we can't afford, the war stories Mr. Zadek tells will not be ours.

Small factors with aspirations of dealing with larger clients and larger volumes need to realize the headaches and dangers that go with that territory. As for me, I'm happy not going anywhere near there. For example, one story Bob told was of an attempted intentional fraud.

This client was phony from the get-go and tried to factor seven customers on his first funding. This guy actually set up seven fax machines with seven different phone numbers, one for each of his "customers" who were very large corporations like Coca-Cola. When the factor faxed the Notice of Assignment letters to these customers, the crook made a very simple but stupid mistake. Upon receiving the letters, he signed and immediately faxed them right back to the factor. Apparently he figured by doing this he would get his advance – over $200,000 – that much faster.

Fortunately the experienced factor smelled a rat. Never in his experience had Notices of Assignment been returned so quickly, especially seven in a row. Most take several hours, often days, to receive. Calls were made to the customers, none of whom had ever heard of this client, and the plot was thwarted.

Small factors are vulnerable to fraud, as are larger factors. However, if we limit our client volumes and advances to quite small amounts, crooks will not be as likely go to the extremes with us this one did, because the money they'd be trying to steal from us isn't worth the effort. I can't imagine a crook going to the trouble of setting up seven phone lines and fax machines to rip me off for a few thousand dollars. Even if he did and got away with it, that kind of loss is not going to put me out of business. It'll make me mad and fume, but at the end of the day the loss will not be catastrophic to the survival of my company.

After hearing a story like this, we may think that fraud is a factor's greatest danger. We may assume that avoiding large-scale fraud by factoring small receivables will protect us little guys from huge losses. Well…yes and no. True, we cannot be defrauded for hundreds of thousands of dollars – but we can still lose plenty of money, whether by fraud, client mismanagement, or a number of other causes.

The greatest risk factors of *any* size face is not fraud: it is over concentration. Factors with too much of their capital invested in any one client, customer, or even invoice run the risk of serious or even catastrophic loss.

Most of the factoring companies of any size who go out of business do so because they take a hit from a client or customer in whom they are over concentrated. If you intentionally limit the size of your client and customer credit limits, and the size of invoices you buy – and most important, *abide* by those limits – your chances of a catastrophic loss are diminished to nearly zero. Yet we often hear of factors taking big hits and going out of business. It happens all the time. A large factor who had been in business for many years, took a $4 million dollar loss and went out of business. It happens to the best of them.

Whatever you do, no matter what size your operation is, avoid over concentrations. Don't invest more than you can afford to lose in any client, customer, or invoice. That simple procedure does not cost a penny, yet it can save you thousands upon thousands of dollars – and even save your company.

If you ever have the opportunity to hear Bob Zadek speak you should do so, regardless of the size of your factoring operation. And if you are thinking about graduating to larger clients and receivables at some time in the future, his seminars and legal documents are well worth every penny you pay for them.

Realize that in the bigger league of six and seven-figure transactions, risks are involved that go well beyond the scope of the material you'll find in this book and other materials from Dash Point Publishing. This material is written for small factors who do not factor large volumes. If you intend to enter those deeper waters, you need financial capability, adequate legal representation from someone like Bob Zadek – and the stomach for the risks involved with transactions involving a lot of zeros.

Personally, I like working with little guys. They suit me just fine. I also like the idea of never paying five figures in legal fees.

+ + +

A True Story about ACH Transfers and Bankers

Quite some time ago when I paid clients with checks, a prospective client from another state asked if I could make ACH deposits into his account instead of sending a bank wire or an overnight check. At that point all I knew about ACH was that it stood for "Automated Clearing House," and that it was a common method for companies to directly deposit payday checks into employees' bank accounts, rather than handing out paychecks. It was an electronic transfer of funds from one bank account to another.

His request led to an education about bankers for me.

As I thought about this alternative means of transferring factoring funds, I saw its advantages. Up to that time I had been providing funds the traditional ways – using FedEx, wiring funds, or depositing a distant client's advance or rebate check in a local branch if there was one near me. The first two were fairly expensive for the client (I charge $20 for either, plus the client pays to receive a bank wire on the other end). Depositing checks in local branches was time consuming: filling out checks, endorsing them, preparing deposit slips, driving to the various branches, waiting in line, and finally driving back home. The more clients I funded that used other banks, the longer this was taking.

Using ACH seemed like an excellent idea and a much better alternative to the time consuming process of check writing. In fact it seemed like a practically free bank wire. Certainly my large national bank, whom I'd been with for nearly 10 years, would have no problem allowing me – a *stellar* customer – to use this (I assumed simply alternative) means of transferring funds to my clients' accounts. It's just like writing a check, only done electronically. Right?

Wrong.

"Our local branches don't handle ACH account requests," I was sweetly (but ominously) told. "You need to apply for this through the online banking center." I didn't like the sound of the words "apply for." I just wanted an easier way to get money to my clients. Why would I need to "apply for" that? What's more, going elsewhere within Big National Bank meant I lost the friendly and familiar smiles of all the tellers I knew so well. Undaunted in my ignorance, I moved forward.

I applied online for ACH as instructed, and after waiting several days received this reply: "Our Business Risk Management Center is unable to approve your request at this time." End of online message.

I couldn't believe it and called the cheerful young voice for online banking questions. She confirmed my rejection. "But…" I stammered, "I've been a customer here 10 years! I've had all my business accounts, personal accounts, my kids' accounts, and home mortgage with you all this time! I'm one of your best customers!" "I'm sorry," she said, "but there is risk involved for the bank with ACH transfers."

Risk? *I'm a risk* to this bank?! In all my accounts of 10 years' standing, when I've never bounced a single check or been a day late with any mortgage payments, *I'm a risk?* Do you know who you're talking to, sister?

No she didn't. And frankly, she didn't care.

"Ok," I reasoned. "I'm a reasonable guy. Maybe I asked for too large of a line." (When you apply for this, you request a daily limit, up to which you can transfer in and out of your account.) "I'll pare my request down considerably. Maybe this will make my account's 'risk' seem less…risky." After all, my application was being reviewed by Big National Bank's "Business Risk Management Center," wherever the heck that was. Certainly not in my local branch. These people would certainly have an eagle eye for risk.

So I reapplied, submitting more documents this time like I was directed. I waited *two weeks* this time and didn't hear anything. And still didn't hear anything. So finally I called this young woman, who was the only contact I had with online banking, which was the only means to this service I had come to believe would save me many hours of time each week. When she answered the phone, I asked if my account had been approved this time.

"Oh," she said. "That just came in today. I'm sorry to say your request was declined." *WHAT?!?* Again?! *"Why?"* I choked. I couldn't believe what I was hearing. "I don't know, sir. I'm not the decision maker. I can only tell you what the decision is."

"Yeah, but does this decision maker know I've been a perfect customer for this bank for as long as I have?" ("…Probably since you were running around a grade school playground at recess." – I thought, but fortunately didn't say.)

"I don't know, sir," was her (mantra-like) answer. "But there is risk to the bank with this service." Being told yet again that I posed a risk scorched what little composure I had left. I lost my cool.

"This is bull*!!" I unfortunately blurted out. No answer. "I guess your bank wants a loyal customer of 10 years, who has brought many clients as new accounts, to take his business elsewhere."

Silence. Finally she replied, "I guess that's your choice, sir."

Yeah, right. My choice. You little grade school Hatchet Girl. My youngest kid is older than you and you just told me I have to make major changes to my way of doing business, to my banking practices, that I'll have to change all my automatic and online and credit card payments, that this will affect most of my clients' bank accounts, and…I was getting really *mad* now. In fact I was mad enough to change banks right then and there. "This is bull*!" I repeated and slammed down the phone.

Now mind you, I'm usually a pretty calm, easy-going person. Most people who know me describe me as "a real nice guy." I've only lost my composure like this one other time in the last 12 years that I can remember. Even when I do get mad, I practically never swear at people. Especially young women who just 10 years ago were running around the grade school playground at recess. But this time, I was steamed.

"What's the matter with these morons at Big National Bank?" I wondered. Then I realized, "You know what? This is *exactly* the ringer banks put most people through when they apply for a small business loan. This is what they've been through when they reach the end of their rope and finally call a factor." Hmmmm. "Only I didn't go through this to *borrow* money," I reasoned to myself. "I don't want to *sell* my invoices. I *buy* invoices."

But that fact meant absolutely nothing to Hatchet Girl or Anonymous Loan Officer at the Business Risk Management Center, wherever that was.

I quickly took this insult to my self-respect as a bank customer, and affront to my dignity as a factor, as a challenge. "By God, I'm a *funding source*. People come to *me* for money. If these idiots who've banked my money for 10 years don't want my business any more, who does?"

Immediately I thought of the manager of a nearby regional bank whom I'd met at a networking group about a year before. She'd referred a couple factoring deals to me since then, and each time made it clear she'd love to have my banking business... but moving banks had always seemed more trouble than it was worth. Until this moment.

I picked up the phone and called. "Linda, does your bank offer ACH transfers?" "Yes we do." "Will I be approved for them if I apply?" I was learning the terminology. "Why don't you come in and we'll see," she answered.

So I went in a couple days later. Now that I had calmed down since my conversation with Hatchet Girl, I asked, "What is this big risk I pose to a bank by wanting to do this? I just want an alternative to writing checks."

She replied, "ACH is an electronic transfer using the bank's money. These transfers are made through the Federal Reserve Bank and go directly from our bank to your client's bank. That means you're transferring money with no float and the transfer of funds is immediate. You could transfer funds you don't have in your account, and disappear the next day. Therefore the bank looks upon this daily transfer as a loan for which you must qualify. You need to meet the requirements for a loan: business financials, tax returns, personal credit report, the whole bit."

Ok, that explained the reluctance of Big National Bank's Business Risk Management Center, wherever that was. Even though I saw this as just a different way of writing checks, the Anonymous Loan Officer at the Business Risk Management Center saw it as a loan for which I didn't qualify. That made me a risk despite my 10-year perfect multiple checking accounts history and 100% on-time mortgage payments. The Anonymous Loan Officer probably didn't even know about those. If he did, he certainly didn't care.

So I applied with Small Regional Bank not only for ACH transfers, but – what the heck – I'll throw in a request for a small line of credit while I'm at it. It's done on the same form, besides. Linda quietly took my information and submitted my request, then I waited a few days.

I was turned down again.

At least this time the loan officer from Small Regional Bank had the decency to call me. She told me her name was Janet, asked several questions about my business and experience – and even about the factoring books I've written – and then turned me down herself.

As this (sickening) conversation ended, I asked what would happen if I just requested the minimum daily ACH transfer possible, $10k per day – and dropped the line of credit request. She said she'd need to see more documentation. I agreed, prepared what she wanted (and threw in two of my books for good measure), and took them to the branch the next day.

Now…here comes the part you need to understand about banks and how they operate. A couple months earlier, Dave, my personal banker at Big National Bank, had left his position there. I was sorry to see him go as he had helped me several times in the past. In a remarkable coincidence, Dave had just started working for Small Regional Bank – right here at my neighborhood branch, no less. He knew my long history at Big National Bank, that I was a good customer, and even that I was a decent human being…which I was beginning to doubt, with all this rejection I'd just experienced.

I gave him the requested paperwork along with the books. He asked if I wanted Janet to give the books back when she finished them. "If she turns me down again, yes," I said with a chuckle (but was actually dead serious).

Then I asked him to put in a good word for me with Janet. "Dave, you know I'm not going to abuse this. You know what kind of a bank customer I am. I just want to save myself a lot of time by making electronic transfers from my computer, instead running all over town making deposits for clients." He nodded in understanding.

Then, curious about all these loan refusals which were taking their toll on my self-esteem, I asked Dave what the real problem was here. He said that banks typically look for a 3 to 1 ratio with these types of transactions. That is, for every dollar you want to "borrow" – in this case, that I want to send in daily ACH transfers – the loan officer wants to see 3 dollars in your account and/or as equity on your balance sheet. My company was too highly leveraged (translate: I didn't have enough cash on hand or equity on my balance sheet) to qualify.

Oh. So that's it. *Now I understand.* My perfect 10 year history meant zilch.

I wondered if Hatchet Girl knew about needed ratios. Had Anonymous Loan Officer at the Business Risk Management Center, wherever that was, ever explained them to her? "No, I doubt it," I thought. "She probably doesn't even know what a ratio is."

I was steeling myself for what I was sure would be a final rejection from Janet. But a few days later she called to say my application was approved. I was both stunned and grateful. I felt like an unworthy yet incredibly fortunate serf who had been bestowed undeserved favor from the Queen Herself. I fought the urge to grovel on the ground and kiss the feet of my benevolent benefactor. And as I hung up the phone, I stepped back momentarily from this image and wondered, "My gosh, what's happening to me?"

The next time I was in the bank, I asked Dave if he had put in a good word for me with Janet. He quietly nodded. And though he didn't say so, the realization hit me: *"That's why I was approved."*

So now I can make electronic ACH bank transfers, at least up to my maximum daily amount, which will save me hours of time. I will no doubt have days when the total needed for transfers will exceed my approved limit; when that happens I'll have to delay some transfers a day or do them the old way. But at least I can make ACH direct deposits. Finally. I feel like a worthy human being again, though humbled by this experience of multiple rejections.

Why have I told this story? There are two lessons here.

First, as a factor needing regular cooperation from your bank, you must understand how banks work. Financial ratios can mean more than your history, especially with large banks in which decisions are made by people far removed from your friendly local branch. And even more, a good word from the right person can change a decision that might otherwise go against you.

Second, when clients come to you, remember that most arrive with their self-esteem bruised and battered by bank rejections, just like mine was. But unlike me, they don't have a Dave to put in a good word for them. Thus they come to you seeking the cash they sorely need but can't get from Big National Bank's Business Risk Management Center, wherever that is. And they've dealt with multiple frustrations from several Hatchet Girls of their own.

So be gentle with them. Do your best to help them. If you can factor their receivables, routinely provide excellent service. If you do, you will appear to be riding in on a white horse and will have their utter loyalty.

And if you decide you want to transfer funds with ACH – which *will* save a lot of time – come armed with a very strong balance sheet and a lot of liquidity. If you don't, be ready for a curt and impersonal rejection – probably from someone who not all that long ago was running around a grade school playground at recess.

Epilogue
A few years later...

After banking with Linda's bank for a couple years, I needed an increase in the daily limit I was allowed for sending ACHs. Again my history with the bank was impeccable and I hoped getting a small increase would be simple and not involve the trauma I experienced a few years before.

I was in for another lesson.

It so happened that a very small client of mine who also banked there had recently converted a few factored checks and became impossible for me to reach. Apparently he pulled a few shady things with the bank as well because during the course of their underwriting my ACH increase request, I was asked what I knew about this client and his business. I thought the question a bit unusual but answered quite honestly.

I said he had been my client for a short time and briefly described what he had done, making it clear I had done nothing wrong: he was dishonest and took my money. I had a small write off from his account and while I wasn't happy with this person, I had moved on and had no financial difficulties whatsoever since his account was quite small. The underwriter thanked me and ended the conversation.

A few days later, Linda called me to give me the news about my ACH increase request. Expecting her cheerful voice saying it was approved, instead her tone was somber. "Jeff, I'm afraid I have some bad news." "They didn't approve it?" I gasped, flabbergasted yet again.

"Well, unfortunately it's worse than that," she slowly replied. "What could be worse than that?" I wondered for a split second. I found out with her next words.

"They have withdrawn your ability to send ACHs." Withdrawn...my ability..."You mean I can't send ACHs at all any more to any client, for any amount?"

"That's correct," she answered quietly. I was speechless. "*Why?!?*" I finally managed. She said, "I don't know. But their decision is final." Feeling as if a knife had pierced my heart, all I could muster was, "You realize this means I can't bank with you anymore." "Yes, I understand that, Jeff. I'm truly sorry."

She *was* sorry, I could tell. While she couldn't give me the reason (if she knew, which I suspected she did), I was sure my association with this shady client spooked the bank. There could be no other reason. Despite the fact I was completely innocent of any wrongdoing and never less than a stellar customer there, I was being shown the door.

The bigger issue to the bank, apparently, was the fact that I was a factor – which some banks consider a high-risk industry. This made me a high-risk customer in their eyes despite my perfect record.

They didn't want me sending "their" money to clients of any size, even ones this small. "How many other dishonest clients does he have?" they probably wondered. Clearly their tolerance for risk here was zero, so their solution was to just cut me off completely, knowing that I'd be forced to take my business elsewhere. That probably suited them just fine.

It certainly didn't seem to bother the underwriter in the slightest; after all, Linda was the one who had to tell me, not he. The higher ups at the bank were clearly most concerned with risk control, not my good record or needs as a customer.

My once friendly Small Regional Bank suddenly felt just like my first Big National Bank – detached, stone cold, and completely indifferent to my banking needs as their once loyal customer.

I immediately began to search for a new bank. After interviewing a few and finding they wouldn't accommodate all my factoring needs, I spoke with a different large national bank who has its own factoring arm that buys the receivables of large clients.

Unlike the other banks with whom I'd spoken, I didn't have to explain factoring as the representative was already familiar with it (how nice for a change!). What's more, being approved for ACHs was much easier here.

The only catch was depositing third party checks at the local branch. They required that I provide a paper copy of the Power of Attorney in my contract when making every branch deposit, which was both a hassle and pretty ridiculous to my thinking. I could picture my daily banking routine: if I deposited ten checks for ten different clients, I'd have to bring copies all ten contracts – every day!) I said surely there must be a better alternative. What about a lockbox?

To my relief, I was told that we could set up a lockbox to accept third party checks just fine, and realizing that my daily drives to the bank were over, I happily agreed. It's been one of the best decisions I've ever made for my factoring business.

I've been with this large bank ever since and have been quite satisfied with their services. Their online banking capabilities are robust and user friendly and I have a personal banker I can call any time. I've learned to lay somewhat low and just quietly run my factoring business without calling attention to my account, and after several years now it has been an excellent relationship. I frequently refer other small factors to this bank.

Final Footnote

I learned later Linda was as frustrated dealing with her own bank as I was, and left for greener pastures shortly after the unpleasant task of giving me her bad news. Clearly I wasn't the only customer she knew who left as a very unhappy camper.

What did Linda do after leaving the bank? To my great satisfaction she started her own small business. Unfortunately she hasn't needed factoring, but she knows where to find me if she ever does.

+ + +

The Secret to Getting Paid
Taught by Alan, the Pit Bull

Some time ago I booked a new client who was referred by a broker. Like many clients, this person has furthered my education in the factoring industry. Most of the small clients I have teach me something, but compared to others, Alan has made a lasting impression. He has shown me how to handle one of the most important issues any factor, large or small, needs to manage: getting paid.

Like most factors, I have had clients – more than I care to tell you – who have given me an education in how NOT to run my (or any) business. Those are the clients who want to bend the rules, who cop payment checks and see nothing wrong with it, or who bounce from one crisis to another like the steel ball in a pinball machine. Such people are just not on top of running their business, let alone keeping track of their receivables.

But Alan is. In fact, he is more than on top of his A/Rs – he's all over them. Like a pit bull. When someone owes his money, he clamps his teeth on their shin and doesn't let go.

Like most businesses who factor, he provides 30 day terms to his customers. He runs a small company with a few employees, and his customers range from small businesses to large corporations that are household names. He spends a lot of time in the field and pretty much runs his business from his cell phone. Yet he watches his receivable payments like a hawk, and if someone is late – even one of the big names – he swoops down on them, talons extended, and doesn't tolerate any excuses.

His philosophy towards his customers is simple: "Before I work for you, we make an agreement. I do a job you need, and you pay me in 30 days. Then I do my job, and you pay when you agreed. If you don't, I'm done working for you."

He is all over his aging reports like white is on paper because he wants to know who's gone past 30 days. He calls every single one at day 31, then he reports back to me when they're going to pay...which is invariably right away.

Is he mean? No. Is he pleasant? Well, not especially. He is **persistent** and **consistent**, which are the keys to dependable, timely payments from creditworthy customers who take longer to pay than they should. If a check is not received a few days after his first call, he calls back and lets them know 1) he hasn't received payment and 2) he is not happy. A check is always received within two weeks of his first call.

I'm sure the payables people know him all too well, and don't want to talk to him. That provides excellent incentive for them to pay his bill right away when they receive it. I doubt his invoice goes to the bottom of their stack, because they don't want a phone call from Alan telling them to do their job. He's not a horrible, nasty person; he just makes it very clear what the terms of his service are, and expects the customers to keep their side of the agreement, just like he has. If they don't, they're done. Period.

For most small factors, collection calls (or whatever you choose to call them) are one of the less pleasant aspects of factoring. Yet they absolutely cannot be overlooked. Your work as a small factor is made immeasurably easier when you have a client like Alan who is not only consistent about following up with slow payers, but tenacious.

I learned some time ago not to rely on most clients to do follow up calls like these; they are too busy, it's not a job they enjoy, and/or their personality is such that being hard-nosed with customers is not in their nature. They are afraid of alienating a customer and losing the business. Most clients are usually more than happy to let you be their collections department, as long as you're professional about it and don't bully their customers.

Professional follow-up calls are one of the most important services you can offer as a small factor. It's also one of the most important tasks you must constantly stay on top of, just like Alan does. Do you need to be nasty? No. Do you need to be persistent and consistent? No question.

I like Alan's approach. He's direct, he lays it out in plain English, and he sticks by his guns. He's confident enough in himself and his business to know if he drops one customer because they don't pay when they should, he'll be able to find another business to replace them. And he does.

Alan's collections are proactive, not reactive. Many clients wring their hands when customers are slow to pay. They treat these customers with kid gloves, and almost apologize when they call a customer to see what's happened to a payment that's 30 or 45 days late. In many cases these hardworking people are being taken advantage of by their customers, who use them as their personal bank. These hesitant clients are not in control of this part of their business.

Alan has provided the model I hold up to them when we talk about collection efforts. I say, "You know, I have another client who is always paid in 45 days or less, and usually less." The others are in awe and want to know his secret. "Simple," I tell them. "Do what he does. Call every customer who hasn't paid you at 35 days, and get the date when your check is going to be cut. If they don't pay according to terms, stop working for them or put them on COD."

Unfortunately many are reluctant to do this. They say they're afraid of losing business or that a huge corporate customer will ignore them or won't keep them as a vendor, which may occasionally be true. But I think more often they just don't want to take the time, or don't want to seem like a hard nose. They're too nice.

Sad to say, when it comes to getting paid being nice is often ineffective. Not that you have to be mean to get paid; just persistent and consistent.

Like Alan, the pit bull – who knows the secret of getting paid.

+ + +

The International Factoring Association

Founded in 1999, the goal of the International Factoring Association (www.factoring.org) is to "assist the factoring community by providing information, training, purchasing power and a resource for the factoring community." It highlights developments and changes in the industry and provides a forum for educational meetings and seminars. IFA members have group buying power in negotiating for goods and services.

Membership is open to all banks and finance companies that, regardless of size, perform financing or factoring through the purchase of invoices or other types of accounts receivable. All members must adhere to the IFA's Code of Ethics found on their site. To join the IFA, download the membership application and submit it via email or fax. You'll need to confirm you are a funding source and not just brokering transactions.

The membership directory, available on the website, lists all members and includes their company information, specialties, and links to their web sites. The database is searchable by Category, State/Province, Country, and Keyword. This allows you to search for factors in a specific industry or areas of the country.

The website's Vendors section lists vendors of interest to the factoring industry including attorneys, UCC search firms, funding sources, factoring software companies, and many more. The Vendor area is also searchable by Category, State/Province, Country, and Keyword. In addition to providing a list of qualified vendors, you will also see IFA Preferred Vendors. These companies offer discounts or preferred services to IFA members.

Member services include IFA's magazine, *The Commercial Factor*, published six times yearly (see below), a website forum, an annual convention, and numerous workshops throughout the year on subjects of interest to factors of any size and niche. Also on the website you'll find a Watch List (entries are made by members about clients or prospects to avoid), which should be routinely checked as part of your underwriting as you consider prospective clients.

Annual membership dues are based on your company size and are very reasonable. Members also enjoy discounted prices on all IFA's conferences and workshops.

Training

The Small Factor Academy (www.SmallFactorAcademy.com) is an interactive training website that provides numerous progressive lessons which teach how to begin and run a small factoring operation. Using as references the author's books and ebooks described below, as well as other resources, these online videos walk you through each aspect of setting up and operating your small factoring business.

Based on material that was originally presented in two-day live workshops, this training is now offered only through this website; live workshops providing this material are no longer available. Those who register for the course receive additional discounts on products offered by the author.

Publications and Websites

The Commercial Factor. As mentioned above, this magazine is the publication of the International Factoring Association. Published six times yearly in both electronic and printed versions, IFA members are subscribed to the magazine automatically as part of their membership. Previous editions, dating back to the first one written in 1999, are available as PDF files via a link to each edition on IFA's website.

FactoringInvestor.com. While not a magazine like IFA's, this website is chock-full of articles written by both the site hosts and several factors about subjects pertinent to the factoring industry. Generally intended for factoring brokers, new factors can also learn from the great amount of information here.

The site includes an archives page with links to all past articles. You'll also find a bookstore with ebooks written by various writers about the cash flow industry in general and factoring in particular.

The hosts also offer their *Directory of Factoring Companies and Service Providers* which lists over 60 factoring companies with their email, phone numbers, and websites. The directory identifies listed factors who are or provide:

- Factoring Funding Sources
- Invoice Buyers
- Medical Factoring Specialists
- Construction Factoring Companies
- Staffing Factoring
- Freight and Transportation Factoring
- Small Business Factoring
- Non-recourse Factoring
- Preferred Transaction Types and Invoice Sizes
- Broker-Friendly Factoring Companies
- Master Consultants Willing to Mentor New Brokers

Cash Flow Exclusive. This is a monthly electronic magazine whose website is www.CashFlowExclusive.com. Aimed primarily at brokers, it addresses many forms of alternative financing which are both business-based and consumer-based. Thus its articles cover the following cash flow instruments:

- Business Based:
  - Accounts Receivable Financing / Factoring
  - Delinquent Debt
  - Equipment Leasing
  - Purchase Order Funding
  - Business Notes
- Consumer Based:
  - Consumer Receivables
  - Contest Winnings
  - Inheritance Funding
  - Lawsuit Financing
  - Life Settlements
  - Promissory Notes
  - Structured Settlements
  - Sub-Prime Auto Financing

SmallFactor.com is hosted by the author and is a portal site with links and resources for smaller factors. These links are to the resources mentioned in this chapter as well as to:

- software
- factoring exchanges
- due diligence providers
- legal services
- factoring franchises

DashPointPublishing.com is also hosted by the author. From this site you can purchase the many products mentioned throughout this book including the books and ebooks below. Also available here are the legal products from attorney David Jencks. The site offers numerous bundled products that are less expensive when purchased together than when bought separately.

Books and Ebooks
The Small Factor Series

Book 1
Factoring Wisdom:
A Preview of
Buying Receivables

Short Sayings and Straight Talk
For New & Small Factors

Book 2
Fundamentals
for Factors

How You Can Make
Large Returns in Small Receivables

Book 3
How to Run
a Small Factoring Business

Make Money in Little Deals
the Big Guys Brush Off

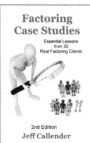

Book 4
Factoring Case Studies
(2nd Edition)

Essential Lessons from
30 Real Factoring Clients

Book 5
Marketing Methods
for Small Factors
and Brokers

Tools from the Trenches
To Make Your Factoring Business Thrive!

About This Series

The Small Factor Series is designed to:

1. Provide a succinct introduction and summary of the books in this series as well as other writings by Jeff Callender.

2. Introduce readers to the investment of factoring small business receivables.

3. Provide a step-by-step manual with complete instructions for small factors.

4. Provide 30 real-life examples of factoring clients from the files of people who have been investing in small receivables for some time.

5. Describe and analyze numerous marketing methods to bring in new business which have been used by the eight contributors to the book.

Each book in the series is written to address the above points:

- Book 1, *Factoring Wisdom: A Preview of Buying Receivables,* introduces and summarizes the other books with brief excerpts from each, and arranges them by subject matter.

- Book 2, *Fundamentals for Factors* introduces potential factors to the business.

- Book 3, *How to Run a Small Factoring Business,* is the step-by-step manual.

- Book 4, *Factoring Case Studies* (2nd Edition), describes experiences of 30 real clients of small factors, which illustrate the many lessons and suggestions made in Books 2 and 3.

- Book 5, *Marketing Methods for Small Factors & Brokers,* includes contributions from seven small factors and an experienced broker.

Other Books by Jeff Callender

Factoring:
Sell Your Invoices Today
& Get Cash Tomorrow

How to Obtain Unlimited Funds without a Loan

Written to introduce factoring to small business owners, this book compares factoring to traditional lending, shows how it can help a company's cash flow, and guides readers in determining if factoring can improve their business.

The above books are available in the following formats from DashPointPublishing.com:

- Paperback
- PDF
- Kindle
- iPad & Android

Ebooks by Jeff Callender

Accounting Methods
for Factors and Their Clients

By Robert Vasquez and Jeff Callender

This ebook describes how to establish and maintain proper bookkeeping records for a factoring company and factoring clients. You'll learn how to use GAAP-approved procedures and make sure you're doing it right. Following these step-by-step instructions starts you on the right foot.

How I Run
My One-Person Factoring Business

Want to get started running a small factoring business by yourself? This ebook shows how the author successfully began as a one-person operation, and the everyday tools you can use now to do the same.

How I Run
My Virtual Factoring Office

A virtual office means you can work from just about anywhere you want. Learn the common tools and technology the author uses (available to anyone) to run his virtual factoring office. Enjoy the comforts of home – at work!

"Top 10" Ebooks by Jeff Callender

"Top 10" Ebooks for Factors:

Top 10 Insights
about Factoring Prospects

Questions to Ask
and Truisms to Remember
When Considering Potential Clients

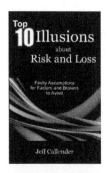

Top 10 Illusions about Risk and Loss

Faulty Assumptions for
Factors and Brokers to Avoid

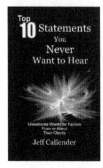

Top 10 Statements You Never Want to Hear

Unwelcome Words for Factors
From or About Their Clients

10 Key Points to Look for in Factoring Software

Consider these 10 issues
before purchasing software
for your factoring operation

"Top 10" Ebooks for Clients:

Top 10 Quotes
on the Benefits of Factoring

Statements from Business Owners
Who Factor Their Receivables

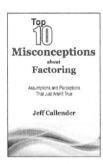

Top 10 Misconceptions
about Factoring

Assumptions and Perceptions
That Just Aren't True

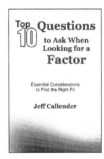

Top 10 Questions to Ask
When Looking for a Factor

Essential Considerations
to Find the Right Fit

The above ebooks are available in the following formats from DashPointPublishing.com:

- PDF
- Kindle
- iPad & Android

Conclusion

This book and the others in this series give you the tools to begin factoring small transactions and helpful resources to further expand your knowledge and thus your business. Following the Cardinal Rule of Money, factoring can be an enjoyable, good, and profitable business, with the satisfaction of knowing you are providing a valuable service your clients need and appreciate.

Best wishes in your factoring adventures!

Acknowledgements

Thank you to **Nicole Jones** for her proofreading skills and contribution to the section on Social Networking. She also created the ebook versions of books in the *Small Factor Series* and all other titles, and did all the work to make these available to the world. Her consistent cheerfulness, multiple talents, and exemplary work ethic have my permanent admiration.

Thank you also to **Anne Gordon** for her proofreading skills, generously sharing her wisdom and experience in the factoring world, and keeping me on my toes running my business. Her insights and acumen are both needed and highly valued every day.

Thanks as well to **Don D'Ambrosio** for his contribution to the section on press releases. His business insights, collegiality, friendship, and sense of humor are good fortunes I thoroughly enjoy.

Finally I owe a debt of gratitude to **Stewart Martin**, Attorney and Counselor at Law, for the chapter in which the legal structures of participations are discussed.

Cover image credit: © Luca De Polo/123RF.com

Important Notice

Also by Jeff Callender

Paperbacks and Ebooks
The Small Factor Series includes 5 titles:

1. *Factoring Wisdom: A Preview of Buying Receivables*
   Short Sayings and Straight Talk for New & Small Factors © 2012
2. *Fundamentals for Factors*
   How You Can Make Large Returns in Small Receivables © 2012
3. *How to Run a Small Factoring Business*
   Make Money in Little Deals the Big Guys Brush Off © 2012
4. *Factoring Case Studies*
   Essential Lessons from 30 Real Factoring Clients
   1st edition ©2003, 2005; 2nd edition © 2012
5. *Marketing Methods for Small Factors & Brokers*
   Tools from the Trenches to Make Your Factoring Business Thrive!
   © 2012

Factoring: Sell Your Invoices Today & Get Cash Tomorrow
   How to Obtain Unlimited Funds without a Loan © 2012

eBooks
For Factoring Clients:

Accounting Methods for Factors & Their Clients	© 2012
Top 10 Quotes on the Benefits of Factoring	© 2012
Top 10 Misconceptions about Factoring	© 2012
Top 10 Questions to Ask When Looking for a Factor	© 2012

For Factors:

Accounting Methods for Factors & Their Clients	© 2012
How I Run My One-Person Factoring Business	© 2008, 2012
How I Run My Virtual Factoring Office	© 2012
Top 10 Insights about Factoring Prospects	© 2008, 2012
Top 10 Illusions about Risk and Loss	© 2008, 2012
Top 10 Statements You Never Want to Hear	© 2008, 2012
10 Key Points to Look for in Factoring Software	© 2008, 2012

Spreadsheet Calculators
APR and Income Calculators © 2002, 2012

Software
FactorFox Software © 2006 – current year

Websites
www.DashPointPublishing.com   www.SmallFactor.com
www.DashPointFinancial.com   www.SmallFactorAcademy.com
www.FactorFox.com   www.FactorFind.com

About the Author

Jeff Callender had an unusual start to his business career. Though he is the son and grandson of businessmen, he began his working life as a pastor.

After earning a college degree in Sociology and a Master of Divinity degree, he served three churches in Washington state over 14 years. While he found ministry rewarding, he realized he had an entrepreneurial spirit which gradually pulled him toward business.

He left his career in the church and about a year later stumbled onto factoring. He began as a broker but after numerous referrals were declined only because of their small size, he started factoring very small clients himself. His career as a factor – and as a pioneer in the niche of very small receivables factoring – was thus born in 1994.

He has worked with a great number of very small business owners in need of factoring. He wrote his first book, *Factoring Small Receivables*, in 1995, and since then has written numerous books, ebooks, and articles, and spoken at many events in the factoring industry. His writing and two decades of experience have established him as a leading authority in the niche of small business factoring.

Jeff is the President of three companies he started. Dash Point Financial provides factoring services to small business owners throughout the U.S. It also provides the nucleus of his experience for writing. Learn more at DashPointFinancial.com.

Dash Point Publishing publishes and sells his books and ebooks, as well as those of other authors who write about factoring. His paperbacks are available from DashPointPublishing.com, as well as Amazon, the Kindle Store,

Apple's iBookstore, and other online ebook sellers. Dash Point Publishing's website provides additional materials such as legal documents for smaller factoring companies.

FactorFox Software offers a cloud-based database solution for factors to track their client transactions. Originally based on his own company's back-office operational needs, readers of his books will feel right at home using the software in their own factoring companies. It has become one of the top platforms for the industry and is used by factoring companies throughout the world. More information can be found at FactorFox.com.

Having grown up in southern California, Jeff now lives in Tacoma, Washington with his wife, dog, and two cats. He has a grown son and daughter.

Made in the USA
Middletown, DE
30 April 2023

29780596R00199